Flamenco LEGEND

IN SEARCH OF CAMARÓN DE LA ISLA

Flamenco LEGEND

IN SEARCH OF CAMARÓN DE LA ISLA

MARCOS

TEMPUS

Cover illustrations: Camarón de la Isla ©José Lamarca; flamenco dancer © Ilian Iliev/Lebrecht Music and Arts.

First published 2007

Tempus Publishing Limited
The Mill, Brimscombe Port,
Stroud, Gloucestershire, GL5 2QG
www.tempus-publishing.com

British Library Cataloguing in Publication Data.
A catalogue record for this book is available from the British Library.

ISBN 978 07524 3992 1

Typesetting and origination by Tempus Publishing Limited
Printed in Great Britain

Contents

For Rancapino, a singer whose voice is the essence of flamenco and in memory of one of the art's great maestros, Pepe Martínez and Juan Rebolledo, a true aficionado

Acknowledgements

I would like to thank the many people whose commitment and dedication has made this ambitious project possible. Nic *la Faraona*, my rock who sacrificed much and gave everything to make the book happen. Dr Roy Lobb, with whom I spent some great nights in Seville drinking *cubatas* of rum and coke all those years ago and who I can never thank enough for his generous support. Thanks to Mario Basilisco for finding me so much rare archive footage of Camarón from his 'secret cupboard' and for all his help and advice with the editing and translating of the vast body of material I had amassed over the years. A special thanks to Carmen González who encouraged me to burn the midnight oil when I started to flag and whose hard work on the transcriptions and translations was invaluable. Also at Coventry University I would like to express my gratitude to Professor Karen Ross for supporting the initial research and to Andrew Beck for documenting the important photographic material. Heartfelt thanks to Karenanne Herbert for patiently combing through the manuscript and coming up with some very useful suggestions, Sarah Franklin for being an absolute star for her sterling work as the deadline loomed and Caroline Jones for her meticulous editing. I would also like to thank the *Ayuntamiento de San Fernando* for their kind permission allowing the reproduction of the *Ruta de Camarón*. Thanks also to Olvido Salazar-Alonso at the Instituto de Cervantes for her assistance tracking down some vital contributors.

Gerald Howson for writing the most outstanding book on flamenco in the English language. Miguel Ángel Ruiz Rosado, a true *Gaditano*, for our long friendship and his encyclopaedic knowledge of Cádiz province and Spain's rich history. For Cynthia, my late mother who encouraged me to become a flamenco guitarist and who adored Camarón and my sister Claire who collected much material for me about the singer over the years. Tony and David Shepherd, two fine musicians, for their support over three decades. Tony Clinton for taking the time to teach me those essential flamenco rhythms all those years ago and my BBC producer Ross Heaton and fellow presenter Leon Foster-Hill for putting up with a very stressful six months! Ian Spence for tracking down some very useful material on his Andalusian forays. My thanks also to Tony Sellors and Lawrence Pollard at the BBC whose talents over the years have helped me make some great programmes about flamenco music and its artists.

In Spain I am indebted to so many people but in particular to those *Gaditanos* Jesús, Juan, Manolo, Alfonso, Augusto and the proprietors of *Bar Gades*. To Pepe Manteca for all his hospitality and for creating Bar Manteca, the most flamenco bar in Cádiz. The *Peña de Camarón* in San Fernando, Real Betis football club and that yellow submarine better known as Cádiz football club for entertaining me while writing this book. My utter gratitude to Leovigildo Francisco Aguilar Burgos at the *Candil* journal in Jaén, for producing and sending me such a valuable resource over the years and also the singer from that province, Rosario. All the gang from the old days when the *Bar los Pollos* was thriving in Seville's Gran Plaza including Ricardo, Emilio, Juan and Angeles and the guitarist Juan Manuel Tudela. Thanks to Pepe and Angeles at the '*Tasca*' for my many happy years in Jimena de la Frontera and to Antonio for running one of the best bars in the village over the years, while not forgetting *Bar Marilyn* and the gypsy Gabriel for his *cante*. A special thanks for those special times with Nino, the ultimate *Camaronero*, in Morón de la Frontera for those great days spent in the company of Paco del Gastor and El Andorrano. Not forgetting Rafael Riqueni and Vicente Amigo, two of the finest guitarists I have ever met and Martin Palmer for believing in the project and Sophie Bradshaw for seeing it through. Finally my thanks to all those people, too many to mention here, who have given me important recordings and artefacts relating to Camarón.
'Ese Kai. OÉ.'

The author and publisher gratefully acknowledge permission granted for the use of extracts from the following publications:

Gay y Blanco, P., (1999) *Gypsies in Madrid. Sex, Gender and the Performance of Identity.* Oxford, Berg.

Graham, H., (2005) *The Spanish Civil War. A Very Short Introduction.* Oxford, OUP.

Pérez-Reverte, A., (1995) *The Seville Communion.* London, Harvill Press.

Stainton, L., (1998) *Lorca. A Dream of Life.* London, Bloomsbury.

1

Hasta Siempre Camarón

On the radio, Camarón still sang of wine and longing, and behind the bar the waiter, in
white shirt and black tie, clapped quietly in time to the music.
Arturo Pérez-Reverte, *The Seville Communion*

Barcelona, Friday 3 July 1992

The eight o'clock evening flight for Seville had just left with an unusual
cargo: a coffin containing the body of a gypsy, whose left hand displayed a distinctive tattoo. Inside the casket lay a flamenco singer, universally
hailed as the greatest ever by the critics and his fellow artists, returning to
the city that had seen many of his finest triumphs and heard him perform
at his very worst. The tattoo, a crescent moon bordering the Star of David,
would soon become synonymous with a middle-aged man whose image
would be re-branded from a drug addict to a national treasure, allowing in
Spain the previously unthinkable possibility of a novel trinity alongside the
Pope and the Virgin Mary. His death marked the end of the country's most
visible gypsy, the creation of flamenco's first superstar and a new saint. From
now on, people would only remember him at his peak: a bony diminutive
figure dressed in a sharp black suit that covered an elegant *camisa gitana*, his
curly hair immaculately permed and the ability to sing with the precision
of a metronome. Local bars still displayed photographs of his marriage to a
beautiful sixteen-year-old gypsy schoolgirl who was known as 'the spark'.
They would never see their idol in a wheelchair, dying and emaciated in a
Catalan hospital.[1]

The body of José Monje Cruz, better known as El Camarón de la Isla would land at the newly improved San Pablo airport, as the city of Seville was enjoying playing host to the world for the Expo '92. The *Sevillanos* had spent the last few years gossiping about the ill health of Camarón and rumours were rife concerning his abuse of cocaine and heroin, repeated failures to appear at festivals and the possibility that he had contracted Aids. In recent years his concerts had achieved notoriety, more for the outbreaks of violence amongst the audience and the brevity of his performance, than his singing. The newspapers had ceased writing about his mastery of the flamenco repertory, to concentrate on unsavoury incidents, including the story of a gypsy woman who had sunk a meat cleaver into a policeman's head at one of his concerts in the autumn of 1990. In the early seventies he had been described as 'looking anything but a flamenco singer' with his 'long, curly blond hair' and 'Carnaby Street'clothes. Yet within two decades he would be facing ruin when he received a demand for ten million pesetas of back tax from the Spanish treasury. Only ten months before, the people of southern Spain's biggest city had heard and read about how poor Camarón's performance had been for the sell-out opening concert in the Expo's splendid newly built Cartuja concert hall.[2] His remarkable voice had also been expected to open the Olympic games in Barcelona, but had last been heard at a Madrid school in January. On the Thursday night, having seen images of Camarón's widow leaving the hospital in Catalonia, where the singer was receiving treatment, people from all social classes made thousands of telephone calls across Spain saying three simple and until then unthinkable words, 'Camarón is dead'. By Friday these agitated callers were able to read the eulogies in the Catholic and right-wing daily, *El ABC* and observe that the unaligned and intellectual national newspaper, *El País*, had chosen to dub him the 'Picasso of flamenco song' and print his photograph on their front page. By Sunday, reports of the extraordinary turnout for his burial dominated the front pages of the Spanish press, sharing the column inches with the French lorry drivers' strike, a possible referendum on Maastrict and another success for the cyclist Miguel Indurain. Journalists would record that a crowd of 100,000 people, including gypsies, plump middle-class women and of course the drug addicts and traffickers who are often seen at such events, would gather to honour their hero.[3] Camarón was going home to San Fernando near Cádiz in southwest Spain for the last time. His body would be collected at the airport by his close friend and fellow gypsy, the guitarist José Fernández Torres, better know as 'Tomatito', the little tomato. This was just the beginning of a new chapter in the Camarón story that would see him ascend to even greater fame in death than he ever achieved in his short and tragic, yet eventful life.

Cádiz, Friday 4 March 2005

In the bar, La Penúltima, the guitarists Paco de Lucía and Tomatito were always accompanying Camarón, as the bar's owner Carlos, was constantly fiddling with stacks of compact discs as he found yet another flamenco album to help him get through the day. As the *cante* or flamenco song blared out from tinny speakers, with the sleight of hand of a magician Carlos produced a large octopus from his tiny curtained-off kitchen and we were all invited to tuck in. The octopus has been cooked in paprika and olive oil, following a recipe created by a Galician girl who frequented the bar. More communal food arrived in the form of an enormous seafood paella, courtesy of a neighbour José, while the bar's resident guitarist and mates decided it was time for a flamenco session. They wanted to hear a few *falsetas* or licks from me as they had heard about my concert tour as 'Marcos' and so I desperately tried to warm my hands and the guitar by the fire. Here, in deepest southern Spain, nobody was really in the mood for flamenco as the only thing preoccupying the locals was the unusually cold weather. They kept asking how, so far south, could so many of Andalucía's roads be cut off due to the heavy snowfalls and would the olive crop survive?

A poster of Christ on the cross from the 1997 Easter Holy Week, which hung above the urinal door, gazed down on the customers as they downed the local *Barbadillo* Cádiz wine. Allusions to the old Spain were everywhere, including a photograph of General Franco in his prime hanging from the bar bell. A plastic model of the *Generalisimo* also formed part of the kitsch proudly displayed behind the bar, but nobody here liked Franco; it was all part of that unique Cádiz humour. Protected from the bitingly cold Atlantic wind, the locals placed their drinks on the barrels that colourfully proclaimed *Tío Pepe* in that striking red and black logo. They peered out through the traditional iron grills that framed the windows, just hoping something interesting might happen to pass the time. A caged canary sang its heart out as the customers expressed concern that Cádiz football club might never make it back to *La Primera*, the top flight in football. Outside, despite the weather, small boys kicked footballs up against the walls of Cádiz Cathedral while a guitarist played the *Romance Anónimo* for the twentieth time that day as the occasional tourist passed through the Caleta.

The smell of the cooked octopus and garlic filled this tiny bar where German tourists curiously poked their heads in to admire a faded yellow and purple old *torero's* cape, which openly displayed the evidence of where the bull's horn had punctured the cloth. For the tourists this must be the real Spain, because the locals were playing a track of Camarón where he sang about hitting an old man who had bumped into him in the street, only to cry tears of blood when he was told a year later that it was his own father.

An old lady, who came every Friday, quietly entered La Penúltima and Carlos knew exactly what she wanted. On the bar he carefully balanced a sausage across the lips of a small terracotta dish using two cocktail sticks and poured in some pure spirit alcohol. He ignited the fluid with his lighter and carefully rotated the sausage with all the skill of a *cordon bleu* chef until the *tapa* was ready, then blew out the flames and offered her the smouldering and part burnt snack. She was not interested in the *cante* or flamenco song, but of course she had heard of Camarón and knew a friend who went to his funeral, but that was a long time ago and anyway, she thought to herself, why should anyone have sympathy for a gypsy who took drugs. She would not go to the film *Camarón la Película*, which would be screened at Cádiz's *Multicines* on the first Friday in November 2005 to the accompaniment of the deafening sound of workers' drills. The film, based on the singer's life, would be shown in a cinema that resembled a building site whilst the management proclaimed business as usual! She certainly would not see the other new release called *La Leyenda del Tiempo*, which took its inspiration from Camarón's life, but went beyond fictional biography to explore the experiences of a thirteen-year-old boy who stopped singing flamenco when his father died. The elderly woman remembered visiting her aunt in Camarón's home of San Fernando in the late fifties, where a very young gypsy boy disturbed their quiet chat over coffee and *churros*, delicious fatty and sweet Spanish donuts. The boy, who was singing unaccompanied, had attracted a large and vociferous crowd by reciting the old flamenco songs she had never cared for.

Seville, Friday 4 July 1992

We may never know what thoughts were occupying Tomatito's mind as he approached Seville airport. He had spent the past seventeen years as Camarón's loyal guitarist. Throughout that troubled first week of July, he was one of the few people close to Camarón who maintained a dignified silence. He was undoubtedly overcome by a sense of the loss of a great friend with whom he had laid the foundations for the *nuevo flamenco*, that vibrant, open and creative flamenco which flourished after the death of the Dictator General Franco. Having also spent time with Camarón's family over the past few days he may well have been considering the future of the singer's widow, Dolores Montoya, and her four children; with the question of the ownership of the rights to Camarón's vast recording output being discussed publicly. Or did Tomatito simply recall those moments when he travelled to the outdoor flamenco festivals all over Seville province with Camarón, in the white Mercedes that became their temporary home? Regrettably, Tomatito's memories, laced with gypsy pride and grief, were shortly to be interrupted and overshadowed by an unfortunate moment at Seville's airport.[4] Before the funeral cortege could set off, a representative of the *Guardia Civil* tried to explain to Tomatito that a police vehicle would lead the funeral cortege towards San Fernando. This was undoubtedly a snub as throughout Spain, when the various religious icons emerge from buildings, people and vehicles follow, they do not lead. Tomatito made his feelings known, that the police should also follow, but was ignored; further examples of the authorities callousness and overbearing policing at this delicate time would surface the following day.

Camarón's body was duly transported to the town of San Fernando, which had been in mourning since the news of his death early on the morning of Thursday 2 July. His coffin had arrived at the Zuazo Bridge, under which he used to swim as a child in the hot summers of the sixties. He would be carried to San Fernando's town hall for the wake and then watched overnight by flamenco's greatest artists. The shops would remain closed, as would the entrance to Camarón's birthplace, and the town hall would lower its flags to fly at half-mast in respect for its future chosen son.

Any journey in search of the person who was the real Camarón de la Isla has to start in the quiet town of San Fernando or the 'island' from where he took his artistic name. This remote town, also known as 'Lions Island', has an illustrious history, being located at the foot of Spain bordering salt flats on one side and the Atlantic Ocean on the other. The Cape of Trafalgar lays just a stone's throw away and San Fernando's inhabitants still boast of the defence of their island against Napoleon's invasion. The town is joined to Cádiz by only a thin strip of land, on which stands the historic roadside inn that launched the career of Camarón. Only here, on the official plaques that mark the Camarón trail, will you find the few testimonies left that record his extraordinary funeral and the vast crowd that gathered in the main street known as the Calle Real. For only the second time in the twentieth century did this sleepy town, mostly associated with ship building, due to its special relationship with the Spanish Armada, witness a major funeral; the previous occasion being the burial of General Varela before Camarón's first birthday. The quality and grandeur of the town's buildings testify to its status as a once great port that dominated southern Spain in the eighteenth century. Its streets are lined with an uneasy mix of neoclassical and modern buildings, featuring many shops and bazaars selling cheap goods imported from China. Today, San Fernando continues to be known for the historic and well-established naval base that prompted the English writer Gerald Howson to call it 'a sort of Spanish Aldershot'![5]

On the eve of Camarón's funeral, San Fernando was about to witness an extraordinary burial and outpouring of grief. Scenes that would eclipse even the pageantry and military power displayed outside Cádiz's great cathedral to mark the passing of fellow musician and Andalusian, Manuel de Falla. Camarón's burial would be an event that matched the tension which gripped Spain as news spread of the death of the Dictator General Franco in 1975. A cult was about to be born which, within a decade, would produce a gypsy icon whose image would be as recognisable as the *Galácticos* of Real Madrid football club or any rock star; in short a new Che Guevara would be created as the art of flamenco gained its first martyr. The commoditisation of Camarón would soon take the exploitation of his image to a level unforeseen during his illustrious singing career. While his premature death would be attributed to his smoking and drug abuse, few people would reflect on how he was also the victim of a system that failed to nurture this talent. His tragic story would be that of a flawed genius, rebel and revolutionary who became not just flamenco's first martyr but its greatest ever artist.

Hampshire, England, Monday 29 June 1992

As Camarón lay dying in a Badalona hospital in Catalonia, I was far from the intense summer heat of Andalucía; touring the southern leafy shires with fellow guitarist David Shepherd. I was known as 'Marcos', a flamenco guitarist who played gigs across Britain and Europe with a battered guitar that had an open crack down one side and was held together with a tapping plate. The most respected guitar maker in Spain, Manuel Reyes of Córdoba, who made guitars for Camarón's guitarist Tomatito, had built this one for me in 1975. I had travelled by coach to the heart of the decaying fascist Spain with hundreds of pounds sewn into an old jean jacket, intent on ordering a new guitar. It would have to be a flamenco guitar made from sweet-smelling cypress wood and distinguished from a classical model by its rich golden body, achieved by staining with French polish mixed with saffron. For me, Seville would come to mean the smell of aromatic plants, the unforgettable scent of the *azahar* 'the blossom of the orange tree' and the odour of jasmine in the night clashing with the smell of ten thousand bars all cooking fish in olive oil.

As flamenco artists, Camarón was our god and we had all his albums to prove it. The mere whisper of a new release would be enough to prompt a visit to Spain to buy one of the first copies, and in May 1992 we heard news of the release of *Potro de Rabia y Miel*. An album, which due to his ill health during its recording, had taken so long to find its way into the shops. The peace and tranquillity of England's rural roads was soon subjected to 'our José's' latest offering which, like all his previous projects, was groundbreaking and would take us weeks to assimilate and decode just what he was now doing with flamenco song and rhythm. Neither the quality of the cassette copy nor the car stereo was able to do justice to this magnificent new creation. We were simply in awe of the innovative guitar playing of Paco de Lucía and Tomatito as they accompanied the unique voice of Camarón on yet another exciting *bulerías*, the most exciting form of gypsy song. What could be wrong now that Paco was back on board teaming up with his old gypsy friend and former recording partner? Camarón sounded back at his very best as he sang about selling fried fish in the streets; sadly I did not need newspaper cuttings from Spain to tell me how ill he was.

I had spent September 1990 in Seville covering as a journalist the artists performing in flamenco's great showcase, the *Bienal*. If you are on the bill at this month-long event then you have truly made it in the demanding world of flamenco. I was one of only 130 people, many of them flamenco singers and guitarists, to attend a concert given by Tomatito in the stunning theatre named after the Spanish playwright Lope de Vega. The *Bienal*, as well as being a major flamenco competition, also brings together the cream of the art; sadly few aficionados are usually inspired enough to attend a concert of solo flamenco guitar and with the guitar taking centre stage that year, attendance was very poor.

By eight o'clock, this venue, which lies at the heart of the land laid out for Seville's first World Exposition in 1929, was very quiet and populated by mainly the guitarists who would be playing there later in the week. How different this would have been if Seville's flamenco loving public had known that Tomatito had a rather special guest singer lined up. To say 'lined up' would be to misunderstand Camarón's nature as he had only promised to pop in if he was passing! During the guitar recital Tomatito introduced his surprise guest, his long-standing friend Camarón and I was immediately shocked by his very thin and gaunt appearance. Camarón, resplendent in a bespoke suit and shirt of handmade lace had a presence that could be felt before he even sang a note. My eyes were drawn to his legs, which looked as thin as matchsticks; he had clearly lost a great deal of weight. His extended *bulerías* had moments of magic which inspired his accompanist, but Tomatito's face also communicated his concern that the maestro's grip and command of the *cante*, and the purest examples of flamenco song, were fading.

Cádiz, 4 March 2005

On a bitterly cold day in early March the clear pure sunlight for which Cádiz is so renowned shone through the side window of the La Penúltima, an historic bar right in the heart of the port of Cádiz opposite the city's magnificent cathedral. The sun's powerful rays illuminated the thin paper of a very basic A4 poster which announced: '*Casting para largometraje documental "La Leyenda del Tiempo", Buscamos hombres de 50 años en adelante aficionados al cante flamenco'*. Camarón's stature had reached a point where two films, inspired by his life, were being made and now they were looking for fifty-year-old flamenco fans to be extras. This tiny bar, overlooked by the golden dome that crowns Cádiz's cathedral, was packed with the usual regulars: the homely Paco who worked for a pest control company, Curro the joker and local government administrator and Ramón the lift engineer, a true *Camaronero* who openly displayed his admiration with the solid gold bust of Camarón which hung from his neck. They were all very aware of the two film crews in town, working on the productions aimed at recreating the myth of a flamenco singer and his performances whilst many still carried fresh memories of him. Thirteen years after his untimely death, the gypsy from San Fernando who initiated a flamenco revolution was about to be immortalised on celluloid and his amazing story revealed to an international audience on the big screen. The regulars at the 'one before the last' bar would have passed their screen test with flying colours as they knew all the flamenco singers and their songs backwards and they could still remember the many occasions when they had seen Camarón with his family, parking his green Land Rover at the 'Pay and Display' car park. One of Camarón's nephews was a frequent visitor to the bar and often enjoyed a Friday afternoon session with his mates after a busy week in the building trade. Spain is renowned for its bars on every corner, whose owners one should never ask for the 'last drink', but always request *la penúltima*, the one before the last, unless of course one is about to depart this earth.

Wiltshire, England, late afternoon, Wednesday 1 July 1992

Gazing at the Temple of Apollo in Stourhead Garden I thought back to how, a year after seeing Camarón sing in the wonderful Teatro Lope de Vega that lies close to Seville's María Luisa park, I had queued unsuccessfully to get tickets to hear him perform again: at the inaugural flamenco concert in the newly constructed auditorium for the 1992 Expo. It seemed I had not missed much as the press described the concert as 'a complete failure' with Camarón's performance and his command of flamenco's rhythm, the *compás*, being heavily criticised. Since then, there had been endless rumours relating to the health of this great singer: his addiction to heroin and cocaine; four packets of *Winston* cigarettes a day; and that was on top of the alcohol! Camarón was known to say that before he could sing he had to have a glass of something, followed by a cigarette, just to 'warm the voice'.[6] There were even stories circulating that he was seriously ill. However there was only one thing that outsiders could be sure of: he was still facing a one-year jail sentence for his part in a road accident in 1986, in which two people were killed. This accident had left him seriously injured and had affected his appearance, leaving him with a flattened nose.

Further evidence of his decline came with the footage of Camarón shot by the Spanish director Carlos Saura for his film *Sevillanas*, which presented a now hirsute Camarón looking very ill and wasted. Then came the dedicated video short, filmed to promote the Expo '92, where Camarón appeared as a Christ-like figure with a full beard and stripped to the waist. I had also heard of his journey in April 1992 to the Mayo clinic in Minnesota USA, for a miracle cure which really meant radiation therapy, but who could say what was really happening to Camarón except his wife Dolores Montoya and his lifelong friend and mentor Rancapino? Also aware of his condition were his manager and bodyguard for the past decade, José Candado, and his guitarists Paco de Lucía and Tomatito, who had spent so much time with him in the studios during 1991. Even Camarón's own record company felt the need to issue a statement on his return from the United States, stating that he had conquered his drug habit and had been advised by his doctors to rest for three months. Rumours about the health of Camarón were nothing new. Much earlier in 1984, he had sent a message to his public by calling his album *Viviré* ('I will live'), and this latest crisis seemed to follow a familiar theme. A theme that also had echoes from his 1986 record in whose title *Te lo Dice Camarón* ('You say this about Camarón'), was even more direct. The reaction from the critics had been mixed as they questioned the quality of his voice, but again he hit back in fine style with live performances that took the white towns, perched high in Andalucía's sierras, by storm.

His image had benefited greatly from a PR campaign designed to challenge the popularity of French group, the Gypsy Kings, who performed a different type of flamenco to that found in the provinces of southern Spain. Using a creative spin involving a well-known London studio, Camarón's record label would successfully guide his latest album *Soy Gitano*, into the Spanish charts. This release in 1989 captured the popular imagination, creating the impression that he had recorded the entire album with the Royal Philharmonic Orchestra in the capital city. It provided the perfect photo opportunity: of Camarón seated on the famous Abbey Road steps outside EMI's studios, in spite of the fact that much of the album was recorded in Seville and the final mix completed in the lesser-known Livingstone Studios. The travel journalist, Howell Llewellyn, was one member of the press who not entirely convinced when he posed the question: 'What was an institution of the Royal Philharmonic's prestige doing laying down the string section for a collection of gypsy racial affirmation songs?'[7] Camarón, now dubbed by the French press as the Mick Jagger of flamenco, was also portrayed in the print media as recording at studios synonymous with the Beatles. Comparisons of Camarón with the lead singer of the Rolling Stones would result in Mick Jagger giving Camarón his best linen jacket as a token of his admiration. On another occasion Jagger had gone as far as suggesting that they should swap underwear, so that some of Camarón's brilliance might rub off on him![8] With headlines like this it was not surprising that the album *Soy Gitano* fully restored his reputation and went on to become flamenco's best selling record.

Having reached such heights was it really possible that on 2 July 1992 Camarón was dying in the Germans Trias i Pujol hospital in Badalona near Barcelona, following kidney failure? The treatment had failed, with the cancer engulfing his lungs and spinal chord, spreading to his legs. Late in the afternoon of Wednesday 1 July, as Camarón faced his last night,

David and I prepared for a recital; spending our free time learning the new guitar *falsetas* or licks from what was to be his last album, aptly titled *Potro de Rabia y Miel*, a colt of rage and honey. While we practiced, Camarón called for his wife and children to say the last goodbye. He died just after seven o'clock on the morning of Thursday July 2 after asking his uncle in the presence of his minder José Candado, 'Dear Mother, what's wrong with me?'

The next day I received a call from a BBC producer with whom I had worked on a documentary about gypsy flamenco. On hearing the news of Camarón's death, Anthony Sellors had enquired if I could put together a special tribute to Camarón for a programme to be broadcast on BBC network radio. So, sitting by the magnificent lake at the National Trust property of Stourhead in Wiltshire, I gazed at the Pantheon Temple and mentally went through my Camarón record collection reflecting on my twenty years of listening to the man from San Fernando. The first track for the programme had to be Camarón singing the *alegrías* from his home province of Cádiz at an outdoor flamenco festival that he would have arrived at with his guitarist Tomatito in that battered Mercedes. On the back of the Stourhead programme I quickly jotted down a very special memento: 'The tragic death of Camarón instantly evoked memories for me of a very hot day in July 1989 when I travelled to the town of Los Palacios to hear him sing beneath the stars. During the afternoon, as the mercury climbed to 48 degrees centigrade, the bars remained deserted, but by midnight the atmosphere was transformed, as car loads of aficionados began arriving in their thousands. They had come to experience that special *duende* and magic that only Camarón could bring to the *cante*. By three o' clock in the morning the customary jostling for tickets and arguing over seats was settled as Camarón, with his loyal partner Tomatito, emerged on stage to thunderous applause. He was always known for his mercurial performances, but as the audience sipped ice-cold sherry they understood that on this occasion he was particularly inspired. Camarón was on top form, with Tomatito's guitar accompaniment as slick as his outfit. We'll hear an *alegrías* from the era when these two maestros topped the bill at every major outdoor festival'.[9]

I did not consider it appropriate to mention in the script the rather unpleasant nature of some of the audience who had imbibed a little too much cold *fino* on that very hot night. It was a Saturday night and they had been fired up by the constant references in the press to Camarón's drug taking and frequent absences at concerts where his name appeared on the bill. There were also the underlying racist attitudes to gypsies that could still be found throughout Andalucía; there was bound to be some reaction to such a high-profile artist appearing in a small town near Seville. Earlier in the evening there had been some good-humoured barracking of the gypsy singer Chocolate, whom members of the audience wanted to sing the popular style of *bulerías*. Chocolate was not prepared to have his repertoire dictated to him and dug his heels in by singing the slower and more darker styles of *seguirillas* and the *fandangos grandes*. A difficult moment had passed, but Camarón's appearance provoked a more hostile reaction from a small number of youths who shouted abuse about his drug addition, picking up and hurling rocks and scattering the wooden fold-up chairs. For a few moments the situation became very ugly and had the potential to develop into the type of violence that had occurred at Camarón's concerts elsewhere.

La Línea, Cádiz, 17 October 1986

Camarón's neighbours were used to reading about him in the daily newspapers, watching his performances on television and seeing him on the cover of Spain's leading colour supplements. Now he was back on top of the world of flamenco with the album *Te lo Dice Camarón*, but even they were surprised to see a brand new Range Rover parked in the Calle Teatro. Evidence of Camarón's earning power had been widely talked about, and under the careful eye of the agent Jesús Antonio Pulpón, his fees were about rise to 300,000 pesetas a performance.[10] Here was further evidence of a flamenco artist who was doing very well and had purchased a new English vehicle that carried much status. It promised to be a typical October afternoon in southern Spain as Camarón's vehicle travelled along the notorious 'highway of death' that goes all the way from Barcelona to Cádiz, finally snaking along the Costa del Sol and the Costa de la Luz. Inside the car were his wife and three children, Rocío, Gema and Luis who, as they approached Chiclana, were unaware that they were minutes away from being involved in an accident that would not only result in the deaths of two people, but would lead to a series of events that would prove damaging to the singer's image and declining health. Camarón would soon be concerned with far more than the injuries sustained to his skull and his flattened nose.

The singer had not been at his best for several days and was entering a period where, it was claimed, he never travelled without a medicine cabinet of drugs and he would be soon taking Mogadon and Rohypnol and sleeping for days at a stretch.[11] If we were to look into the car's footwell, would we see, together with a scrunched up packet of Winston cigarettes and a handful of coins, a small bottle containing methadone syrup? We can be fairly sure that as Camarón changed gear and gazed briefly downwards he would have reached for his preferred brand of cigarettes, which were partially covered by the silver *duros*. Within days, the talk in bars from Seville to Madrid would link Camarón's name with a synthetic and highly addictive drug whose effect lasts longer than heroin. This 'medicine' was soon to receive considerable notoriety amongst the public; the majority of whom verbally convicted the singer without any evidence that Camarón had been unfit to drive. The drug became inextricably linked in people's minds to the drowsy state that Camarón was accused of being in while at the wheel.[12] Once again, others would claim to know more about his personal life than the man himself, with the prejudice against gypsies enough to convince the public that Camarón was guilty as charged.

San Fernando, Cádiz, 11.53pm, Friday 3 July 1992

As Tomatito and the funeral cortege drove south, San Fernando's second day of mourning was ebbing away against the background of a vivid sunset. That remarkable sunset was then followed by an equally impressive and luminous half moon just like the tattoo on Camarón's hand, a coincidence that was not lost on the reporter Amelia Casilla who had been sent to the southern port as a special correspondent for the Spanish newspaper *El País*.[13]

Before the clocks struck midnight, a coffin draped in the gypsy flag was carried into San Fernando's Town Hall signalling the start of a further day of sombre reflection, wails and sobbing. This was a gypsy funeral and the authorities had clearly expected trouble since the Special Operations Brigade had been drafted in at three o'clock in the morning; crowd disorder would occur on the steps of the Town Hall as the coffin was taken in. Ironically, while many gypsies would find themselves excluded from the burial ground, an elite band of them brought calm to the scene and helped lay out the chapel as both Paco de Lucía and Tomatito had to fight through the crowd to place the coffin in position.[14] Gazing at the casket with Rancapino and Pepe de Lucía was Manuel, Camarón's oldest surviving brother, and his other brother Jesus El Pijote. The gypsies would later guard the funeral car as it made its way to the church and cemetery. Inside the Town Hall there was a chaotic scene with so many people wanting to pay their respects. Each person made the sign of the cross as they approached and then kissed the coffin. A single red carnation was laid on the closed cask, framed by countless wreaths. Many of the mourners who filed passed the coffin were not gypsies, but sobbing middle-aged Andalusian women. The famous bullfighter Curro Romero mourned the loss of his friend throughout the night, watching over the body with Tomatito who could not stem his tears. Camarón's world famous guitarist, Paco de Lucía, was seen looking out from the corner of his eyes; communicating fear and tremendous loss. Was Paco terrified because some among the crowd outside had already hurled abuse at him? Had they been provoked by hearing accusations that he was responsible for depriving Camarón and his family of the royalties created during the golden years of their partnership? What made them even more incensed was the portrayal of Camarón as a near illiterate gypsy when it came to matters of negotiating record deals. This was an issue that the *Guardian* newspaper in Britain was to revisit twelve years later on the release of the film *Camarón, la Película*, when it reported that Camarón's widow Dolores Montoya 'claimed that Lucía had cheated him of hundreds of thousands of pesetas in royalties from the records'.[15]

While Camarón's early death created a number of potentially dangerous rumours concerning Paco de Lucía and Camarón, Carlos Lencero, who wrote many of his lyrics, would later play down this story. For Lencero it was simply a question of Camarón not being the type of person to worry about the paperwork, or even record what the contributions to his albums were.[16] Paco de Lucía had just lost his own idol after spending a very difficult year recording and editing Camarón's last album. This had been a labour of love, as Camarón had struggled to lay down useable versions of the new material in single takes, and skillful editing was required to produce this eloquent swansong. Now, Paco found himself vulnerable to attack whilst being propelled into an unusual atmosphere of hysteria with the local police completely out of their depth. He faced the difficult position of having to attend the funeral, despite becoming the focus of grief which turned to anger and hatred amongst some of the crowd. He found himself at the centre of an ugly controversy more common to the world of rock and blues, and this was just the first day.

After a night of unrelenting mourning, the coffin finally emerged into the very bright sunlight for its journey to the church service and then onto the cemetery. This was to be an ordeal for Camarón's widow that was to end just after one o'clock on that very hot Saturday afternoon. The casket, which was carried by more than twenty people, was immediately surrounded by thousands of mourners as San Fernando became the scene of wild hysteria and a cathartic outpouring of grief. The pall-bearers formed an A to Z of the luminaries of flamenco, including Camarón's close life-long friend and fellow singer Rancapino; his guitarists Paco de Lucía and Tomatito; and his childhood hero, the bullfighter, Curro Romero. As the coffin made its way to the cemetery, the crowds lining each side of the street maintained a very respectful silence only broken with the occasional chants of '… Camarón', '… Camarón'. Many punched the air with their arms as others used the palms of their hands to reproduce one of flamen-co's hypnotic beats. The reporter from *El País* would comment on how many Camarón lookalikes there were, with their trademark permed hair and gold chains. Amelia Casilla even went as far as comparing the scene to a painting by Romero de Torres, an artist well known for his eccentric and surreal portrayal of flamenco dancers and guitarists in such works as his *Musa Gitana*. San Fernando had been transformed into a town animated by Torres' clichéd images of Andalucía and its flamenco people.

The flamenco writer José Luis Ortiz Nuevo eloquently described the range of people who had come to say goodbye when he wrote that all walks of Spanish life were represented, from car parking attendants from Seville to the *Chirigoteros* of Cádiz with their distinctive brand of humour. The presence of *Chirigotas*, a type of choir who sing satirical songs in harmony accompanied by drums and whistles, was not surprising as Camarón had been an icon to them. General Franco had once banned their appearance at the Cádiz Carnival in 1938, before the end of the Spanish Civil War. Ortiz Nuevo also compared the people's veneration for the coffin with the bibli-cal portrayal of the taking of the body of Jesus, but the armed police did not share this adoration. He commented on just how touched the *Guardia Civil* was with Camarón's death; on the morning of the funeral, they coldly announced their intention to fine and prosecute any drivers caught speeding![17]

Earlier, one of Camarón's brothers, Jesús El Pijote, had passed the coffin to Rancapino and then to Tomatito who wore sunglasses and a brightly decorated gypsy shirt as he finally took his place towards the rear of the casket. Tomatito took the weight on his right shoulder and left hand, know-ing that inside was the body of a gypsy who had revolutionised flamenco and, in the words of the author Félix Grande, had 'suffered for us all'.[18] The police gazed at the scene with great apprehension, they were not pre-pared for a crowd like this, whilst politicians including the President of

Andalucía, Manuel Chaves, were now merely spectators. Thousands of his fans, many of them gypsies, waited out in the strong sun only to be told that they would not be allowed to enter the burial area and this decision provoked scenes of enormous tension.[19] Instead, many stood with their flowers at the cemetery gates, while those gypsies who had come from Evangelical churches had little interest in attending the more orthodox service. They had earlier been given a gesture from the second priest, Amos Rodríquez Rey, who had held out his arms to them when the sign of peace was given in the mass.

The remarkable scenes at Camarón's funeral had been seen by millions of people across Spain as the drama was played out on television news bulletins and special programmes. Who could forget seeing San Fernando's Calle Real, so packed with mourners that all you could see from a first floor balcony was a sea of faces and the coffin as it rose above the heads of the crowd? The chaotic scenes of the police struggling to cordon off the hearse and the route to the car were etched into the memory of the Spanish people, as was the extraordinary spectacle of so many people in the crowd raising their hands towards the casket whilst crying. As hundreds of photographers jostled to get the best angles, the palm trees remained motionless beneath the strong sunlight. The shutters on the bazaars and 'everything for 100 pesetas' shops, normally heaving on a Saturday, remained closed. Outside the town hall, Cádiz's great singer, Chano Lobato, looked shocked as Tomatito took up his position as a rear pall-bearer to take the coffin on its final journey. The crowd in short sleeved shirts and tee shirts, including women with children in their arms, gazed into space, while a boy climbed a tree for a better look; men and women fanned themselves, sobbing. Gypsy associations from all over Andalucía came to pay their respects; a banner from the gypsies of Palma de Río proclaimed that Camarón would always live in their hearts.

The intensity of the women's wailing grew as the coffin proceeded down the street; some amongst the crowd had tried to break through the cordon to catch one last glimpse of a small piece of history. Rancapino was forced to wipe the tears from his eyes, while El Pijote just gazed down at the floor. The gypsy flag was removed to reveal a highly polished wooden cask decorated with a crucifix, crafted in gold. As the coffin headed for the church of El Carmen, where the mass was scheduled to take place at half past ten o'clock, the police attempted to control not just the crowd, but the growing media scrum; microphones with cubes advertising the various radio stations of Spain were blindly thrust anywhere, in the hope of obtaining a vital clip from Camarón's family and his artistic admirers.

At the cemetery, where two of Camarón's other brothers were also buried, his widow Dolores Montoya continued to sob as the sound of earth falling from a shovel hit the wooden cask. The eminent flamenco writer José Luis Ortiz Nuevo, had managed to get close to the graveside and graphically described the moment when the coffin was lowered into the grave and covered with pieces of warped wood. Although reflecting on the sterile nature of the wood, the strength of the cries all around the cemetery informed Ortiz Nuevo that Camarón would live on for centuries.[20] The sobbing of Camarón's widow blended with the shouts of protest from the crowd outside who wanted to enter, but was held back. The face of Dolores Montoya, better known by her nickname of 'La Chispa', showed all the trials of the past sixteen years of marriage as the thud of the final clod of earth marked what would now become a new site of pilgrimage and the birth of the new and very different Camarón as a flamenco martyr. When the coffin was finally lowered into the pit, the tension became too much for La Chispa who left the scene with a group of women and delivered a strong message to the press. For the writer Paco Sevilla, some aspects of the passage of the coffin to its resting place had been undignified: 'Many among the hundreds of reporters and photographers were harassed and beaten, their equipment smashed. Camarón's wife, La Chispa, was widely quoted as screaming at the press amid her tears and anguish, "Shove it up your arse! My husband never wanted anything to do with you."'[21] The occasion had also become too much for Tomatito who had left earlier. The flamenco journal *El Candil*, reporting on the event months later, chose a more romantic approach to Camarón's departure: comparing him to a star of the cinema that had died young, a James Dean who had lived his life in the fast lane.[22] Interestingly, their reporter caught up with some of the singer's fans who were keen to tell the world outside of San Fernando that they should listen to the real Camarón; not the artist who made so many records with Paco de Lucía, but the voice to be heard on early 45s that Camarón cut with Antonio Arenas in 1968.

A week after Camarón's death, two producers, Allison Hughes and Mercedes de Prado, working for Spanish National Radio, started editing audio clips for a special tribute to Camarón for the English Language Service; a broadcast that was heard by aficionados worldwide on the short-wave bands. The audio clips they selected were very representative of the feelings of those who had gathered in San Fernando to spend two days mourning the loss of their idol. Fans and flamenco professionals were united in their sentiments: 'I can't believe it. Camarón hasn't died. He's gone to rest. His soul is as young as ever and lives in the heart of flamenco'. 'This is the one singer who could have happened in flamenco *cante*. There won't be another until God knows when'. 'We could already see that he wasn't well when we told him, "Stop, stop little man"'. 'God has taken Camarón so he'd sing for Him'.[23] The last comment prompted a somewhat humorous cartoon by Ricardo Martínez and Nacho Moreno in the Spanish daily *El Mundo*, which depicted Camarón seated in his usual singing position, clapping his hands ready to sing as God accompanies him with a lyre. Camarón exclaims 'Yes you can play like God, but like Tomatito, forget it'![24]

Now a new audience across the world was learning of the death of this remarkable gypsy: two fifteen-minute reels of magnetic tape revolved, informing listeners that Camarón had dominated the front pages of the Spanish press for three days, and Spanish television had even gone as far as to interrupt scheduled programming to re-run footage of his concerts. There were already plans in place to commission the statue that now stands opposite the Venta de Vargas in San Fernando.

Audiences for this programme were to learn a lot more than how Camarón had changed the course of flamenco's history, how he had modernised the *cante* and, more importantly, how for gypsies his death had elevated him from a successful popular hero to a saint. Interestingly, the producers of this programme hinted at Camarón's martyrdom when they suggested:

> but how much pain, or even luckless joy can a person take? What is the toll of this desperate duty? The life of a flamenco, whether he or she be a professional artist or not, is always maintained on the fringes of society, apart from the people who live by day, for the deep intimacy of this song needs the protection of night.

Despite these heartfelt words for the producers of the programme, the cause of his death was quite simply lung cancer and they were not prepared to speculate on air beyond what was written on his death certificate.

The earliest suggestions of Camarón's martyrdom could also be found in the leader column of the leading Spanish daily *El País* for Friday 3 July. The editor chose to focus on three stories, Sarajevo and Milosevic; reform of the EU and Maastrict; and the death of the 'Picasso of the Cante'.

These emotions were echoed in Britain the following week by James Kirkup's obituary in *The Independent*. For Kirkup it was:

> the cult of death that overshadows all passing fads and fashions in Spain, as can be seen in her morbidly ecstatic religious fiestas and dramatic passional processions at Eastertide; and in the vast convulsions of grief at the death of the great flamenco singer and guitarist Camarón de la Isla at the early age of 42. The whole of Spain has been devastated.

Camarón was only forty-one when he died and, as we will discover, did not 'start working the Chiclana bus, performing for a few pesetas to help the family budget' as Kirkup claimed; but myths have always attached themselves to Camarón. Kirkup's homage rightly claimed Miles Davis and Chick Corea as just two members of his illustrious fan club. The *Guardian* newspaper summed up the situation by simply saying: 'it is rare for a flamenco singer to attain the status of a national hero. It is even rarer for a gypsy to be the subject of universal mourning'. By Sunday 5 July, news of his death had reached the *Japan Times* which chose a more direct top line to bring its readers the news: 'Singer Camarón de la Isla, whose voice touched the depths of Spain's tortured, melancholic flamenco music, died Thursday in Barcelona'. The writer and flamencologist Félix Grande, reflecting the thoughts of the growing band of *Camaroneros*, summed up that tragic and tearful day of Saturday 4 July when he proclaimed, 'He was dead but not dead'.[25]

Within ten years Camarón would become more than just a saint; a Christ-like figure depicted with a beard that grew out of his chin at a horizontal angle. The gypsies had indeed, as the singer Enrique Morente commented, been given their first deity. Of more concern would be Camarón's emergence as a commodity, with his image selling everything from cushions to key rings and from cigarette lighters to ring tones. A devoted fan, Juan (a painter and decorator from Cádiz), told me years later that Camarón was now a 'gypsy prince, a god and now even more revered than the footballer Maradona'. For Juan, his drug addiction was irrelevant: 'I value Camarón neither for his life nor for his drugs. I value Camarón for his singing and his art'. Our conversation felt so distant from those summers in San Fernando where, as a schoolboy, Camarón could swim untroubled under the Zuazo Bridge. It seemed even further removed from the Spain of General Franco when, as a small child, he would dodge the *Guardia Civil* to sing in the local roadside inn, the Venta de Vargas.

2

A Gypsy of Cádiz Bay, 1950–1967

De Madrid al cielo, pero por La Isla se corta camino.
Juan Vargas

San Fernando, Cádiz, August 2000

A reel of magnetic recording tape had lain concealed in a drawer inside San Fernando's famous roadside inn, the Venta de Vargas, run by the avuncular Juan Vargas. For over three decades, the reel of four-track tape, protected by a rusting tin and placed inside a box, had remained untouched.[1] Thirty-three years earlier, María Picardo had relaxed in this inn with the young Camarón, whose company she enjoyed. After all, it was her bar and Camarón was a good neighbour from the Las Callejuelas district of San Fernando and a frequent under-aged visitor to the *Venta*.[2] Soon, with the money that Joselillo Picardo had obtained by pawning an item of jewellery, Camarón would be heading for the lure of Madrid and its more sophisticated nightlife; with just a potato *tortilla* or Spanish omelette to keep him company on the journey.[3] He would no longer be stoking the fire in his father's forge before an all-night session on his guitar, as he entertained the customers who played cards and dice until seven in the morning.

The patrons of this establishment were more interested in the delicious thin wafers of *jabugo*-cured ham and the *tortillitas de camarones* that were always on offer, than a reel of tape. The quality and flavour of María Picardo's 'flamenco style' food was known well beyond the province of Cádiz and the house speciality was always shrimps with onions, cooked in flour with just a hint of parsley. In a couple of years the tape would be unearthed by María Picardo's nephew Manuel and found to contain a precious moment from the very hot summer of 1967, before Camarón ceased to be the gypsy boy singer that the drunken *señioritos* would send for to perform and later pay him 100 pesetas at the end of the night. Wrapped in an oily textured plastic, the recordings offered a unique insight into the teenage Camarón before he embarked on the career that would ultimately lead to his martyrdom.[4] During that summer of 1967, although he had already performed as a singer in a pub in Málaga, Camarón had little sense of where his forthcoming move, from the sleepy town of San Fernando to the bustle of capital city life in Madrid would lead him.

The owner of the inn, Juan Vargas, was typical of most men in the sixties: having a keen desire to own his own tape recorder, with which to preserve for posterity the legendary stars who, like the giant of flamenco singing Manolo Caracol, were regular late-night drinkers in his unique establishment which had been granted a twenty-four hour licence.[5] Juan had obtained the Phillips recorder from Holland and it came with instructions on how to make recordings of professional quality.[6] The release of these lost songs in February 2005 was to further enhance the mythical status that had grown up around Camarón, and also offer some vital evidence in any thorough search for the real Camarón de la Isla. After the sessions were completed, Juan Vargas hardly ever bothered to play the tapes again even though the sixteen-year-old Camarón had been very keen to have the recordings. He had left in a hurry for Barcelona without this testament to a time in his life when he was happy and at ease with himself.[7] The tape was finally handed over to Camarón's producer, Ricardo Pachón, and the writer Enrique Montiel, who carefully peeled away the plastic like an onion skin, to reveal the concealed treasure that was later described as a miracle.[8] Frozen in time was not just the young Camarón's voice but also various flamenco artists whom Juan Vargas had recorded from the radio. Having obtained the tape Pachón and Montiel then eagerly set off for Seville in search of a machine that could play the reels and found a collector of old equipment who assisted them in dubbing the four hours of material into a digital file.[9]

The launch of *Camarón en la Venta de Vargas* by the Universal record company on Monday 21 February 2005 would give some journalists another opportunity to rehash the many myths about the life of Camarón. It was time to retell the story of the gypsy boy from a poor family who was forced to sing on trains and buses for spare change to support his large family.[10]

But on the album, we did at last discover the real Camarón: he demonstrated just how at ease he was at singing the old songs of flamenco to the accompaniment of the crickets in the trees around the Venta de Vargas. As well as his voice, the sound of a lorry passing the front door heading for Cádiz city centre was now preserved for posterity. It was the summer of 1967, and Camarón was about to swap his worn corduroy jacket for a sharp grey suit and embark on international tours as a member of the Dolores Vargas company. He would appear alongside legends including the dancer La Singla and the singer Juanito Valderama. As the reels of Juan Vargas' tape recorder rotated, Camarón sang his heart out, accompanying himself with a guitar on occasions in this bar dubbed 'the temple of flamenco song and sherry since the thirties'.[11] The recording proved that Camarón was not 'an unpolished diamond', as Antonio Sánchez Pecino had described him when he arrived in Madrid.[12] Antonio, the one-time cloth salesman, amateur guitar player and father of Paco de Lucía would later snap up Camarón's signature for an extended recording contract; despite insisting that he was 'very young and green and by no means a complete cantaor'.

The Venta de Vargas had been Camarón's second home for as long as he could remember. He was always comfortable in its traditional bar: decorated with paintings depicting bullfighting scenes, shelves buckling under the weight of hundreds of bottles of *fino* and *manzanilla*. Sat on one of the inns' distinctive green wooden chairs and gazing at the framed photographs of San Fernando's estuaries he would dream of becoming a *torero* and fighting a bull in the local ring. He had spent his childhood singing all night until six in the morning in the patio, to receive his reward of *veinte duros* from the wealthy clients.[13] But there were occasions when, although he was in need of funds, he would not sing for money. A local butcher once offered him fifteen pesetas to sing some *cantes* but Camarón declined the offer, only to have to borrow seven pesetas for the fare to Cádiz to visit his friend and mentor Rancapino.[14] As a child Camarón spent many hours practicing to become a matador, dressed in a polka-dot shirt and spearing a makeshift bull with two horns mounted on a bicycle wheel that was driven towards him. On one occasion, when he was only twelve, he borrowed without asking Rancapino's bullfighting suit, so that he could play a joke posing as a bullfighter. The inseparable pair were frequent visitors to the corrals where the fighting bulls were kept and they would both practice their skills with the *muleta* while dreaming of the *estocada*. If he could not fulfill his dream of becoming a *torero* and triumphing in the *corridas*, as bullfighting constantly dominated his thoughts, then he would make it as a professional flamenco singer. As a child his obsession with bullfighting was illustrated by the hours he would spend posing for photos dressed in the classic 'suit of lights' and as a teenager he participated in several bullfights. Later, as a young man, he would often play-act in the street: beckoning an imaginary beast towards him. Ultimately after an unpleasant encounter with a bull, his involvement with the art of *la Lidia* would be left to his friendship with the bullfighter Curro Romero. This love of bullfighting and flamenco was natural for a gypsy born into a poor family. Camarón's fate had been sealed the day he was born and as a gypsy what other routes to fame and fortune were available to him other than the bullring and the flamenco nightclub.

San Fernando, December 1950

José Monje Cruz, later to become better known by his nickname of El Camarón de la Isla, was born on 5 December on the ancient and historic Island of San Fernando; a port that benefited greatly from Andalucía's busy trade in the eighteenth century. His mother, Juana Cruz Castro, gave birth to eight children during her troubled life; all of whom developed the skills needed to sing the *cante* or flamenco song. She was born in 1916 and represented a very important link to the artists who performed the flamenco songs that flourished in the nineteenth century, while his father, Juan Luis Monje, was also a competent singer. Camarón was her seventh child and his appearance as 'a blond and pale boy, almost transparent like a shrimp' was to prompt his uncle to give him, and the world of flamenco, a name that would ultimately redefine the art.[15] In his last interview for Spanish television Camarón explained why he was named after a 'shrimp':

> I was given the nickname by my uncle, who was very witty and called 'Joseico'. He was an old gypsy from San Fernando and he nicknamed us all. He nicknamed 'La Perla de Cádiz', he called me 'Camarón' and he gave nicknames to all my brothers. He gave me the nickname of Camarón because I was very fair-haired. He was always saying Camarón, Camarón and so Camarón it was.[16]

The tourist brochures are keen to remind us that San Fernando is closely linked with Spanish naval history and derives much of its character from its churches modelled on the baroque style, that stand close to its estuaries. If you take the M-010 bus from Cádiz, passing the Cortadura and follow the railway line, you will be greeted first by a contemporary fountain fashioned out of rusty metal, before you reach the more mature neoclassic architecture that influenced San Fernando's buildings. The writer, Gerald Howson, worked in San Fernando during the late fifties and spent much time observing this town of eight thousand inhabitants. Howson recorded several graphic details of San Fernando's army and naval culture, with its 'barracks, factories, military drilling-grounds, whitewashed churches and a pleasant main square walled on one side by a huge yellow late Renaissance Town Hall'.[17] But he also unintentionally hinted at a key location for the start of any search for Camarón. Howson reported that: 'In another district, long since abandoned to the very poor, tumbledown courtyards and sheds cluster around the small red bullring and swarm with gypsies, beggars and thieves'.[18] Camarón's father, Juan Luis Monje, was one such gypsy who had moved his forge close to San Fernando's bullring. The forge had originally been at No.5 in the Calle Orlando, but he later moved to the Calle de la Amagura where it has now been lovingingly restored.[19] As well as its gypsy heritage, Howson also pointed to San Fernando's links with two well known classical myths: informing his readers that the island had also been called the Isle of Erythia or even *Aphrodisias*:

> Here Perseus came to the grove of the hideous Gorgons and slew Medusa, whose gaze turned everyone who saw her to stone; and here, in the performance of his tenth labour; Hercules slew the three-bodied giant Geryon, and drove away the Red Oxen, after dividing Calpe and Abyla – the 'Pillars of Hercules.[20]

Away from the myths, we know that gypsies had arrived in Cádiz Bay over a thousand years before Camarón's birth, but the terrain and the people of San Fernando were shaped as recently as two centuries ago; by the powerful economy created by the fleet of Spanish Armada. Many of the tourists who go on the 'Armada Trail' that provides San Fernando with much needed income from visitors, are unaware of the town's historical salt industry. An industry which provokes nostalgic images of all those hot summers: drying the sea salt which lies on the mud waiting for the winter harvest.[21] Camarón is now one of the town's main tourist attractions, rivalling even the sixteenth-century San Romualto castle and the Royal Naval Institute with its important observatory. Against this historic backdrop of one of Spain's poorest regions, which was still recovering from the devastating harvest of 1945, the first of Camarón's forty-one years was about to unfold.[22] His relatively short life would bridge the austere years of Franco to the vibrant, permissive and open Spain; from the impoverished and demoralised country that existed under the dictator in the fifties, to the growth of the new liberal Spain of Juan Carlos II in the late seventies and early eighties.

Camarón was born at number 29 Calle del Carmen in the district of Las Callejuelas. A house which the writers Luis Fernández Zaurín and José Candado Calleja interestingly pointed out was also the birthplace of the Lion's Island's other famous singer, El Chato de la Isla, who left Cádiz for the lure of Madrid, as Camarón would in time.[23] But the nickname of 'la Isla' had long been linked to some of flamenco's greatest singers, including El Viejo de la Isla and another singer from the nineteenth century, José López Domingo, whose name appeared on posters around the turn of the century as El Niño de la Isla.[24] The island's houses around the working-class district of Las Callejuelas were populated mainly by fishermen's families and the descendants of retired seamen. No.29 was the location for a very basic home where geraniums grew out of rusting paint pots and old boilers on the patio. Traditional iron grills protected the windows while the *azulejos* or tiles, which are synonymous with this region, decorated the frames of the doors. The walls of its collection of out-houses were painted with whitewash, while sheets of corrugated iron offered protection from rain that could be very heavy in December and January. Blinds were stretched across the patio to form a roof, keeping out the very strong sunlight, while close by the sound of the hammer beating an anvil would have been heard reverberating to the accompaniment of Camarón's father's singing at his forge at 21 Calle de La Amargura.

Camarón was never in any doubt that his great gift of singing came from his mother but the loss of his father, who was also a singer, would remain with him:

> In our house everyone sung, but not professionally. My father sang his gypsy *soleá* and *seguiriyas* but his asthma was choking him. He didn't get it at the forge. He got it earlier, during the years of hunger working on the streetcars in the day and nightshifts in the rain, and so, often soaked to the bone.[25]

It was here, in the San Fernando of the fifties, that the young *Pijote Chico*, as he was initially called after his elder brother, first heard the singing of his mother whom he adored.

My mother sang with incredible personality. I could say l learned everything from her – from her, and from all the old artists. Everyone on the island learned from those who passed through and stopped at our house. Many nights I stayed up all night to listen, concentrating on the details. I've done the same old thing all my life, learning from the old artists, going back to the sources.[26]

Camarón would later describe his mother's voice as having a unique quality and monochrome footage of Juana la Canastera singing on the local beach leaves little doubt as to who was the most formative influence on his singing career. To watch the expression on her face as she sang *por bulerías* with such impeccable phrasing is to rediscover the young Camarón and understand where his trademark melismas originated. He inherited his mother's gift of singing and shortly before he died said 'you can learn to dance, you can learn to play the guitar, but singing is something you are born with. I think in my case, when I was born, I was born singing instead of crying'.

Camarón was also heavily influenced by his childhood hero, the singer La Perla de Cádiz, who on a visit to hear him sing in Madrid exclaimed that he had taken all her songs and could now sing them better than her![27] Camarón never forgot his debt to La Perla, and on his *Te lo dice Camarón* album of 1986 he paid tribute to her and his other hero Antonio El Chaqueta. His words expressed his sadness that the flamenco clubs, or *peñas flamencas*, did not have any photographs of his two childhood heroes on their walls. This situation has subsequently been rectified with a very large building just off Cádiz's seafront dedicated to the memory of La Perla de Cádiz.

San Fernando, Wednesday 9 November 2005

I went in search of Camarón's birthplace in the Calle del Carmen; although no longer the poor neighbourhood of Las Callejuelas that it was in the fifties, it has not benefited from the gentrification that other parts of San Fernando have experienced in recent years. Everyone had their own story to tell about Camarón and it appeared that the citizens of San Fernando could not agree on the exact location of his birthplace. Did the house lie off the right-hand side of the Calle Real, looking across the estuaries, or was it on the left; nobody seemed to know? The birthplace of San Fernando's most famous son was not as well known as I would have expected and after several wrong turnings which took me past a driving school and a grocery store trading under 'El Carmen', I headed for a bar. I asked for directions over an *anis del mono*, that strong spirit made from aniseed in Badalona that comes in the ridged bottle with a charming red label depicting a half man and monkey.

You could easily walk past the unremarkable residence of 29 Calle del Carmen, if it was not for the impressive ceramic plaque that declares it part of the official *Ruta de Camarón* with an explanation that this is the house where he was born and how his blonde hair led him to be named after the Spanish word for a shrimp. The plaque also features a sculptured relief of Camarón as he sings beneath the crescent moon, his left hand outstretched in the characteristic way as he emphasised the emotion and passion of his words. I had discovered the modest dwelling with its door inset, protecting it from the strong autumnal sun and framed by painted stone rectangle. Beneath numerous electric cables and high above the door was the number twenty-nine, painted over in whitewash. As I looked away from the door, down the road towards the estuaries that this area is renowned for, I thought back to Camarón's childhood and how he used to like to swim under the Zuazo Bridge. An old man wearing a beret similar to the one Camarón's father used to wear interrupted my daydreaming. He just wanted to know why I was looking at the building, but he knew anyway as a few people usually came here looking for Camarón's birthplace. Having satisfied his curiosity he shuffled off down the street in his slippers to have his usual morning *carajillo*, a black coffee laced with Spanish brandy and sometimes *anís* to wash down a portion of *churros* oozing with fat.

I had learnt that there was very little of Camarón to be discovered close to the house where he was born, apart from some tacky souvenirs. It would soon be time for lunch and I was in the land of the finest fish: *choco en amarillo* or cuttlefish in a saffron sauce; deep fried dogfish or hake in a batter made from cumin, oregano, garlic, vinegar, olive oil, a hint of sherry and that local sea salt. Most species of fish were on offer at the busy restaurant in the heart of Cádiz's narrow streets at the Plaza de las Flores. I decided against a trip into Cádiz and headed for one of Europe's finest beaches, the Playa de la Victoria, to enjoy some fresh sea urchins with a plate of salty palm hearts, while taking in the view of the vast Atlantic Ocean as I sipped on a cool *rebujito* made from dry sherry and Seven-up.

Andalucía, 1950–1967

Camarón's birth in 1950 marked five years of peace in Europe after the conclusion of the Second World War and fourteen years since the outbreak of the Spanish Civil War. It was now time for the Jesuits, who greatly influenced government thinking, to attempt to rebrand the image of the New Francoist Spain.[28] The conclusion of the Second World War in 1945 had seen the knives coming out for Franco, with France closing its border with Spain and the United Nations calling for its members to shut their embassies in the Iberian Peninsula. Six years after Franco's triumph, would Spain continue as a dictatorship or would the Bourbon monarchy be restored? The answer to this question would lie in the very skillful work that a Jesuit-influenced government would do to airbrush the image of the New Spain of the Dictator.[29]

As Camarón's parents were preparing for Christmas 1950, and another child to feed, General Francisco Franco's position was looking far more comfortable. A deal had been done with the father of Spain's current King to have the young Juan Carlos attend a Spanish school, enabling Franco to hint that the boy would eventually succeed him and that Spain was a type of monarchist state.[30] France was also back on side and by the early fifties Spain offered useful location opportunities for military bases, two of which would be built in Andalucía – Rota in Cádiz province and Morón de la Frontera in Seville. The only concern of Franco was to keep the army chiefs sweet; while the wellbeing of the country at large was a very low priority. The plight of the Spanish people at this time has been highlighted by the historian Juan Lalaguna, who painted a grim picture of the first decade of Francoist Spain, often dubbed 'the Hungry Years':

> There is no dearth of examples, especially south of Madrid, of the scale of scarcity and deprivation unparalleled in Spain's living memory. The long-suffering mass of landless peasants were not even allowed the forlorn hope of escaping to the towns and cities. During those years, it was the people from the towns who tried to move back to the country in the hope of at least procuring the basic means of subsistence. One of the foremost economic exponents of the new regime wrote, in 1941, that the per capita income of the population had sunk to nineteenth-century levels. Despite food rationing from 1939 to 1951, even the basic necessities of life, such as bread grain, were in dire need.[31]

Despite this depressing portrait, Enrique Montiel, who was a contemporary of Camarón, described the San Fernando of the fifties as quite prosperous; 'La Isla in 1950 was a medium-sized city and was, in a certain way, well-to-do. The state owned company Bazán possessed various dry-docks in

the area that ensured plentiful jobs, and the San Carlos Naval Works manufactured motors and weapons for the navy'. As Montiel points out, there
was always the salt works where Camarón's father also found employment
when he needed it. Other commentators have even viewed his father as
being part of a 'gypsy aristocracy', because he was a blacksmith who owed
his forge while his wife's skills at making baskets enabled the singer to be
born into an elite group of gypsies.[32]

Montiel claims that the local kids were happy because of the pleasant environment of salt flats and estuaries that surrounded them. In need
of cooling down in the hot summers that raged during his childhood,
Camarón had already noticed a certain roadside inn as he carried his towel
under his arm:

> When I was ten years old, many days I went to take a swim by the Zuazo
> bridge that passed in front of the tavern. Little by little I earned Juan Vargas'
> trust. He really liked the way I sang, and from time to time he'd have me
> earn a few pesetas singing at the tavern. The civil guards didn't let me work
> because I was too young, but if someone wanted to hear me at any hour, he'd
> send for me.

Although Camarón claimed to enjoy these diversions from school, he was
later to complain, in the lyrics of his song *Otra Galaxia*, that while the
other children were studying at school his childhood was spent at the forge
working on the anvil with the nail and hook. Camarón did attend a private school run by Carmelite brothers, but he found himself relegated to
the basement, coming from a family who were unable to afford the fees!
He received a basic education that included being prepared for his first
communion. School held little interest for him as he was fascinated by San
Fernando's rich environment and would even bunk off school to play in the
slaughterhouse.[33]

Camarón had been visiting the roadside inn know as the Venta de Vargas
from 1958 and in that year met the singer Alonso Núñez Núñez, better
known as Rancapino, who was to be a very important influence and lifelong
friend.[34] Juan Vargas had bought the building, built in 1924 and formerly
known as the *Venta Eritaña* from a bullfighter from San Fernando called
Perico el Tato in 1935.[35] Unusually for the Franco period, the inn had permission to be open and sell alcohol twenty-four hours a day and was almost
a training school for flamenco song, where gypsies regularly performed for

the *señioritos* or toffs for a few *pesetas*. The *Venta* was allowed such privileges, as it was a well-established stop for people travelling to Cádiz and its status was also derived from having a toilet and a telephone! On most nights Juan Vargas, dressed in his trademark tie and cardigan, would entertain the customers with his own songs. Camarón's first visits to the Venta de Vargas would be very risky in this climate, where *Guardia Civil* ruthlessly ruled Andalucía and would have come down very hard on a young gypsy earning money by singing in a licensed establishment.

By singing from the age of eight in this famous inn, Camarón came into contact with many of the great gypsy singers of the time, including Fernando 'Terremoto' and El Borrico. He was very much a child prodigy, having already made his singing debut on Radio Cádiz, but at the tender age of nine he was to encounter the ultimate gypsy singer: Manolo Caracol, who had won a prize for singing at the 1922 Granada Concurso when only thirteen. Caracol was much more than a giant of flamenco, as he had dominated Spanish cinema throughout the forties and early fifties. Born in Seville, Caracol was also the legendary partner of Lola Flores, another screen star, and everyone from bullfighters to politicians would queue up to have their photograph taken with him. In 1959 Manolo Caracol was at the height of his powers and his meeting with Camarón was to prove memorable for all the wrong reasons. Camarón took his recollections of his first meeting with Caracol in 1962 to the grave:

> when I was little, Juan Vargas told Caracol to take me to work in Madrid, and Caracol said, No, this little blonde can't sing. And I don't know what else. But it stayed engraved in my mind, and I could barely sing for him when he came to see me later in Madrid, night after night, also dying without ever being able to get me to sing in his tablao.[36]

Servando, a former professional singer from Cádiz now in his late seventies, still remembers what a precocious talent Camarón was as a young boy, with the ability to sing like a sixty-year-old man. Servando told me one of his most vivid memories of an incident that occurred when he was having a drink with José Barita who used to take fighting cocks to the Americas. As they shared a bottle of wine a very young Camarón turned up and was immediately asked to sing a *fandanguito*. As his mother Juana waited, Camarón was promised a few pesetas for his art while the two men tucked into a plate of seafood that the young singer had been offered and had declined. Within minutes Servando and José Barita would be on their way to hospital to have their stomachs pumped out as Camarón went home with five pesetas in his pocket! Shortly after this Camarón was rarely to be seen in Cádiz and San Fernando without the company of Rancapino and they would often be spotted in Manzanares in the bar *El Burladero*. An establishment owned by the well-known Agustin 'el Melú' whose sister had links to flamenco's queen of the dance, Pastora Imperio.

Camarón's destiny would not be blown off course by the snub he received from Manolo Caracol, as he would put his talent to the test entering a flamenco singing competition in Montilla, Córdoba. He gave a very good account of himself and as he left his school days behind him, there could be only one direction for his trajectory. He had already gained so much experience knocking around with the cool Rancapino, who wore shades when singing, and El Pinto who taught by example. By 1963 his unpleasant childhood experience with Caracol was, for the moment forgotten, as he began to establish himself by giving performances at the *Teatro de las Cortés* in San Fernando with his older brothers, watched by a very emotional mother.[37] In 1963 he travelled to Andalucía's biggest event of the year, the annual Spring fair in Seville, which attracts thousands of visitors and the finest flamenco artists to its hundreds of *casetas* or temporary elaborately decorated marquees. Rancapino, his ever-present companion had gone with him to sing in the *caseta* of the Venta de Vargas. Camarón was now mixing with some of the all-time great flamenco artists, including the gypsy singers Antonio Mairena and Juan Talega and the awesome Lola Flores. Within four years, such was his talent that he would be working in Madrid and undertaking a tour outside of Spain in Cairo.[38]

As the first blossoms of the spring of 1964 appeared, people in many parts of Andalucía were starting to talk about a blond gypsy boy from the island of San Fernando who had an outstanding talent. Yet it was to be another two years before his professional career really started to take off with regular engagements. His charisma and potential as a rising star was also picked up by the director Rovira Beleta, who cast Camarón in the 1964 film of *El Amor Brujo* featuring master of the dance, Antonio Gades. It was to be the first of several films that he would appear in although, due to his premature death, he would not be featured in Carlos Saura's *Flamenco*, a historic snapshot of flamenco's greatest artists in the early nineties. By 1965 Camarón had found more stable work in Málaga with the company of Miguel de los Reyes and in 1966 he became an established member of the *cuadro* of

Miguel de los Reyes, working in the *Taberna Gitana de Málaga*, where he spent some crucial time with another of his formative mentors, the singer Antonio el Chaqueta. Camarón greatly admired El Chaqueta and paid him the ultimate compliment on his album *Te lo Dice Camarón*, by demanding to know why there were not any photographs in the flamenco clubs of his late hero.

In January 1966 Camarón faced a major setback when he was told of his father's death and returned to San Fernando. Camarón believed that his father had died from an asthma attack, but Enrique Montiel has suggested that it was alcohol that finished him off. Juan Luis Monje had been a much-loved gentle person who was often seen in the squares of San Fernando looking for work. As well as being a devastating blow, his father's death would mean that he would emerge as an important breadwinner for the family as he needed to work to support his mother and her large family. He would now combine singing with working in his father's forge, while his brother Manuel emerged as his new father figure. His mother Juana survived this difficult period by finding extra work 'cleaning stairs' and 'sweeping some bars of San Fernando'.[39] Soon Camarón, through his very special talent, would be bringing home 'more than a day's pay' which some have estimated at a remarkable two to four thousand pesetas a day; an incredible amount for Spain in the late sixties![40] The claims that he liked to spend as quickly as he earned were not evident in these early days as he used to save his money and hide it under the guttering in the forge.[41]

North London, 25 February 1967

Having started my education in a similar way to Camarón, being taught by the nuns of the La Sante Union Convent, followed by the less kind Christian Brothers at Saint Aloysius, I was about to embark on an adventure that would ultimately lead me to Camarón and Spain. Owen's school in 1967 was dominated by a guitar culture with Bert Jansch and John Renbourn as the two key luminaries of the acoustic guitar, and I just had to be part of it. They became my role models, but a flamenco maestro would shortly replace them and there would be no more time for *subbutteo* table football. After many years of begging for a guitar to play, I was duly rewarded with a Russian instrument bought in Camden Passage for a fiver. It was difficult to master and lessons at school were not helping so I was sent to a master of the flamenco guitar for private lessons with a new guitar. And on a cold February day, I was introduced to the basic chord shapes for flamenco and a new love affair that was to change my life.

These were exciting days as I turned up each Sunday, after serving mass and doing two paper rounds, to learn the intricacies of the flamenco guitar including its techniques and the all important *compás* or rhythm. These early lessons with Tony Clinton and his Spanish wife Josephine in a North London basement were to launch me on my journey in search of Camarón.

As Camarón was preparing to settle permanently in Madrid, Tony was showing me how to play *alegrías*, Camarón's favourite flamenco form that originated in his home province of Cádiz. I was about to swap my Bert Jansch records for albums of the flamenco guitar maestros, as Niño Ricardo and Sabicas became my idols. Soon the *cante* or flamenco song would become an obsession as I listened to the songs of Camarón on worn-out and badly scratched vinyl discs. His voice would transport me from a council flat in North London to the heart of colonial Seville and the Spain of General Franco; to discover the home of the Spanish Armada and the cove of Trafalgar where Napoleon met his defeat in those waters off the ancient city of Cádiz.

Back in the swinging London of the sixties, seasoned professionals from Spain, and Englishmen with Spanish pseudonyms were still performing at Antonio's Restaurant in Long Acre and the basement bar of the Chandos near Trafalgar Square would soon have a resident flamenco guitar player. The Spanish refugees from Franco's regime had originally settled around Notting Hill, in areas like Westbourne Grove and Westbourne Park and enclaves of flamenco had been established in the most unlikely places. In the early day flamenco fans would go to the Linden café in Notting Hill Gate, Hemmings in the King's Road or Torinos in Soho. London aficionados received a boost in 1951 when Antonio Mairena sang to full houses at the Stoll theatre. Mairena had come as part of the Lusillo ballet company and was to certainly enjoy himself in the capital. From 1954 the Margarita in Cork Street had echoed to the sound of flamenco with Rafael Rodríguez and Alberto Vélez as regular performers. Gerald Howson had told me that 'it was run by a man called Blanche who employed a dancer who was half Chinese and had studied flamenco in Madrid'.

Howson fondly remembered those tiny pockets of flamenco in London before he left for Spain in the fifties:

> The espresso coffee bars created a free and easy atmosphere where artists like
> Enrique Bequerano [the cousin of Mario Basilisco's uncle Lionel] and myself

would visit and start performing. If we had a singer with us then there would be some *cante* and nobody objected. We might even get paid though we were not that good at flamenco then, but nobody else knew about it either. Rafael Rodriguez worked at the Acapulco and his guitarist was another Englishman called Freddie Phillips. After recovering from my jaundice I visited Rafael. He asked me whether I could accompany and I replied a bit. As a result we worked at the Acapulco for a year and then moved on to another club in south Kensington and Knightsbridge. It was a very smart club visited by film stars and I played there once a week with Paco Victory and other singers'.[42]

I would become familiar, as a child, with all these names and the stars of the touring companies who all wanted to play London in the sixties. This was the golden era for the dancers Antonio and Pilar López at the Savoy and Cambridge theatres, who would soon be joined in the swinging capital by artists from Madrid's Zambra club with the singers Manuel Vargas, Pericón de Cádiz and their guitarist Andrés Heredia. It was also the time of a Dr Alec Martínez, a true flamenco aficionado, whose London home was frequented by numerous artists including the singer Antonio Mairena who returned to record an album there.

By the sixties, flamenco in London had found a new home at the Troubador club, where I was to play many years later on my return from seeing Camarón perform in Spain. A man had approached me during the interval, as I took a break from playing a set at this legendary folk venue. He introduced himself as Glyn Davies who, as Gonzalo Díaz, had launched the first flamenco sessions at the Troubadour in the early sixties!

When Howson finally left San Fernando he painted a picture of the London flamenco scene as he went in search of a singer: 'I went to his house, in the sordid slum by Westborne Park, and together we took employment – he the cantaor and I as the guitarist – in a coffee bar frequented by Greeks, Turks, Arabs, German au-pair girls, and Spanish exiles and expatriates, near the Tottenham Court Road'.[43] Howson may have considered Westborne Park a slum but he was even more concerned about the Cádiz guitarist and friend he was leaving behind:

who lived in a room twelve feet by ten feet, including kitchen, with a piece of rotting boarding for a window and crumbling brick-dust for its sill; who slept in the same bed with his father, who was ninety, his mother, who was seventy-eight, his wife, his three daughters and his son.

At the same time Camarón was growing up in very similar conditions sharing a cramped bedroom with seven other siblings.

San Fernando, August 1936

To go in search for the real 'El Camarón de la Isla' one must revisit the world of his parents: his mother Juana Cruz Castro, the *canastera* who weaved baskets and other objects from reeds and his father, Juan Luis Monje, the blacksmith. They would have lived through the horrors of the Spanish Civil War, or revolution as some historians preferred to call it. As gypsies they would have regarded the conflict as '*una guerra de los payos*', a white man's war that they preferred to keep out of. The early days of the uprising were particularly unpleasant in Andalucía, southern Spain, as the historian Paul Preston had noted. Preston viewed the 'agrarian war in the south' as the fiercest conflict of the Spanish Civil War because once the fighting had started there would be no control over the 'social hatreds' that lay just beneath the surface and the region would soon witness some 'horrific cruelties'.[44] At the outbreak of the Spanish Civil War Camarón's mother was twenty-three years of age and his father twenty-five.

Before examining the fate of prominent gypsies, at the time of the uprising in that summer of 1936, it is important to understand the social and economic situation that the Second Republic faced on coming to power in 1931. Certain gypsies, known for their flamenco artistry and the trades of the smithy and the slaughterhouse, would face execution at the hands of the Nationalists. At the bottom of the pile were the agricultural workers of Camarón's region of Andalucía who were paid just enough to exist and suffered all the insecurity of the typical day labourer. Over two-million of Spain's workers who toiled the land did not own any land of their own and in the Andalusian capital of Seville things were at their most extreme, with five per cent of the landowners owning seventy-two per cent of the land.[45] Add to this the power of the church and army and one cannot imagine the plight of farm workers or gypsies in 1920's oligarchic Spain. The historians Broué and Témime have documented a stark portrait of the country that Camarón's parents grew up in as children; 'Spain, at the beginning of the twentieth century, was an anachronism of the West: she was an oasis of tradition in an increasingly uniform world, and her masters were proud of having presented her *Hispanidad* in spite of modern political and socio-economic trends'. For these authors, Spain at the turn of the century continued to be a 'Semi colonial Country' and 'was a basically agricultural country' with 'more than 70% of her active population was engaged in agriculture. The Spanish peasant used the same implements as his forebears in the Middle Ages: throughout most of the country the hand plow was preferred to the horse plow'.[46]

While Andalucía's farming remained primitive, its political conscience was far more developed as the residents of the village of Casa Viejas in Camarón's province of Cádiz in 1933 demonstrated. The background to the most brutal repression of a peasant uprising that led to many fatal casualties could be traced to the suffering of the previous year. Preston's research had revealed that during 1932 'four out of five workers in Casas Viejas were unemployed for most of the year, dependent on charity, occasional road mending and scouring the countryside for wild asparagus and rabbits'. Steep rises in the price of bread would be the final catalyst that would finally convince the workers that the earlier call for a revolution by the anarchist trade union was justified. They were to encounter a vicious and bloody response that resulted in the deaths of twenty-four villagers.[47] While the Anarchists had been successful in encouraging the peasants to revolt; their reward would be further hardship and the burning of their houses. As the Rebels landed in southern Spain this tradition of militancy would be found particularly in two areas renowned for flamenco and home to gypsies – Triana in Seville and San Fernando in Cádiz. Triana, which proudly lies on the east side of the River Guadalquivir facing Seville, saw its people bombarded with cannon fire and then slaughtered by the knives of the soldiers of the Moroccan Legion. The long established gypsy and working class community in Granada also fought hard on the night of 20 July.[48] Visiting Granada's architectural jewels today including the Alhambra, it is hard to imagine the brutality that was required to finally suppress the largely unarmed residents of the El Albaicín.

Andalucía had proudly displayed her tradition of anarchism that flourished throughout her regions but the ideology of Communism also had a foothold in Málaga, Seville and more importantly Camarón's backyard where its membership was very strong. Southern Spain would only be involved in the war for a matter of days but it would have to endure the terror that followed for decades. Despite this disruption the leading flamenco artists of the thirties continued to make records during the last years of the Second Republic and throughout the Spanish Civil War. The recording studios in Barcelona and San Sebastián would resonate to the golden sound of the voices of Antonio Mairena, Tomás Pavón, Manolita de Jerez and the darling of her generation, La Niña de los Peines.

Banks of the River Guadalquivir, Seville, Tuesday 14 July 1936

On a very hot July afternoon, the tug *Pastor y Landero*, festooned in the green and white flag of Andalucía, was navigating southern Spain's great river, known by the locals as the Río Betis.[49] Her sails were also white to match the green rigging and she attracted much attention from people on either side of the riverbank. Angel Sody de Rivas recorded that on board were the guests of Don Blas Infante Perez and members of the *Junta Liberalista*, celebrating their success in promoting regional ideas for an Andalusian statute based on assurances made in the Spanish Parliament in 1933. The Andalusian Assembly had met for the first time on 5 July, but the party was blissfully unaware of a flight that had left London's Croydon Airport on 11 July.[50] While its pilot, Captain Bebb, was also unsure about the exact nature of his mission, within days, his flight would change the lives of the guests on the tug and create the unique conditions that allowed Camarón to conquer the world of flamenco when General Franco's grip on Spain finally weakened. Bebb's confidential mission was to fly General Franco from the Canaries to Morocco to enable him to take control of the army of Africa and invade Spain.

Ángel Sody de Rivas later revisited the events of that summer's day in Andalucía, as the locals enjoyed the sunshine on the land surrounding the waters of the great river Guadalquivir. Diego del Gastor, one of the great gypsy guitarists, was sitting on the banks of the great river that flows through Seville, unaware of the tragedy and bloodshed that was about to unfold.[51] In time he would become a role model for Camarón and a musician much admired by Camarón's eldest son, Luis.[52] Diego appreciated how happy the tug's passengers were from the songs that were being sung on-board and the *sevillanas* that were being danced. Soon he would be facing execution because, unusually for a gypsy at this time, he held certain political views that brought him to the attention of the Rebels who took Seville's neighbouring town of Morón de la Frontera at midday on 25 July.

Cádiz, Triana and Morón de la Frontera, Tuesday 9 July 1936

The reaction of the trades unions in Cádiz to the Nationalist uprising was to start a general strike on 19 July, as they had heard of how neighbouring Algeciras had fallen with the workers unarmed. Within a day, all resistance in Cádiz was crushed as the army changed sides, but things were different in San Fernando where:

the crew of the destroyer *Churruca*, which had taken a *tabor* of Moroccans to Cádiz on the nineteenth, revolted on the twentieth and shot its officers. Then the crews of the *Almirante Valdes* and the *Sánchez Barcaiztegui* followed suit and left Melilla for Cartagena. In San Fernando, the crews of the two gun boats and a cruiser were eventually crippled by coastal batteries, and the *Almirante Cevera*, immobilized by repair, and the *España*, out of ammunition, were recaptured from the sailors in Ferrol'.[53]

Camarón's parents found themselves very much in the middle of a war that did not concern gypsies, as low ranking sailors began organising themselves and executing their officers. This resistance was to temporarily hinder the Nationalists, by disrupting reinforcements and communications, as Camarón's parents waited to see which group of *payos* would ultimately take control of Spain.

Morón de la Frontera, which would soon be next on Franco's list of towns to crush, is the most flamenco place I have ever visited. For the majority of its people flamenco really is a way of life and the music can be heard blaring out from transistor radios on every street corner while it appears that everyone can sing, dance or play the guitar. It was on a very hot summer's day in Morón that I spent hours playing Camarón 45s in a garden where the plants and trees had stood for centuries. Later that day I would meet the town's famous flamenco artists for the first time, the guitarists Paco del Gastor, Juan del Gastor and Dieguito del Gastor with the singer Andorrano. They were all related to the Morón's most famous resident, Diego del Gastor who would only narrowly escape death when the Nationalists took control of his town during the war. This was the Morón that boasted the legend of the cockerel and was renowned for its limestone. A town that was very difficult to conquer, as the Romans and the Arabs had discovered to their cost. It was also during that hot July of 1936, that the troops of General Franco would also face their fiercest test, as it would take more than the radio propaganda of Queipo de Llano to break the *Morónenses* or *Aruncitanos*, as they prefer to be called.

The people of Morón had become aware of the landing of the Rebels from Morocco on the morning of 17 July. They had been shocked to hear of the taking of Seville by Queipo de Llano, who had arrived in the capital unannounced and then proceeded to take the workers strongholds of San Marcos, San Julian, La Macarena and finally Triana. They were soon to discover that Comidant Castejón, who led the *Quinta Bandera* of the legion

that had so ruthlessly butchered the workers of Triana, would be assigned
to take Morón. Castejon had earlier resorted to very extreme measures to
capture Triana that could have been avoided if the unions had taken Seville's
airport, and prevented the landing of the troops from Africa. Broué and
Témime have spoken of the 'Moors' reputation for cruelty' as 'rumours of
their arrival spread terror' and the result was a massacre with the slaughter of 9,000 workers.[54] The journalist Bertrand de Jouvene witnessed the
atrocities for *Paris-Soir*:

> with a fierce war cry, the men charged into the streets of the district. Then
> came a relentless mopping-up operation with grenades and knives. There
> was no mercy. When I managed to steal into the ruins the following day, I
> saw men clutching each other, both of them transfixed by bayonets and long
> switch knives.

Not surprisingly it was left to the flamenco capital of Triana to give the
Rebels a bloody nose as the district proudly held out for over a week.

In Morón de la Frontera an advance party of Rebel troops arrived on
the morning of 24 July having overcome the town of Arahal to be greeted
by *Moronenses* on the town's rooftops and towers. Despite fighting hard the
Rebels had taken control by midday on 25 July and this signalled the start
of the looting, raping and the daily executions that would continue until
the end of the war.[55] With the Nationalists now in control, the fate of the
gypsy guitarist Diego del Gastor was uncertain as he was placed on a list
of suspects as the author of an anti-Nationalist poster. Diego, a man whose
only interest was the flamenco guitar, was seen by an army patrol drinking
in a bar with friends who were members of the Socialist UGT union.[56]
The following day he was arrested with two other men and detained for
twenty days. Despite being urged by his brother to plead guilty so save his
own life and send his fellow prisoners to the firing squad, Diego refused and
declared that they were all innocent.[57] As a gypsy and a flamenco, Diego
was not a member of any political party, but he was a well-known free
spirit who sympathised with those who held radical ideas. He successfully
avoided death, but the authorities confiscated all of his property including
his home.

One of flamenco's greatest ever stars; the gypsy dancer Carmen Amaya
also suffered difficulties in the north of Spain at the outbreak of the war.
She was performing in Valladolid when the army commandeered her car.[58]

Carmen Amaya was one of the lucky artists who did manage to leave Spain by first travelling to Portugal, but many of the flamenco touring companies were stranded out of Spain as the war broke out. One such group was the *Compañía Teatral Alcoriza*, who were performing in Morocco along with many other famous flamenco artists.[59] Their guitarist, Gabriel Ruiz, managed to escape to Paris via Port Bou: 'in that same Moroccan city, fleeing from our cruel and horrible war, were La Argentina, Pilar López, Luisita Esteso, some famous bullfighters, and other well-known names that I can't recall'.[60] The creator of the modern flamenco guitar, Ramón Montoya, was another gypsy who found himself in Paris as these events unfolded. Montoya was recording a new blueprint for the flamenco guitar while the Nationalists eliminated all opposition in Andalucía.

Although the workers in Andalucía had some success in taking over many of the big estates and meting out some rough justice to the wealthy landowners, it would not be long before a region known for its strong anarchist tradition would be captured by Franco's Nationalist troops. Franco and his generals realised early on in the war that the illiterate workers of Andalucía needed to be crushed as they offered a threat. As the historian Helen Graham noted:

> During August and September 1936, Franco's forces swept up through southern Spain *en route* for the central capital city of Madrid. In its wake the repression escalated as the Army strategically butchered and terrorized the pro-Republican population, especially the rural landless. For this initial phase of the Civil War in the south was also part of the 'solution' to pre-war conflicts. It was a war of agrarian counter-reform that turned Andalucía and Extremadura into killing fields.

With Seville under the control of General Queipo de Llano, violence was unleashed across Andalucía: 'In villages across the rebel-held south there was systematic brutality, torture, shaving and rape of women in the aftermath of the conquest. Sometimes villages were literally wiped off the map by repression'.[61]

The workers of Andalucía's regions were quickly crushed and Cádiz fell, despite the success of its general strike early in the war, and the victors were soon to reinforce their victory by renaming Cádiz's streets: the Calle Sagasta would now be named after Queipo de Llano, the so-called 'Radio General' who had terrorised the people of Seville with his propaganda broadcasts. Cádiz's Plaza de Las Flores would now be called Plaza Topete but few *Gaditanos* would publicly acknowledge the changes. In Cádiz province the Rebels would soon take the mountain villages, including Jimena de la Frontera.

On 1 April 1939 General Franco announced his victory and the end of the war but, as the writer Paco Sevilla has commented, his regime was not initially good news for flamenco artists:

> It is not clear whether the successes of large touring companies and the dif-
> ficulties facing gypsy artists in the bars and cafes were directly due to the
> environment created by the Franco regime or merely coincident with it, but
> under Franco signs appeared for the first time in bars and taverns reading: '*Se
> prohibe el cante!*' (The Singing of Flamenco is Prohibited.)

Tom Scott-Robson was to highlight the concept of the flamencos not being able to practice their art freely in their homeland in the BBC film *Where the Unspeakable is Sung*, which he directed in 1969. The guitarist Manuel Morao, dancer El Farruco and the singers Chocolate and Fernando Terremoto are filmed playing cards in a bar which doubled as their office, waiting for a telephone call from a member of Andalucía's large landowners inviting them to perform in a great house away from the eyes of the law. The script explained that 'banned from working in their own environment the gypsy musician has unconsciously slipped away from his own people and acquired a new status of uncomfortable respectability'. Wild and boisterous flamenco gatherings were no longer tolerated under Franco, and the stars of the time, Fernanda de Utrera and Antonio Mairena were filmed performing in a controlled environment to the Spanish middle classes sipping sherry. In this fascinating film, that also boasted unique footage of Aurelio Sellés in his eighties and Camarón's idol La Perla de Cádiz, the audience were given an intimate insight into the difficult world of the jobbing guitarist in the late sixties.

Ironically, by the early fifties Franco would be happy to national-ise flamenco and sell it as the music of all Spain, not just Andalucía, in a bid to attract tourism and vital foreign currency. This cynical act combined with the aid he was to receive from the United States through the Marshall Plan was superbly satirised in the 1952 Spanish film *Bienvenido Mr. Marshall*. Its plot had the locals of a sleepy Spanish town hundreds of miles from the south, hoping to get their hands on some GI money.

They decide to redesign their buildings and change the clothes of the inhabitants to create an attractive Andalusian town where everyone dances and sings flamenco. In this classic of neo-realism cinema, despite even the local priest mastering the *compás*, the United States GI's drive straight by the town taking their money with them! Another classic film, *The Spirit of the Beehive*, set in a small Castilian village in the 1940s, illustrated the stifling psychological state of the Spain that Camarón would inherit and how everyone was under suspicion in the newly imposed fascist state. This highly ambiguous 1973 film avoided the censors scissors, despite Boris Karloff's Frankenstein being a symbol of the 'monster' Franco and the little girl Ana, who meets the 'monster' in her dreams, being symbolic of the country of Spain. The censor would miss the obvious signs of a political statement in a film that showed Franco's portrait hanging above the figure of Christ in the classroom and later his image on a postage stamp burning on a letter. There are few better illustrations of the accusatorial and claustrophobic atmosphere that personified the Franco years in which Camarón grew up as a child perfecting his *cante*.

Cádiz province, summer 1989

Jimena de la Frontera is served by the remarkable railway that links Bobadilla to Algeciras. It was built by the company of the British philanthropist Sir Alexander Harrison in 1890.[62] Jimena has a very tidy and well-run station where the stationmaster will not open up the booking office until he knows there are only minutes until the train is due. He will then don his ticket office manager's cap and sell you a ticket and then, only moments later, complete with his green flag and whistle, ask you to produce your ticket before you board the train! This stunning village perched on top of a steep hill which, as its name suggests, was once used by the Arabs to signal any threat to their frontier, is now home to many English people who find it very convenient for commuting to work in Gibraltar. Jimena's Arab castle fell to the Christians in 1434, but in 1936 it was to witness another bloody assault from Franco's Nationalists. It is also a town that still bears the scars of the Civil War; a fact I always ponder as I gaze down on over the sierras rich in oak and cork trees and wonder what fear went through the Jimenatos as they saw the arrival of the Nationalist troops in the lower town and knew it would be only a matter of time before they arrived at the top of this hillside town. There is only one road in and out and, although the Jimenatos had managed to survive the Roman invasions of many centuries earlier,

Franco's troops inspired by the ruthless General Queipo de Llano would be a very different matter. Jimena is one place in Spain where they have always talked about the once taboo subject of the Civil War and a local historian once succinctly titled his book 'a history according to Cain and Abel'. It was a war that literally set brother against brother and destroyed families as thousands were shot in the 'white towns'. Jimena's bars, usually frequented by the drunken English, remain not the best places to be seen reading the ABC, a right wing daily, as the Jimenatos have much to thank Felipe Gonzalez's Socialist government for.

It was here, in this town that an old friend of mine, Juan Rebolledo, the president of the Jimena's flamenco club, was not allowed to attend school under Franco, but forced to cut cork in the forests and his hands bore the scars till the end. As a young man in the fifties he was forced to migrate to West Germany for work, as did many of his fellow Andalusians, only to be greeted with appalling racism as they sought to make a living. One of Camarón's brothers, Jesús El Pijote was also compelled, through economic circumstances, to emigrate to Germany in the late sixties when the singer was performing at the Torres Bermejas tablao in Madrid, but he did not stay for very long. Only in the New Spain of Felipe González, when Spain's Prime Minister sought to reverse the effects of the Franco years on Andalucía, did Juan finally enjoy his latter years: opening a clothes shop and selling goods at the local markets of the surrounding villages. Juan would be surprised by the growing number of English residents in Jimena enabling the village to mount an annual international festival as holiday homes and tourism vie with honey, cork and the delicious pinonate cakes that the Jimenatos are justifiably proud of.

Conil de la Frontera, Monday 9 September 2002

During my search for Camarón I decided to visit the birthplace of his father Juan Luis Monje, the blacksmith from Conil de la Frontera. After surviving the walk along the dangerous road from Cabo Roche, where you have to dodge every car that comes along by jumping into the ditch, I arrived in the very genteel and middle-class town of Conil. It turned out to be as far removed from the gypsy forges as possible, having been colonised and gentrified by Germans. It seemed inconceivable that Camarón's father had his roots in this town as German appeared to be a more useful language than Spanish and surf boarding the only activity that would motivate anyone here. But I was close to Barbate de Franco and La Almadraba on the coast where in May and June the fisherman, covered in blood, slaughter hundreds of tuna fish by stabbing knives into their gills in a ritual known as the *levanta* that has been maintained for a thousand years.

The Phoenicians initiated the origins of this art of fishing with fixed nets but now even this tradition in Camarón's homeland is under threat. It is an art that has seen men wait every summer for the arrival of the tuna that pass this area, as they migrate from the Atlantic Ocean towards the Mediterranean Sea, in order to lay their eggs in the warmer water. The people of La Almadraba dedicate their lives to these two months of the year and their campaign usually starts under the strong May moonlight when shoals of tuna arrive. It seems that soon there will be little use for the special net known as *el copo* that can hold the vast weight of the tuna, because stocks are dwindling as a result of overfishing. As the quantity of kilos being caught each year declines is it possible that soon the bars of this area will no longer be able to serve *mojama*: the delicious tuna cured and dried in the sun?

One relatively new custom that is sure to survive is the 'burial of the mackerel' in Cádiz's historic flamenco quarter, the Barrio La Viña. This annual event, which takes place in August and has celebrated its twentieth birthday, is typical of the city that claims 'it smiles'. It is of course a creative mickey-take of the better-known 'burial of the sardine' and involves parading through the streets a giant polystyrene model of a mackerel in a basket-shaped boat followed by some rather curious mourners. The four-and-a-half metre long fish usually sets out at early evening from the Caleta beach followed by a group of people who are all dressed in black. These mourners, including men dressed as widows and priests, are joined by the general public who are encouraged to bring their pets. They are helped along the way by a silver band who accompanies the irreverent and satirical Cádiz song form known as the *chirigota*. The best time to hear these songs is during the *carnaval* that is celebrated in February with the influx of thousands of visitors to Camarón's homeland. Cádiz's *carnaval* began in the seventeenth century inspired by the tradition of another seaport, Venice. It became a victim in 1937 to General Franco's orders as he feared the lack or respect for authority displayed by Cádiz's citizens, but in characteristic style the *gaditanos* got the better even of the *Generalisimo*! There is no better place to be in February to see Cádiz people dressed as minstrels, musketeers and even beers; but make sure you take a wig!

Dreaming about next year's *carnaval*, as I passed miles of sandy beaches, I found very little of the heritage that would produce the talent of Camarón

in an area overrun by Germans who have imposed their culture. Before I
left I witnessed one incident that really summed up the cultural divide when
I saw some tourists given the customary free saucer of salted *altramuces* or
lupins that are an excellent accompaniment to ice-cold beer. Unfortunately
nobody had informed these visitors that, as with so-called monkey nuts that
come in their shells, you only eat the bit inside! The technique being to bite
off the end where the lupin was joined to the stem, hold the lupin close to
your mouth, squeeze hard between your thumb and forefinger, and it will
pop out of its skin and be easily eaten. Having great difficulty digesting
their *tapa* the tourists bravely continued chewing not wanting to offend the
goodwill of the bar owner!

Andalucía, 1950–1958

When Laurie Lee returned to Andalucía, and in particular Cádiz province,
in the fifties he also reflected on the ability of the locals to be good hosts
despite the hard times;

> There are bars in Algeciras where a glass of wine and a plate of shrimps cost
> only two pence; where a bootblack has only to see you to press drinks upon
> you; and where processions of strangers are for ever offering you glasses of
> cognac with proud gestures of courtly friendship. Any attempt to return the
> favour is discouraged by a shocked shaking of the head. You are a traveller,
> they say; it is our privilege to make you welcome[63]

However, despite these displays of generosity to be found in Cádiz's ports,
Juan Lalaguna highlighted that inland it was the large landowners of
Andalucía who were getting fatter by the day, while their workers had to
be content with starvation wages. He also observed that that industry was
also at rock bottom without the sufficient food being produced from the
land to fuel its workers, but a change was about to come in the first year of
Camarón's life with a bumper harvest in 1951.

Remarkable changes were also to come during Camarón's teenage years,
as Spain was to be dragged kicking and screaming into the twentieth century. By the time he was nineteen and beginning to look more like a rock
star with slick greased-back hair, Spain, and in particular his Andalucía,
had taken the leap from an almost medieval existence to a model more
common to the rest of Europe. But there was a price to pay for one of the
key elements that would reinvigorate the sluggish and impoverished state

that advertised itself as 'different'. The two-year- ld Camarón would have been unaware of Franco's desperation to broker a deal with the USA and get some vital cash from the '*los yanquís*' that might yet save his tottering fascist state. Franco got his cash, and the United States got their bases including Rota and Morón – an agreement which would also have a profound influence on flamenco; as the gypsy guitarists Raimundo and Rafael Amador traded flamenco licks and *falsetas* for the blues riffs from the GIs and the *blues de la Frontera* were born. The end of food rationing also marked better times while Camarón was a toddler and by 1955 even the UN's half-hearted gesture against Franco was rescinded.

By 1958 Camarón's career was already being shaped as he began singing in bars and at fiestas for *parné* in San Fernando and throughout Cádiz province. This tradition continues today and was how a current star and *Camaronero*, the young singer El Potito, was discovered at a very early age. Throughout the main cities of Andalucía, singers with less talent will pitch up outside a restaurant and sing a *rumba* or *bulerías*, usually accompanying themselves on the guitar. The back of the instrument is then thrust at the tourists with the singer holding the neck in the expectation of cash – after all the audience have had the benefit of the *cante* whether they understand or even want it!

Camarón had understood where his future lay from an early age:

> To be honest, I was going to be a bull fighter, but I obviously found singing easier because I would go to a *tentadero* and I would start singing and the crowd would shout for the fair haired boy to sing and I would sing there and get money and food for it and from there I got invited to parties where I was the singer and in this way I found it easier to become a singer.

Camarón did go on to fight bulls on several occasions when he was young but did not become a professional *torero*. He had to settle for being the friend and admirer of one of the greatest bullfighters ever, Curro Romero. Soon there would be no time for bullfighting as a move to Madrid would ignite a flamenco revolution and send the singer on a journey that could only end in tragedy.

3

Castles of Sand, 1968–1978

No Hay Lenguaje Como el Cante
Álora Flamenco Festival poster

The year 1968 was to be one of the most important years in the life of Camarón as he took a decision that was to launch him on a journey: to international stardom, a glittering recording career, drug addition and ultimately his premature death. Madrid, the capital city, with its numerous and thriving flamenco *tablaos* or night clubs had traditionally been a magnet; pulling in young flamenco talent from southern Spain. Camarón's outstanding ability and growing national reputation prompted his decision to make a permanent move to Madrid where he would live in the Calle Barquillo and work nightly in one of the best *tablaos*, Torres Bermejas. His apprenticeship in the capital city would equip him with the ability and the reputation to record an album that would influence the course of flamenco's history and development. Soon he would be appearing nightly in a crowded smoky club, crammed full with tables and with very cramped back stage conditions. The Argentinian photographer, Pepe Lamarca, would create Camarón's new image with a series of inspired shots. In one he would resemble the character Mick Jagger played in the film *Performance*, dressed in a 'wet look' jacket covering a tee shirt with his hair backcombed. He would also be presented in casual clothes, relaxing with his guitarist Paco de Lucía in a pose that concealed the rift that would develop between them.

Camarón would meet Paco de Lucía, a guitarist with exceptional technique, in the hot and clammy atmosphere of Madrid's nightclubs and
form a partnership that would reinvigorate the flamenco song that was in
decline. The dominance of Antonio Mairena, the ageing gay gypsy who
was best known for his collection of cravats and singing while standing up,
would soon be at an end. Mairena had become boring, taking himself too
seriously, and Camarón would soon eclipse him with a string of creative
albums. The chemistry between Camarón and Paco de Lucía, who subsequently emerged as a guitarist of world status, was extraordinary and would
find an outlet in Madrid's recording studios. Camarón always remembered
their encounter, when he was working at the Madrid nightclub, with great
affection:

> Paco's father came often to Torres Bermejas. One day his son came with him.
> We understood each other immediately. He liked the things I did and I liked
> the things he did. Was I interested in working with him? Wow was I inter-
> ested! He was incredible! Every time we worked together we got along so
> well we understood each other by telepathy.[1]

One of the best insights into Camarón's life during these early, heady Madrid
days came from an unexpected source going public a year after the singer's
death in 1992. Paco de Lucía, his guitarist for the nine albums recorded
between 1969 and 1977, provided a rare and fascinating account of their
troubled relationship, which illuminated the many stories about Camarón's
professional life in Madrid which began when he was only eighteen.[2] Well
before Camarón's decision to live and work in Madrid, Paco de Lucía had
encountered what he described as a 'fourteen year old stranger'.[3] In 1964
Paco could not foresee that he would go on to accompany Camarón on a
set of albums that would provide future artists with a rich and unmatched
body of work. He also could not have foreseen that the death and funeral of
this little gypsy boy would haunt him for the rest of his life. It is clear from
Paco's account that Camarón was already as a teenager, an exceptional talent and worthy of the costly fare for a gypsy to travel from San Fernando
to Madrid to attend an audition to secure a recording contract. Paco de
Lucía's account of Camarón's ill-fated trip reflects how the *cante* was stagnating in this period; dominated by the academic approach of Antonio
Mairena. Camarón had visited a studio where Paco was recording an album
with the commercial flamenco artist Bambino whose catchy *rumbas* were

very popular in the sixties. According to Paco, Bambino wanted him to accompany Camarón for the benefit of the director of the Columbia record company. Interestingly, Paco had already alluded to having a special affinity with Camarón by constructing this initial encounter as the start of a special relationship. In his interview he explained that the other guitarists were too tired to bother backing Camarón but 'I was sixteen and maybe out of solidarity accompanied him'.[4] This is a very curious statement as one of the other guitarists, Paco del Gastor would only have been nineteen and more importantly, unlike Paco, was a gypsy. Camarón would have interpreted this early encounter differently but it would not have influenced the decision to sign him up for a record deal. The record boss was not impressed with Camarón's traditional *soleá*, saying 'that sort of music didn't sell and no one was interested in it'. He was of course right because as the decade progressed even gypsies became bored with flamenco. But Paco de Lucía was captivated and promised to cut an album with him. However another five years would elapse before the release of *Al Verte las Flores Lloran* and another year before they would meet again.

Before their very well chronicled meeting in Madrid when Camarón broke all ties with Cádiz and switched her clear air and pure sunlight for the smoke filled nightclubs of Madrid, Paco recalled another meeting where he really came under the spell of Camarón. It was in Jerez at a party, while they were both enjoying a *copita*, that Paco recognised the real qualities of Camarón's singing, including his metronomic sense of time. For Paco, 'He had it all. I became a *Camaronero* for the rest of my life'. Paco had bumped into Camarón in the early hours of the morning:

> He was with another gypsy of the family of Parilla, and we began drinking together. In the morning Camarón told me that we would go to Parilla's house because he had a sister who was very nice. So we went to this house of a very pure gypsy flamenco family. We started to play and Camarón started to sing, and when I listened to Camarón that morning, I got crazy. Never had I heard singing like I wanted to sing more than the singing of this guy! Never! And at that moment I said, 'now we go to Madrid to my house and we really prepare to record'.[5]

Paco would later reflect on this meeting when he commented that he 'couldn't comprehend such perfection in his singing, such precision of tone, such mastery, such taste. He had it all.'[6]

Paco's account of their time together in those golden years from 1969 to 1978 reveals an important clue as to why their relationship, no matter how close, would also be troubled. Paco described Camarón as 'a good person, kind and noble, but we had little in common'. Interestingly he avoided addressing directly any issues of ethnicity and did not mention that Camarón was a gypsy and that he is a non-gypsy or *payo*. The potential underlying tensions of this question of race were touched on inadvertently and explored in a more peripheral way when Paco expressed how desperate he was for Camarón to come and play football or go fishing with him, but despite all his efforts he managed on only a single occasion to persuade Camarón to come to the beach. Paco was unable to offer any reason as to why Camarón had little interest in these pursuits and hinted that, despite their long friendship, he was never able to get that close. While he clearly became infatuated with Camarón and his prodigious talent, he could not fully enter the world he occupied, despite moments of camaraderie over a game of pool, which broke the monotony of the nightly performances at the *tablao* Torres Bermejas:

> We spent a lot of time together preparing the records in my house or in my parents' house, doing annual tours for two months in Europe and living in the same room singing and playing all the time with enormous dedication. We were very young, we were live flesh, full of harmony and illusion and we only wanted to create for fun. It was a very beautiful period.

Paco de Lucía was the frustrated singer in awe of an artist who found the *cante* so easy, an obsession that was to lead to a lack of judgment: he released *Luzia* in 1998 with a track dedicated to Camarón; clearly demonstrating his inability to sing flamenco. Camarón's decade with Paco de Lucía laid the foundations of what would become a flamenco revolution, but it also exposed them to criticism from the purists and their work had numerous detractors. Camarón's pioneering albums were not universally accepted at a time when Antonio Mairena continued to dominate and claim that only he knew how the flamenco songs of Andalucía should be interpreted. On top of this pressure Paco also felt that Camarón was insecure and remarked; 'he aged very quickly, he was disconcerting and you never knew if his opinions were sincere'. Paco's prophetic words indicated how flamenco's first universal star was already heading for martyrdom.

Despite considering Camarón to be a prodigy, Paco would also talk about the difficulties that the singer had when learning a new phrase; to the point that even the studio engineers knew the innovation backwards. Yet when it came to laying the track down he would produce a moment of pure genius. Paco's brother, Ramón de Algeciras, did not share this view, describing Camarón as devouring new material. Paco's claim that they made these albums for themselves, and that the first few albums were almost unconscious statements that occurred after all their travelling around together, was undeniably true. Paco was also keen to point out that Camarón always delegated all the arrangements to him. Soon, because of his international engagements, Paco would not be able to undertake the bread and butter work of the festivals with Camarón. His brother Ramón would step in and there was also Paco Cepero, one of the singer's most influential early guitarists.

1968 was to be a landmark year for the seventeen-year-old Camarón, despite already tiring of working in the clubs, as it witnessed the release of his debut record and his first international trip, travelling to Venezuela. Franco's exploitation of flamenco culture to promote tourism was at last beginning to bear fruit, with international audiences packing out Madrid's flamenco clubs, but the extra shifts would also challenge the artists. They would now have to increase the number of performances they undertook in those very crowded and far from pleasant conditions. Camarón's memories of this 'golden period' of his life were not all pleasant:

> every evening I did two sets singing to ten dancing girls. Then, at night another two sessions early on for the foreigners. The Spaniards didn't arrive until two or three in the morning. Then I could sing alone. And then there were the *senioritos*. They invited you to their villas and afterwards kicked you out by the seat of your pants. Most nights though, we artists just hung out together.[7]

I visited some of these flamenco haunts in Madrid during 2006 in search of Camarón: there was little trace of his spirit in Casa Patas where artists and tourists hang out, but his songs were still being sung in venues like Triana and the Soleá where the gypsies worshipped him. Artists from Andalucía were still entertaining the punters, but those born in Madrid just yearned to return to the villages of their grandparents. Camarón's presence would not be found in the Spanish capital because he was never comfortable in the big city environment and hated the routine of the nightly performances.

The clubs led to Camarón recording his first album in 1968 with the Ceuta-born guitarist Antonio López Arenas. The idea of Camarón working in a studio had come from Arenas, who was a well-known figure in the Madrid world of the *tablaos* and had met Camarón while he was performing at the flamenco nightclub, *La Soleá*. Camarón had laid down four tracks that drew on his best styles, the *bulerías*, *alegrías* and *soleares*. Interestingly, one of the *palmeros* engaged to do the flamenco clapping was the other artist from the island of San Fernando, Chato de la Isla.[8] While this album is of historic interest and has been issued many times for the benefit of collectors, it does not match the amateur recording made a year before at the Venta de Vargas.

Antonio López Arenas was also Camarón's touring companion in Caracas and a photograph was published in the Venezuelan press showing Camarón seated alongside Arenas looking wistful and wearing a shirt typical of the time with those very long collars. It also showed that during his one year living in Madrid he had aged considerably. The accompanying article, written by Rafael Ruggeri, remarked on the pair's long tour of Venezuela, where Camarón had remained for six months, and said they might return in early 1975, but by then Camarón would have even bigger fish to fry. He would soon start recording with the legendary guitarist from Algeciras, Paco de Lucía, but first there was the small matter of laying down a few tracks with a much older maestro, Sabicas.

Piccadilly Circus, London, 1968

Within a year of moving to Madrid, Camarón was not only recording his first album with Paco de Lucía, he also became a member of the *Festival Flamenco Gitano* show that used to tour all over Europe. As a young schoolboy, with a few years of practising the flamenco guitar and some public appearances under my belt, I was about to come under Camarón's spell and embark on a journey that would end with me witnessing a live performance from the man from the 'Island'. In 1968 I was blissfully unaware that Camarón's drug habit would begin with the trendy drug of the swinging sixties, LSD. This was the era when the travelling flamenco companies were at the height of their pulling power and when the impresarios Lippman and Rau dominated the concert halls of Europe with a selection of artists brought directly from Spain. It was only a matter of time before the seventeen year old blond gypsy sensation, who had been such a hit in Málaga, would be brought to the attention of British aficionados. Camarón would perform in London, as he had the previous year, in the group of La Singla, a dancer from the gypsy Somorrostro district of Barcelona. Two very significant events would occur during this London visit that were to prove very influential. It was during this tour that Camarón would come to the attention of the Seville based lawyer, Ricardo Pachón, who would prise Camarón away from the clutches of Paco de Lucía and his father to make flamenco's most groundbreaking recording a decade later.[9] Pachón would constantly pester and annoy Camarón during his Madrid years, but his persistence would eventually pay off. Camarón was showing signs of coming under another powerful influence in the swinging late sixties of London as large quantities of 'acid' were in circulation.

One of Camarón's early love affairs was to feature prominently in the 2005 film biopic of his life, after an earlier one night stand, he was found beneath the statute of Eros in Piccadilly Circus. Having been missing for over a day, an exhausted teenage Camarón was finally spotted sitting by the fountain where London's adopted Greek god of love watched over him. The writer José Manuel Gamboa later wrote that Camarón had been partying with the rest of the company when he was enticed to leave with an attractive woman who took him to her home.[10] This would prove to be an early example of well-documented disappearing acts that would soon be worrying festival promoters and his guitarist Tomatito.

Camarón's artistic trajectory was now gathering pace and would be accelerated by the recording of his first record with Paco de Lucía in 1969 and his two-year participation in the leading touring flamenco company, the *Festival Flamenco Gitano*. Paco Rebes, a Catalan artist who had discovered another gypsy sensation, La Chunga, would be instrumental in arranging a contract for Camarón to perform in this group: he would also appear alongside the emerging 'monster' of the guitar, Paco de Lucía.[11] Their unique chemistry on their first album produced a work that remains as fresh and vibrant today and their interpretation of the *soleá* has yet to be matched. It presented the authentic gypsy voice with the innovative playing of Paco, but more importantly it sounded so distinct from the other albums available on the market. One song, *Detrás del tuyo se va*, would connect with a new audience because, although it might still be considered traditional, it had a commercial edge that would bridge the gap between flamenco and popular music. However, not everyone appreciated the music of the so-called 'flamenco tandem' and what this duo were doing to the art of flamenco. Camarón was forced onto the defensive:

I took that *cante*, did it my way, and it caught on. It sold many records, and everybody was singing '*a rin, tin, tin,*' '*a la bimbombera,*' but that stuff is worthless to me … It has been a commercial success, like so many things that have been commercially popular but are worthless … there are many records out there that are worth nothing, but people go crazy over them. A record comes out and they might like one number because it has a catchy tune, yet there is another song that is very good, really good, and they don't understand it, they don't know how to classify it.[12]

Camarón's first album did not sell anywhere near the quantity one might expect, but the album's *tangos* was to become an anthem and was revisited thirty years later by that master of flamenco rock, Raimundo Amador.

The guitarist Mario Basilisco was, like myself, a London schoolboy studying the flamenco guitar, and he remembers seeing a young Camarón in the capital on several occasions during the late sixties. His uncle's house in Hoxton near Shoreditch, also had a reputation for parties which would go on all night and where the artists, including Camarón, would imbibe into the small hours. They would then depart, packed like sardines, in a Ford Anglia. His uncle's house was a regular venue for *fiestas* run every weekend by his cousin Lionel; Mario has fond memories of Camarón's visits and remembers his exceptional singing:

It was heaven and it was at this time that all the artists used to come over from Spain, and somehow all meet up. If my father or brother didn't see them, my cousin Lionel would and they would end up going to my uncle's house and having a party.

For Mario, Camarón was already reaching a peak in his singing and his appearance has never faded from his memory; 'He was slightly built, very muscular, with narrow hips and a wide chest; you could see he was very lean and he had long hair'. Camarón was also to be a guest when Mario Basilisco arrived at the home of his father Carlos in Vauxhall, after a long day working for a firm of Spanish fruit importers:

From the front door there was a corridor of about twenty or thirty feet to the door of the living room, so I opened the front door and I heard guitar playing and I realised it was Paco de Lucía but I thought that it didn't sound like a recording – it sounded like an actual live guitar like it was Paco de Lucía, so I walked those twenty or thirty paces whatever – opened the door to the living room and lo and behold before me I found Paco de Lucía, Paco Cepero, Camarón, Diego Pantoja, Chaqueta and I think also Barrilito, yeah Barrilito'.[13]

This time he also discovered Camarón sitting on the sofa with a bottle of whiskey and, as one of the guests owned the adjacent off-licence, there were always copious amounts of wine and port on tap! Even in these early years and in such exulted company, Mario recognised that Camarón was emerging as the leading singer of his generation, but he felt privileged to have heard him sing in his prime:

> The first time I saw Camarón, he was in London doing a show and the second time was in my house when he was performing at the Albert Hall in *Fiesta Flamenca Gitana*. I saw them perform at the Albert Hall and the next day they were in my flat in Vauxhall.

In 1970 and 1971 Camarón would record two more landmark albums with Paco de Lucía, *Cada vez que nos miramos* and *Son tus ojos dos estrellas*, which is often referred to as *El espejo en que te miras*. Their fourth collaboration *Canastera*, released in 1972, was significant for two reasons. Paco's presence on the cover would be minimised and after this release his photograph would not appear on Camarón's records. Even more noteworthy, was Camarón's creation of a new flamenco style that he introduced on the title track *canastera*. This was no ordinary *fandango* because it was interpreted in a previously unheard way that also required retuning Paco's guitar. Camarón was now at the top of his game and he proved it by taking the silver plate at the flamenco-singing contest named after Antonio Mairena. Mairena's rules had finally been broken and later his body language and facial expression would say it all whenever he was photographed with Camarón.

During 1972 there were two other important landmarks that would confirm and cement Camarón's status as somebody who was much more than simply a flamenco singer. He would make his second appearance on the big screen and his record company would issue a double album of songs culled from his first four records with Paco de Lucía. This compilation signalled to the public that his work was already seen as ground breaking, durable, and of more significance than the work of his contemporaries.

This would be followed by another compilation where his songs were cou-
pled with Manolo Caracol and Fosforito, but it was Camarón's name that
appeared first. The film, entitled *Casa Flores*, starring the queen of Spanish
cinema Lola Flores, would feature Camarón as a bad boy on Madrid's mean
streets. Camarón was portrayed as the height of cool, dressed in a stylish
jacket with epaulets and trendy pockets with zips. There was also another
suggestion of the Mick Jagger image with his trademark slicked-back hair,
as he rode a motorbike singing the film's theme tune *Sere Serenito*. Another
giant of flamenco, Manolo Caracol, had been a film star in the forties and
fifties, but Camarón did not have a strong enough personality and was too
introverted to sustain a cinema career.

In the early seventies Camarón was filmed many times for Spanish television with Paco Cepero as his guitarist. Camarón had already worked with
several players, one of them being the brother of Paco de Lucía, Ramón
de Algeciras, who had accompanied him at live performances until the
demands of working with his illustrious brother became too much:

> Camarón would be singing, say, in Cádiz, and the next night Paco and I per-
> haps giving a concert in San Sebastián, then the next night with Camarón
> somewhere else, and so forth. Finally I couldn't take it any more and had
> to stop accompanying Camarón, so I could concentrate my efforts full-time
> with Paco which kept us busy enough.[14]

These were the days when middle-class producers smoked pipes as they laid
down the tracks but the recordings with Cepero would show Camarón at
his absolute peak. The singer would talk very fluently at this time in contrast
to the mumbled almost incoherent words that he would start uttering in the
late eighties. Often dressed in a smart polo-neck sweater he would, despite
his fame, still find time for the gypsy children of the street who played in
and around abandoned cars.

While Camarón had toured extensively abroad and had appeared in
South America, a very attractive proposition was to arise in 1973: for a gig
in Brazil with Paco de Lucía. The concert proved to be a mix of Paco's
solos and some of Camarón's best songs. Listening to the recital over three
decades later reveals much about the strength and precision of Camarón's
voice, but he suffered the same problem he always hated facing at the summer festivals in Spain. The audience just chattered through his most serious
material, forcing him to ask them to be quiet, and there were the usual over

enthusiastic fans who kept shouting out what style they wanted him to sing. However this touring was not allowed to get in the way of the pair's grip on the flamenco record market, where they had released four records in four years. 1973 would be no different, with the arrival in the shops of *Caminito de Totana* that featured some excellent *bulerías* and some superb *fandangos*.

In 1974 a fresh, young and relatively unknown guitarist, Tomatito, would start to emerge as Camarón's accompanist for live gigs. They had first met the previous year when the 'little tomato' was just fifteen years old. It was a crucial meeting because Tomatito was a gypsy and could bring something different to their sessions that the non-gypsies or *payos* simply did not have. By an accident of fate Tomatito had become a professional guitarist in Málaga, because that was where his father was sent to do his military service, although his preference had been Seville.[15] Tomatito began playing in Málaga's *Taberna Gitana* where he picked up the tricks of the trade from Pedro Blanco, by constantly waking him up and asking him to put on some flamenco records. This flamenco nightclub used to attract some of the big names for its late night performances including Pansequito, and one day Camarón arrived. The club's resident guitarist, El Chino, was away and so it fell to the very young Tomatito to face the daunting task of standing in. Soon he found himself sitting down next to Camarón for a performance in a sports centre. When later asked about this initial encounter, Tomatito has said that if it was to happen today he would have never turned up, even though his ability on the guitar is considerably better than it was in 1973. He now sees it as an incredible act of bravery because, due to his youth, he was not fazed by Camarón's international reputation.

During 1974 Camarón continued his remarkable work with Paco de Lucía, releasing *Soy caminate* where the *bulerías* would continue to set the standard and be unmatched by any other singer. It appeared that this partnership was invincible; they had released a new album every year since 1969 and, in 1975, Camarón had the confidence to dedicate his latest record to his childhood hero. The title track *Arte y Majestad*, another pioneering *bulerías*, was a glowing homage to the bullfighter Curro Romero. Camarón was now emerging as a pop star, communicated not just through his music, but also his choice of clothes and haircut. His distinct style would be fully exploited on his 1976 release *Rosa María* where the title track, based on *tangos*, would create flamenco's first commercial anthem.

Oxford and Seville, 1975–1978

By the mid-seventies, as Camarón's career as a singer radically changing
the art of flamenco was taking off, I was heading for Andalucía to study
with one of the most eccentric and colourful characters in the business.
The concert guitarist, Pepe Martínez, was a short and plump man who
came to Britain every winter in a Renault car loaded down with all the
provisions he would need for three months on the road. He even had the
mechanics at his Seville garage 'fix' his suspension, so that the car's excessive cargo would not attract unnecessary attention from customs officials.
Every part of that car from the boot to an enormous roof-rack was used
to import and export the maximum goods possible, with no room for passengers. The vehicle contained everything from bags of chickpeas, gallons
of olive oil, oversized watermelons, rare woods and usually about nine flamenco and classical guitars. Pepe's first visits to England had been done by
air, with the guitarist convincing the other passengers to take on board a
guitar each!

The cargo for the return car journey through France to the bottom of
Spain would prove even more exotic. Pepe would like to take back the best
of English produce and that included soft tissue toilet paper, caramel biscuits,
the latest electrical goods picked up in Andorra and a completely different
set of guitars to the nine he had brought to England. Once stopped at the
Spanish border and asked by the guard why he was bringing such quantities
of English toilet paper, Pepe merely threw the guard a roll and said 'try it
and you'll see why'. When he experienced difficulties with authority, be it a
policeman who had seen him go down a one-way street the wrong way or
a restaurant owner who was cross that he had gone into the kitchen to see
how they cooked, Pepe's excellent English would immediately evaporate.
The hapless officer or manager would be presented with the phrase 'I iz
Pepe Martínez from Seville where coming your marmalade' as he showed
them the covers of all his albums!

Pepe, although not a big drinker, would always start his morning around
seven o'clock by going to his car and promptly drinking two cans of lager
which he would then throw over his shoulder into some poor soul's front
garden. His real loves were eating and smoking and he was never without
a cigar in his mouth, even when playing, and usually a Cuban *Montecristo* at
that. This is a brief portrait of the *flamenco* that would enter my life and my
house from 1976 until we had a little disagreement over a guitar in 1982.
Shortly after that he suffered a series of strokes and died in 1985.

I had first met Pepe Martínez, one of Seville's finest guitarists, when as a schoolboy I travelled to Oxford to see him in concert on a foggy night in 1970. Pepe had been best mates with the guitarist Ramón Montoya, who had created the modern flamenco guitar and had performed at Buckingham Palace. In 1974 I saw Pepe in concert at Oxford again and he invited me to come to Seville the following summer to study with him. Pepe's eccentric ways were flagged up in a letter I received from him in April 1975:

> I know one pension of friend of mine, very nice, in the city centre, not expenses, the last friend of mine stay in this place last February I remember pay 130 pesetas, approx. I think is no more now, but your thinking in one pound a day, only for the room, each one, naturally.

As a result, my guitarist companion Roy Lobb and I were subsequently given the 'friendly prices'. Having found this *pensión*, which was actually a long way out from the city centre and situated near the Gran Plaza, we climbed the stairs to our room. I immediately went to freshen up and was startled by the washbasin falling off the wall and smashing on the ground. I asked Roy what I should do, to which he replied, 'Tell the bloke'. The proprietor, Antonio, who looked like he had never shaved in his life, merely shrugged his shoulders and said, 'don't worry about it'. Later we went downstairs to discover more about our home for the coming weeks and encountered a patio where, when looking up to the ceiling, you could see the sky. Over the years the rain had penetrated all the walls; rotting the furniture and ancient settees whilst also staining the valuable oil paintings.

We had arrived in the colonial city of Seville at a time when the smell of fascism was still in the air, but soon to be vanquished. Soldiers still guarded the fort that lay on the corner of the called Menéndez y Pelayo and Demetrio de los Ríos. This was the very quarter, which lay close to the Puerta de la Carne, where the writer Pérez-Reverte chose to set his novel *The Seville Communion*. A typical corner of Seville where Pérez-Reverte's Jesuit detective Quart, would suspect the motives of a flamenco-loving nun as he 'ran an eye over the books and tapes' to discover that 'she had mainly baroque music, but there was also a lot of flamenco, both classical and modern, and all of Camarón's albums'.

From this seedy area, Roy and I would travel along the Avenida de Eduardo Dato to the Gran Plaza and discover a popular roast chicken bar, where I would drive the customers mad by repeatedly playing the B-side of a Camarón single.

It was here, on Sunday, that an old gypsy man would arrive with an extraordinary animal act. I was used to seeing gypsies playing trumpets while a goat climbed a set of stairs and then balanced its hooves on a tiny circular stand, but nothing had prepared me for this. A monkey riding a dog with a saddle on it would suddenly come tearing past the customers sat on the roadside tables and chairs. Dressed in a knitted wool outfit it appeared to take great delight in digging its claws into the dog to make it go faster. People would give the man some spare change while the owner of the bar would offer him a steaming glass of the water that the *caracoles* or snails had been cooked in.

Before my visit to Seville's April Fair in 1980, Pepe sent me a letter listing some items that he wanted from England, only this time his request was really bizarre:

> *Mi querido Marcos el ateo*, Just a short letter for another little order … That is for one jok (*chiste*) for some friend of mine; you buy for me, please, in one Boots shop, 2 pakets of preservative (anti conception) the name FIESTA; this preservatives is in one little paket and contains each paket 5 preservatives IN COLOUR assorted (anticonceptive).

Sure enough, Pepe was waiting for me on 19 April on the Seville airport runway shouting and wanting to be reassured that I had brought the coloured Durex. Inside the terminal and in front of his family, I discreetly said yes but he demanded them immediately and then insisted on tearing the packs open and showing them to everyone.

Later that year, when he heard that I was playing on the fringe at the Edinburgh Festival, he wrote 'I know you are very busy with the guitar, and you go again to Edimburgh, with one poet. Why not with Camarón?' This was a gentle dig provoked by his frustration at my constant interest in Camarón and his music. When Pepe had stayed with me in Oxford, during the winter of 1979, I had made sure that every morning he was woken up with the sounds of Camarón's latest album *La Leyenda del Tiempo*, blasting out from the speakers in my bedroom. I knew that secretly he really enjoyed this new direction that flamenco was taking and I had often caught him playing some of the latest guitar licks. Whenever I told him I was going to a Camarón concert he would demand that I drop by for a nightcap of *coñac* and tell him how it went. However, he was not quite ready for the drums and percussion on Camarón's interpretation of *La Tarara* and proceeded to knock down my bedroom door!

Being around Pepe in public could be a little embarrassing, as in Seville's city centre he insisted on wearing pyjamas that he had bought in England. Both his daughters and I found this created a lot of unwelcome attention but Pepe was his own man and demanded to be comfortable. Often he would drive to Seville's magnificent post office in his pyjamas with a car full of signed contracts for his forthcoming tour in Europe. With the amount of miles he did in his travelling home come grocer shop, Pepe needed a new car every couple of years and one day he asked me to accompany him to the Renault garage which lies on the outskirts of Seville near the airport. 'Is my new car ready and remember I ordered silver,' Pepe said to a slightly worried looking assistant. At that time most people in Seville had white or yellow cars, because the strength of the sun would fade brighter colours, but Pepe liked to be different. The assistant came back and said it was ready and Pepe promptly pulled out the complete sum in hundreds of notes. As the assistant looked at the pile of money in amazement we retired to the bar while extra staff were called to count the loot!

In 1975 I agreed to buy a Manuel Reyes guitar through Pepe, which would lead to one of the most bizarre journeys and quests I have ever experienced as I found myself in Bar sur Aube in France in search of the owners of a sports shop! I had paid Pepe the money for the construction of the guitar during the summer and he duly brought it to my home in England in the autumn. I could not wait to play it and quickly got it out of the case and started to test it out. After a little while Pepe said he was sorry, but there had been a little difficulty and he would have to take the guitar with him all over Britain and France on his tour. I was not to worry because he was going to leave it with a family in France where I could pick it up from their shop. He then pulled out from his wallet their business card and then, using zigzag movements with a pair of scissors, cut the card into two halves. I was to go to Bar sur Aube in December and call on Mr and Mrs Blanc and produce the half of the card that he gave to me. The other half of the card, and my guitar, would be in their safekeeping. In the second week of December I received a letter from Pepe writing from Bar sur Aube which said 'You guitar is here in the hands of M. and Mme Blanc and the two half of my visit card. Came here any time for collect the guitar. The guitar is here, in nice place, same my house, and no worry for nothing, O.K?' I travelled all the way to France only to be told the shopkeepers had gone on their Christmas holiday! When I eventually tracked them down and rang their doorbell and told them who I was,

Mme Blanc asked for the card and then went to a drawer to find the other half. Slowly and meticulously she checked several times that the teeth on the two halves of the card fitted like a glove. Six months after paying for the guitar it was finally mine, although when Pepe returned to England the following winter he asked if he could borrow it again!

In 1976 Camarón married Dolores Montoya, who later became better known by her nickname of La Chispa. They were to have four children, although it would emerge on his death that the singer had another daughter from a previous relationship. After Camarón's untimely death, his close friend Rancapino had spoken of how this couple first met as the two singers struggled to survive with their demanding flamenco lifestyle. Rancapino had travelled to La Línea to make a recording when he saw La Chispa and said to Camarón that that little gypsy girl was going to be for him. Camarón's reaction was very natural, in view of La Chispa's exceptional beauty, when he replied that he liked her as well. They were married a year and a half later at what would be described as a major gypsy event. The twenty-six-year-old singer had found the ideal partner in the very beautiful sixteen year old gypsy girl.

While visible proof of La Chispa's virginity would be an essential part of the ritual of her traditional gypsy wedding, Camarón had earlier informed his future bride about a little fling he had undertaken as a young man living in Madrid. In 2005, the film of Camarón's life would controversially feature a woman called Isabel, with whom the singer was portrayed as having had a relationship. In reality, Camarón did have an affair with a woman called Mari Paz by whom he had a daughter who was later named Juana after Camarón's mother.[16] Camarón's growing fame and good looks made him an ideal catch and he found this young middle-class Catalan woman, who later moved to Barcelona, very attractive. His manager and close friend, José Candado, was later to declare that news of this other child of Camarón had only surfaced when details of the singer's will were made public.[17] Camarón took full legal responsibility for the child, who went on to be accepted by La Chispa and her four children and is legally entitled to a fifth-part of the singer's estate.[18] Candado also shed some light on Camarón's attitude to his 'third daughter', when he explained that the singer had concerns over her non-gypsy upbringing which had given her an outlook on life which was in conflict with the singer's belief in traditional gypsy values.[19]

The couple's wedding, which was held in La Línea, was a very happy occasion with the bride looking young and radiant as she fanned herself dressed in an elegant bridal dress. Camarón also looked very dapper in a white shirt with a red satin string bow-tie and pin-stripe suit as the happy couple left the church. Camarón's mother was at peace as her José had found the perfect gypsy girl, with the celebrated dancer Manuela Carrasco and his brother Manuel as the godparents. After the service there was a great celebration with many invited guests who drank Seville's *cruzcampo* beer from plastic glasses underneath a ceiling festooned with *farolillios* or paper Chinese lanterns.

Married life agreed with Camarón and gave his music a new edge. Within a year of his marriage he released the album *Castillo de Arena* that brought together his creativity with some of the licks that Paco de Lucía was serving up on his international tours. Pepe Lamarca's photograph, which was used for the cover of this album, was to be almost as influential in building Camarón's image as the singer's innovations recorded for posterity on the vinyl. The photograph created an image of an artist who existed very much outside of the closed world of flamenco. This side view of Camarón, dressed in a white t-shirt drinking from a glazed and decorated clay pot, was an early example of his emerging iconic status. On the album his *bulerías* continued to break the mould while the *seguiriyas* had an intensity that was unmatched by his contemporaries. There were few signs on this collection that these two artists, who had made nine albums together between 1969 and 1977, were soon to go their separate ways. Paco had, in the February of 1976, conquered London without Camarón: playing to a packed Wigmore Hall audience that included many of the capital's best guitarists. He had continued to build his solo career with a string of appearances on British television and I was to be impressed by his modesty and unassuming manner when we met in the green room. Three years later I would be writing about Paco filling the Albert Hall as he teamed up with the masters of the steel strung guitar, John McLaughlin and Larry Coryell.[20]

While Paco de Lucía was concentrating on his international career, during 1978 his father would make the mistake of leaving Camarón without a recording contract. Others would soon convince the singer that his yearly albums with Paco had become too formulaic. It was time for something new, and a palace revolution that would see Paco and his enterprising father usurped.

4

A Legend of Time, 1979

La vida es un contratiempo
José Monje Cruz

After his marriage to La Chispa in 1976 and the release of *Castillo de Arena* in 1977, Camarón entered one of the quietest times of his life. This unusual period of tranquillity was soon to end with the recording of an album that would mark a watershed in flamenco's 250-year history. In the same way that commentators have spoken of the flamenco guitar before and after Paco de Lucía, the roots of flamenco art, its *cante* or song, were about to experience a revolution that would threaten this very conservative art. Flamenco song, which had been stagnating in the final years of Franco's dictatorship and had almost become the personal property of artists like Antonio Mairena, would finally be freed from the clutches of the reactionary critics. Ironically, this reborn 'Che Guevara' of flamenco was also a master of all the older *cantes* and would frequently race off to a remote village where he had heard that an old singer knew the lyrics to a song from the golden age.[1]

La Leyenda del Tiempo, which went on sale in 1979, was an album that found Camarón in superb form. Much of its inspiration had come from the joints he smoked between takes in the Madrid studio's toilets. His fellow musicians, who included the group *Alameda* and the Amador brothers, chose to stave off the long hours with a seemingly endless supply of fried fish.[2] This was just the start of the singer's need to take drugs both for inspiration and to calm his nerves. Sadly Camarón would soon upgrade from hashish to heroin. He had never been in such a large studio and was used to recording his work within the constraints of only eight tracks. After nine records overseen by Paco de Lucía's father Antonio Sánchez Pecino, Camarón had finally been lured away to the more demanding world of multi-tracking by a new producer, Ricardo Pachón. He was now entering an orbit where other talented musicians just drifted in and out of studios; including the jazz–rock group *Dolores*, who would later tour with Paco de Lucía, and the very talented *palmeros* who did all the rhythmic clapping on flamenco studio albums. None of the musicians, including Camarón and Tomatito, thought at the time that they were about to unleash a ground-breaking record that would inspire a revolution. They were more interested in food and particularly the *mojarrita* that was prepared by Juan el Camas.[3] During the recording they sent for twelve kilos of fish from San Fernando and accompanied it with chickpeas, chard and *pringa*: containing pig's trotters, beef and the all-important type of fat, the *tocino*.

La Leyenda del Tiempo did not just happen spontaneously, but it is also unlikely that this record would have been made had Camarón not been in search for a new recording contract. Although Camarón had been in talks with Manuel Molina about a new album, nothing had been signed as Camarón was in a hurry to return to his home in La Línea. The search for a new record deal created a vacuum and the ideal opportunity for the enterprising producer Ricardo Pachón to make his move and attract Camarón with an exciting proposition. Pachón, who had a reputation built around the production of albums with the gypsy duo *Lole y Manuel*, was keen to show Camarón his arrangement of Federico García Lorca's *Romance del Amargo*.[4] The offer of such innovative material was very attractive and a deal was struck; Camarón leaving for his home with a new contract. This was the start of a journey that would later see him emerge as both popular hero and victim. Camarón would now turn his back on the material of Antonio Sánchez Pecino that owed much to flamenco's past, as he sought to create a new tradition.

The origins of this impending revolution can be traced back to the album *Guitarras Callejeras*, when Camarón had been close to the gypsy Amador brothers Raimundo and Rafael, and he was soon to be surrounded by members of the *Alameda* rock group in Ricardo Pachón's home in Umbrete on the outskirts of Seville. These were heady days in the spring of 1979, when the musicians came together in the picturesque Andalusian countryside dominated by the olive groves and vines that produce the *mosto* wine. Drinking something a little stronger and enjoying themselves, their antics would prompt calls from the *Guardia Civil.*[5] Camarón would come into contact with many talented young musicians, including Kiko Veneno who wrote *Volando Voy*, later to become the official hymn of post-Franco Spain.[6]

In the summer of 1979, the public finally found out what Camarón had been up to in those Madrid studios when *La Leyenda del Tiempo* hit the streets on 16 June. This album, later dubbed the *Sgt. Pepper's Lonely Hearts Club Band* of flamenco by the writer José Manuel Gamboa, was distinct from any previously recorded project although there had been hints of a sea change on *Castillo de Arena* of 1977.[7] Despite being subsequently described as 'iconoclastic' and initiating the flamenco revolution now labelled *nuevo flamenco*, it was to be a commercial flop.[8] Selling at 500 pesetas, the grainy, over-exposed photograph on its cover portrayed a more intellectual Camarón. The skillful cropping of this image presented Camarón not just as a singer, but also as a dignified composer contemplating his music with a half-smoked cigarette hanging from his mouth. Gone was the youthful, t-shirted, fresh-faced gypsy star, to be replaced by a more thoughtful and intense figure. Had this superb photograph by Mario Pacheco not been cropped, we would have discovered a very different Camarón, whose intense gaze was actually focused on his left hand as he fingered a chord on his guitar. With this album, Camarón severed the ties of his recording partnership with Paco de Lucía and his father Antonio Sánchez. He also appeared for the first time with a beard and conveyed another less than subtle message on the reverse of the sleeve, where he was shown fighting a young cow. This was common practice for the many young men who, like Camarón, have aspirations of becoming professional bullfighters; but this image was removed when *La Leyenda del Tiempo* became available as a CD.

So what made this album so different and can it really be compared with The Beatle's *Sgt. Pepper's Lonely Hearts Club Band*? Both albums owed much of their creativity in the studio to the stimulus of drugs. LSD was a very popular drug in the late sixties while Camarón would smoke a considerable quantity of hash during the recording of *La Leyenda del Tiempo*. The Beatles' landmark album would turn pop music into an art form while Camarón's project would also influence the future development of flamenco. If we approach this question simply from a point of view of sales, then there can be no comparison. At the time of Camarón's death, thirteen years after its release, *La Leyenda del Tiempo* had sold a mere 5,470 copies![9] A very small quantity for a record described as the greatest in flamenco's history by *El País de las Tentaciones* in August 1994.[10] Although Nacho Saenz de Tejada did report that another 372 albums were sold during the twelve days after his death, it still remains small beer. It is possible that many more copies were sold at the time, but then later taken back to the shops having been played just once, as the producer Ricardo Pachón recalled in 1993:'I still remember when gypsies returned albums of *La Leyenda del Tiempo* to the department store *El Corte Inglés* saying that the artist was not their Camarón and in that album is José's most chilling *soleá: El Romance del Amargo'*.[11] There are many comparisons that can be made with the Beatles album of 1967. Both were produced with covers that made a fundamental break with the past. Camarón was no longer depicted in the typical flamenco singer pose that featured on his previous albums and more importantly he did not look into the camera and gaze out at his audience. While through the medium of a grey, grainy photograph, the reverse of the sleeve showed Camarón practising his dream profession of being a *torero* as he tested out his cape work. This was just the start of the projection of a very different type of flamenco artist, whose image had much in common with a rock star; the sleeves of Camarón's vinyl long players would later reflect this. Gone were the laminated covers of the mid-seventies, to be replaced by a soft matt and patterned finish, to compliment the burnt out and heavily exposed grainy photograph. While Camarón's record, in common with The Beatles' album, reproduced all the lyrics for the first time, there were even more radical signs of the impending revolution.

Also for the first time, the name of his established guitarist Paco de Lucía was absent and Camarón was no longer *de la Isla* but famous enough to be simply 'Camarón'. Something far more fundamental had happened which did have echoes in the work of the Beatles, as *La Leyenda del Tiempo* was a complete departure from the live performances Camarón was giving in the mountain villages. The album took full advantage of all the possibilities and opportunities that a studio had to offer. In 1979, responding to the developments in popular music, Camarón was about to become the first flamenco artist to exploit contemporary studio techniques. The days of recording flamenco 'in the field' were numbered and Camarón would follow the example of the Beatles and create his music in the studio and not on the road.

The impact of this album owes as much to the skills and vision of its producer Ricardo Pachón and the photographer Mario Pacheco, as to the genius of Camarón. Pacheco had spent several years in London working as a photographer for record houses and had acquired many skills in image creation that were to be employed on flamenco's most distinctive cover. Meanwhile, Pachón had been staying up late following Camarón and guitarist Tomatito perform in the Andalusian summer festivals. Pacheco would go on to establish his own flamenco label in Madrid, built on his success promoting punk and pop bands and the new avenues that Camarón would open up. Pachón would become the real architect of what became known as *Nuevo Flamenco* or the new flamenco movement. Pachón's experiment with Camarón would draw on and encourage a whole new generation of artists who, in the eighties and early nineties, became the vanguard of the new flamenco movement recording on Pacheco's *Nuevos Medios* label. Pacheco's flamenco roots were to be found in Madrid where he had listened to the exotic sounds of flamenco on the radio while his father had worked on the films starring Manolo Caracol. This rich heritage would later provide a sympathetic producer for the creative talents of the gypsy bands *Pata Negra*, *Ketama* and *La Barbaría del Sur*, while Pachón would launch the *Flamenco Vivo* label.

The inspiration for *La Leyenda del Tiempo* can be found in the recordings that Ricardo Pachón made of Camarón singing at festivals during 1978, on his portable Nagra tape recorder with a Newman microphone.[12] This lawyer and amateur guitarist had the stamina to visit far-flung villages including Bornos and Alcalá de Guadaira to record Camarón at his best. He had already worked outside the conservative field of flamenco with the group *Smash* in 1970 and with Lole and Manuel in the mid-seventies, and was now politically and artistically motivated in his bid to create new flamenco, rather than simply produce albums of songs coming from an accepted canon. In several ways it was a strange way to approach making what would essentially be a studio concept album. Now entering his forties, Pachón felt the 'reason and purpose for flamenco had been lost' with the destruction of houses in Triana and the eviction of the gypsies. This displacement of the gypsies allowed the self-appointed guardian of flamenco, Antonio Mairena, to order flamenco song into a 'classic body of work'. Flamenco songs would now be taught in a 'cold way' to the new generation and audiences would now listen to flamenco in a 'formal and depersonalized way' as the festivals began to grow in popularity.[13] Pachón was clearly more than just someone with the capacity to unleash a musical revolution, as was demonstrated much later when he adapted Alberto Korda's iconic image of Che Guevara, to promote Camarón's posthumous *Antología Inédita* album in 2000. Pachón has been identified as the chief architect of this revolution that presented Camarón and his guitarist Tomatito, who was only twenty years old at the time, with the challenge of recording a project that they did not fully understand. Neither did they anticipate the fierce criticism they would attract from the conservative flamencologists or that, even worse the album would be a commercial flop.

Looking back at the recording of the album in 2001, Tomatito talked about his role as Camarón's guitarist on *La Leyenda del Tiempo*. He was just a young and relatively unknown guitarist, barely out of his teens, working with a singer he worshipped. Only Tomatito really knew how Camarón, an artist so enraptured with the songs sung by the village elders, actually reacted to such a ground breaking project:

> I was really scared, these were pieces that were much too modern and I couldn't see the point. José was also amazed and he would say; 'don't suffer Tomate. You will see how tomorrow we'll turn this around.' He could see quite clearly, and now you can see that it was so advanced that now twenty years later you could even release the practice sessions.[14]

Tomatito and Camarón may have been scared by this project but they certainly did not show it, as the photographs of the time record. Tomatito was captured with uncharacteristically short hair, relaxed and stripped to the waist, while Raimundo Amador, who also played guitar on the album, had even unbuttoned his trousers. All this while Camarón calmly smoked *porros* or joints in the studio toilets.[15]

The journalist Diego A. Manrique had reminded Tomatito that, despite the high regard that the album is held in today, two of the live sessions had not been successful. Interestingly, Tomatito did admit to being ashamed of some of their flamenco recordings, but when comparing it with the offer to play with the group Weather Report, he admitted it was a lack of preparation that he would not allow to happen today and that there were aspects that made him embarrassed. How did Camarón react to the critics who claimed that he had damaged a traditional art? Tomatito was convinced that it had no effect on Camarón's self belief:

What Camarón didn't want was the fatigue of touring with a group. He never doubted that he had done the correct thing. Also he dominated the classical better than anyone. He knew all of the old songs. If they told him there was someone old or somebody young in such a village that could sing songs which were unknown he would go.

Camarón's former accompanist, Ramón de Algeciras, had also testified to the singer's interest in tradition:

we played Camarón a tape we had of Niño Barbate singing some excellent old-time cantes. After listening a couple of times, Camarón not only learned them, but invariably improved upon them, adding his own touches and personality. He was like a sponge, but not any old sponge; Camarón is a sponge with genius.[16]

Once again there were echoes of the Beatles, with Tomatito openly admitting that Camarón hated the touring associated with live performances. He also hated the hanging around at the summer flamenco festivals where, because of his fame he would often be the last performer on stage.

So where can we find the inspiration for this remarkable experiment in flamenco music? Should we return to Miles Davis' *Sketches of Spain*, recorded in November 1959 and March 1960? Or should we go back even further to 1956 when *Flamenco Sketches* was featured on his *Kind of Blue* album? The sleeve notes on *Sketches of Spain* had proclaimed 'It is as if Miles had been born of Andalusian gypsies, but instead of picking up the guitar, had decided to make a trumpet the expression of his *cante hondo* [deep song]'.[17] Miles Davis had become obsessed with Joaquín Rodrigo's *Concierto de Aranjuez* but on this album he ventured to the heart of Camarón's world with his stunning interpretation of a *soleá*. Is it possible that Juan Serrano's album *Flamenco Fenómeno*, released in 1966, was an early attempt at pushing at the then rigid boundaries of flamenco? Serrano included, amongst the traditional *toques* his *Flamenco Variations on Autumn Leaves* and *Flamenco Impressions of New York*. Or, should we turn to the gypsy guitarist Sabicas and his remarkable excursion into the world of rock with the release of *Sabicas – Rock Encounter with Joe Beck* in 1970? Here the sleeve notes claimed that 'Rock and Flamenco are both alluring and erotic, loud and have kick, sock and great passion' and that this was 'perhaps the first time an international classical concert performer of world renown has sat down and seriously tried to get into rock'.

Whoever designed the lurid cover for this album, which depicts a flamenco guitarist playing in front of a castle surrounded by a naked woman and some flying mice, had certainly enjoyed more than a joint before penning this one! There is an easier answer with the album *Flamenco-Jazz* recorded by in 1967 by Pedro Iturralde with Paco de Lucía. Dare we also mention, for fear of upsetting the purists, the work in the United States of Carlos Montoya: including the *St. Louis Blues* and his *Moors in Granada*, issued in 1966.

Coventry, Autumn 1979

The young flamenco guitarist and composer David Shepherd had just returned from another trip to Jerez, studying with those renowned guardians of the tradition of the *guitarra gitana*, José Luis Balao and El Carbonero. His lessons had been conducted in the traditional way, the guitar variations demonstrated at breakneck speed. It was taken for granted that he had the ability to imitate the *falsetas* immediately. The local currency in Jerez, as with most cities in Andalucía, was the guitar licks from the Paco de Lucía album *Almoraima*, which had created a whole new school of guitar playing, in the same way Camarón's 1979 album would rewrite the rules of the *cante*. Elsewhere, guitar lessons in southern Spain during the late seventies were much as they had always been, informal affairs where a vague time was set but a price not agreed and the tuition often involved the student showing the teacher a lick he was interested to learn and still having to pay for the privilege! This was not how José Luis Balao and El Carbonero operated; they were amongst the best teachers in the business and taught their own creations. They were also fascinated by David's ability to play the classical as well as the flamenco guitar. This summer was to be a little different as he had bought a copy of *La Leyenda del Tiempo* and could not wait to find a turntable to play it on:

> It was an immensely important album at that time, obviously I would have come to this album through earlier releases of Camarón with Paco de Lucía, again immensely inspiring collections, but albums that really reflected what those two performers were taking to the public at that time. This album is incredibly different, it's a concept album that is designed to be listened fully through, beginning to end. It incorporates so many different and new instruments, the sitar, the keyboard synthesizer, the approach to the guitar, a very tight relationship between the *falsetas* of the guitarist and excellent player Tomatito and the music of Camarón, also the incorporation of Latin-American styles and *compás* into this album. All of those points have been

departure points for a completely new direction in flamenco. People are still referring to this particular album now for new ways to go, new ideas to capitalize on. So it's a vital album for everybody involved in flamenco today.[18]

He had also read the headlines that described the album as a failure, but he was not surprised:

> Flamenco has always been in a state of change and I think it's simply one of those things that there will always be people involved in this art, who prefer what they know and there will always be people in this art that prefer what is coming, what they're inventing today. Right now in the capitals of Spain, in Madrid, in Barcelona, amongst the new generation of players, the new flamenco is certainly flamenco and certainly vital to them. It's a new form of expression, which fills their lives. They can't be asked to express themselves in the way that the previous generation or the generation before did, it makes no sense and it certainly makes no sense to them.[19]

David could still recall how Camarón's 1977 album *Castillo de Arena* had concluded in a traditional way with the *seguiriyas, por cositas malas*. There was nothing here to upset the purists as Paco de Lucía's guitar accompaniment fitted Camarón's singing like a glove. But there were some clues as to the direction Camarón was moving in with the fresh approach he took on the opening *bulerías Samara*. The fluency of his singing was remarkable, but there was something very different about this *bulerías* which indicated that having now mastered the key forms of flamenco, Camarón had to put his own stamp on them and any young singer would now have to get to grips with what he was doing stylistically. The tangos, *Y Mira Que Mira Y Mira* openly displayed the touchpaper for a musical revolution that was about to be lit. The gap between the most recognisable form of music associated with a European country and the type of popular music being created in Britain and the United States was narrowing. The instrumental licks played on the *Laúd* or Arabic lute alluded to flamenco's rich heritage, while taking their cue from Paco de Lucía's ground breaking *Almoraima* album from the previous year. However, the basic *tangos* rhythm could still be clearly distinguished and would not unduly worry those who held chairs in flamenco at Córdoba and Granada Universities and neither would it attract much attention from the conservative critics of flamenco who wrote for the Spanish dailies. *Castillo de Arena* did not even prepare the most diehard *Camaroneros* for his forthcoming record, which would and still does, mark a watershed in flamenco's illustrious history.

Camarón's album of 1977 had listed Paco de Lucía's father, Antonio Sánchez, as the author of the majority of the tracks but on *La Leyenda del Tiempo* it was noticeable that Camarón had turned to a new producer and ended a run of nine albums with a team that had brought him so much success. Ricardo Pachón and his *Flamenco Vivo* production house had done the unthinkable and released a Camarón album without the guitar playing of Paco de Lucía. Paco was busy conquering Europe and the United States; working on his image as a guitarist of world stature, as he forged links with guitar luminaries from the world of jazz and rock, including John McLaughlin and Larry Coryell. Meanwhile in Spain, Camarón's new producer, Pachón, was drawing on the poetry of Federico García Lorca for the *letras* or lyrics of five of the songs on the new album. His most inspired decision being the recording of Lorca's famous lullaby *Nana del Caballo Grande* which he set to the rhythm of the *siguiriyas* played on a sitar.

The opening seconds of the *jaleos* on the album's title track, *La Leyenda del Tiempo*, were revolutionary in themselves, as Pachón chose to fade up the *palmas* or rhythmic handclapping that introduces this work. Before Camarón's voice even appeared we were clearly told, by the introduction of electric piano and a full drum kit, that this was no ordinary flamenco record and that it intended to break all the rules including featuring instruments not traditionally used in flamenco. Camarón's voice was as fresh and inspired as ever, but he now had a new guitarist, who very few people had heard of and who appeared as comfortable at playing rock riffs as the traditional flamenco *falsetas*. By the time the moog synthesiser entered the fray, one could almost hear the critics and some of the guitar teachers in Jerez reaching for their poison pens! With another faded introduction and more Lorca poetry Pachón had clearly signalled his intention to release flamenco's first genuine concept album. The *soleá por bulerías* was classic flamenco at its best with Tomatito's minimal accompaniment allowing Camarón's voice to take centre stage. There was little sign of the revolution here, apart from the way the track was recorded and mixed in Fonograms' Madrid studios, but we were introduced to just how fast Tomatito's right-hand thumb was and the precision of his *alzapúa*. Pachón had chosen to programme a *bulerías* for the *Homenaje a Federico* and there was a hint of Raimundo Amador's variations on the bass underpinning Tomatito's classy licks but the sting came in the tail. Pachón cleverly used a traditional *palo seco* conclusion to this song with the absence of Tomatito's guitar, as Camarón sang a cappella, but he gave it a modern twist by reintroducing the drum kit to ensure the disapproval of the critics. Camarón had few problems recording the *cantiñas* which, in common with the *bulerías*, drew on the *letras* or lyrics of the poet Federico García Lorca that followed. This was the maestro at his best, singing to the rhythms of his homeland in San Fernando learnt from his mother as a very young child. There was nothing particularly revolutionary about recording the footwork of the dancer Manuel Soler, but there was a very innovative feel to the way Pachón had recorded and mixed Tomatito's guitar.

If Camarón's fans had been uneasy with the opening title track, the inclusion of *La Tarara*, again accompanied by electric guitar and a very prominent drum kit, was the final straw that prompted them to return the album in such high numbers. This was their idol unashamedly singing an arrangement which had more in common with a rock song; only the slick and stylish *picardo* runs, some tasty *alzapúa* thumb work and the ubiquitous *tarantas* chord from Tomatito's guitar remained to reassure them that this was a hybrid flamenco project. While Andalucía had a long-established tradition of artists who played flamenco music on the piano, aficionados were not yet ready in the late seventies for instrumental piano breaks on the albums of mainstream flamenco artists. To understand how revolutionary the inclusion of the keyboards and drum kits were, one has to compare this album with the material other flamenco artists were releasing in 1979; close examination reveals an enormous gulf. Comparisons can only really be made with the music being created by bands including *Alameda* and *Smash*. The licks created by the electric guitarist Pepe Roca would make this album more accessible to audiences in Britain and the United States as Ricardo Pachón introduced the unthinkable for a flamenco album, the fade-out to close the A-side. After five ground-breaking tracks that put an ocean between this offering and his previous album *Castillo de Arena*, how many of the few thousand fans that purchased this record in the early days of its release had the stomach to turn the record over and find out what delights Pachón had programmed on the B-side?

Kiko Veneno, who had left Camarón's home province of Cádiz for the magic of the colonial city of Seville, would mastermind one on the most memorable tracks from this album to open the second side. Veneno had worked with the Amador brothers and would subsequently emerge as a key writer for the gypsy group *Pata Negra*. *Volando Voy* would later become a universal anthem that had many sections of Spanish society humming and singing on the coaches and trains as, after all, it was an unashamedly popular *rumba* that had wide appeal. A catchy tune, lively guitar strumming, sugary flutes and bongos could not fail to win over the public as Camarón transported them to Latin America, but what was this track doing on the album of an artist who cherished the purity of his gypsy race and their creation, the *cante*. As the curtain closed on the flute playing of Jorge Pardo, Pachón took us back to the flamenco world of the seventies where styles like the *alegrías* were punctuated with handclaps in counter time very much in the foreground as the art had not yet discovered the *cajón* or percussive box. The next track, entitled *Bahía de Cádiz* gave the impression of honouring the tradition of the *alegrías*, until the arrival of the marauding bass lines of Manolo Rosa began to develop. Then, just as Camarón began to sing about the river estuaries near his homeland in Santi Petri to the backing of a Moog synthesiser, the innovative arrangements of Pachón revealed that this was anything but a typical *alegrías* despite the regular and familiar guitar *falsetas* cleverly putting the listener at his ease. The album was now drawing more on flamenco's roots as Camarón sang Kiko Veneno's arrangement of Omar Kayyam's *Viejo Mundo* set to the *bulerías*. How could the purists object to a number that featured the young Tomatito unveiling for the first time some of his best licks and just how fast the thumb on his right hand could move? Camarón was inspired by his new guitarist and the verses on this track would very quickly become obligatory 'hits' to be heard whenever he performed live. Once again, as Camarón excited his audience with his trademark *lailo lo lailo la*, Ricardo Pachón fully exploited the opportunities for creativity that multi-tracking offered. He then stayed with the rhythms that had evolved around the gypsy forges by fading in *pitos*, or the rhythmic clicking of fingers, to present a fascinating interpretation of the *tangos* as Tomatito again showed what a promising guitarist he was. This track just oozed the atmosphere of a flamenco party with Camarón very comfortable with the style he was to dominate for over a decade, but not all the public were ready for a fade-out studio mix of Camarón's *leilolas*.

They say that in showbusiness you should save the best for last and leave the audience wanting more; a cliché Pachón was very aware of when he programmed seven seconds of silence before introducing the most controversial aspect of the album. Aficionados were initially surprised at hearing the sound of a sitar, an instrument previously not used in flamenco music, as Gualberto García Pérez was introduced to the traditional flamenco lullaby or *nana*. This *Sevillano*, and former member of the group *Smash*, had a history of developing flamenco rock and this album would encourage him to continue the musical experiments with the guitarist Ricardo Miño during the early eighties on the album *Puente Mágico*. This remarkable track, which initiated a major upheaval in flamenco art, was born out of strange circumstances that included no prior preparation or rehearsal. An exhausted hungry and thirsty Gualberto had arrived in Madrid from Seville to meet Camarón. As Camarón drank from a bottle of water the sitarist Gualberto drank a beer whilst ravenously munching on a roll filled with *chorizo* as they quickly prepared for the recording.[20] Little did Gualberto realise that he was laying the foundations for the re-issue of this lullaby ten years later, as Camarón's voice and the strings of the Royal Philharmonic Orchestra would combine to give him a best selling album. Yet another version of the *nana*, this time set to the rhythm of the *siguiriya* with Tomatito's guitar complimenting Gualberto's sitar, would also surface in 2000 as Pachón now portrayed Camarón as the new Che Guevara on the sleeve of *Antología Inédita*. The *Nana del Caballo Grande* was recorded live with the two artists facing each other while the keyboardist Manolo Marinelli marked out a backing track. This awesome track was completed in just one take with both artists under a great deal of pressure facing a studio full of people. Camarón sang with such passion and Gualberto eloquently answered the lines that spoke of a horse that did not want to drink because the water was black amid the branches. This track, with such a remarkable haunting quality, was to present Camarón, then a well man at the height of his artistic powers, as an artist totally focused on producing a new album. Within two years he would take heroin for the first time as he embarked on the first of three albums that would cement his reputation for posterity.

Nacho Saenz de Tejada later quoted the precise number of copies that *La Leyenda del Tiempo* had sold by 14 July 1992 as 5,842.[21] Even allowing for a boost in trade during the two weeks after Camarón's death, the sales of this landmark album had failed to make the 6,000 mark. Nevertheless a new framework, model and context for making flamenco albums had been firmly established. Camarón was to be deeply hurt by the negative reviews that *La Leyenda del Tiempo* received and was determined that his next album, *Como el Agua*, released two years later in 1981, would not be an extreme experiment that pushed the boundaries and attracted adverse critics. Yet Camarón was already emerging as the art's greatest artist and he would later be reassured, as he emerged as the father of new flamenco, that *La Leyenda del Tiempo* was an important gift he had given to the art. Despite the fallout and negative criticism Camarón received from this album, he went on to say:

> I have always tried new and different things and to contribute something of my own, without losing sight of the roots. With every record I bring out, I did the same thing. That's not difficult. I say that everything we do is flamenco because I am above all flamenco, and that's it.[22]

From *La Leyenda del Tiempo* onwards, the Camarón brand would become further established as the singer acquired the ownership of the 'new flamenco'. 1979 had been a momentous year as Camarón also became a father to Luis, his first son who would emerge after his death as a professional guitar player.

5

San Fernando's Rolling Stone, 1980–1987

*Panuelos de lunares que un gitano de San Fernando me quitabas la vida
con un solo 'quejío' y un solo quebranto.*
Juan Gómez 'Chicuelo' and Ginesa Ortega, *mis clavellinas*

The head-on collision that occurred on 17 October 1986, on the N340, was reported the following day in the local press with the story that an unconscious Camarón had been taken to the Hospital de la Seguridad Social de Cádiz. Remarkably, his wife and three children were only bruised, although Spain's leading daily *El País* described Camarón as seriously injured. Later, the accident was to further fuel the gossip regarding the extent of his drug-taking, and the subsequent attitude of the hospital staff indicated that he stood little chance of a fair trial. According to the journalist, Paco Espínola, while many of his fans went to the hospital to support Camarón, the hospital's doctors and nurses became very angry when they 'realised that the accident could have been due to his tiredness caused by a recent dose of liquid methadone found in the car'.[1] Camarón would receive little sympathy at the hearing when his defence argued that an unusual mechanical movement had caused the accident. Was it Camarón's reputation, or that the vehicle had only 3,000km on the clock that influenced the judge to rule out even a cursory examination of the vehicle? The decision to dismiss any inspection of Camarón's Land Rover seemed very unreasonable, with the judge taking the unscientific and perverse view that a new vehicle would be unlikely to have faults.

The eighties had started well for Camarón as he took on his rival, the singer Enrique Morente, in a *mano a mano* at the Frontón in Madrid. These singing contests, which often bring together two singers with contrasting styles, are more like a boxing match with the rival supporters becoming very vociferous and animated as they await the knockout punch. Camarón was emerging as the highest paid artist in flamenco and was paid a million pesetas for this high profile scrap, but the conservative organisers of the first *Bienal de Arte Flamenco* were not yet ready to invite Camarón to their exclusive bash. They preferred more conservative artists like the school-teacher Calixto Sánchez, but the organisers would be forced to invite Camarón in the years to come. At this time the singer had far more important bookings, as he would soon start appearing at sports stadiums in front of 15,000 spectators. Camarón would launch these alternative flamenco spectacles in 1981, at a Madrid sports stadium, and later take his new circus in the company of other artists to Barcelona. His growing fame had also brought him to the attention of the influential filmmaker, Carlos Saura, who was about to shoot the first of a trilogy of flamenco films, the most popular of which would be *Carmen* staring Antonio Gades, Cristina Hoyos and Paco de Lucía. Unfortunately, although Saura filmed sequences of Camarón for his film adaptation of Federico García Lorca's *Blood Wedding*, they did not find their way into the final cut of one of the most enduring flamenco films.[2]

Commercially Camarón was still on top of his game, releasing *Como el agua* in 1981, the first of three highly produced records that would be heavily influenced by the brothers Paco and Pepe de Lucía with whom he had renewed his recording relationship. *Como el agua* would give Camarón a 'hit' song whilst the cover portrayed him as a pop star whose life revolved around the recording studio. Two years later, in 1983, he would release an even more commercial album with orchestral string arrangements and a very catchy *fandango de Huelva*. The dimly lit cover photograph on *Calle Real* presented a more sophisticated and mature Camarón wearing a *sombrero* that gave him an air of mystery.

In 1984 Camarón recorded *Viviré* with the Paco de Lucía Sextet, while away from the studios incidents at his live performances would start to feed the many myths that had begun to surround the singer. This album saw Camarón reach his commercial peak with the stamp of Pepe de Lucía all over the lyrics and arrangements as the singer told his fans, through the album's title, that he would survive. Camarón also became involved in another project of Ricardo Pachón: investigating the origins of flamenco and the lives of its practitioners, for a television series called *El Ángel* that was filmed between February and June but not released on CD until 1993. Camarón stole the show with the most remarkable performance of the *bulerías*, *El Niño Perdido*, which demonstrated that despite his problems he remained the undisputed king.

1985 was not been a good year for the singer as he parted company yet again with his guitarist Paco de Lucía after a disagreement in New York; it would be another two years before they were united by a concert in Madrid.[3] Camarón was also facing a public debate over his revolutionary treatments of the *cante* that was picked up by the media, who printed articles with some aficionados defending his work. His growing band of fans considered him to be in a different league to his rivals as he ranked with the greats, including Manuel Torre, Manolo Caracol and Antonio Mairena because he did not simply copy the old ways but created his own.[4] While he continued to dominate the art, his problems away from the stage were growing and his declining health was further compounded with his teeth continuing to decay. In her radio tribute to Camarón, Allison Hughes, the presenter of the English Language Service on Spanish National radio, graphically highlighted how the singer's increasingly erratic behaviour was being perceived:

> His absences contributed to the growing black legend that surrounded him. Camarón had a drinking problem and he was a widely known heroin addict. His face became progressively more gaunt and cavernous. His eyes had a lost look about them. Like other *cantaores* before him, Camarón was pushing himself to unbearable extremes.

But were others also expecting too much with his naturally shy nature making it increasingly difficult for him to cope with the level of expectation that went with his fame. Paco Espínola's assessment of Camarón's situation in the mid-eighties was blunt and revealing when he stated that Camarón was feeling 'very ill' and proclaimed him as bankrupt.[5] Camarón's financial situation now contrasted greatly with that of Paco de Lucía, whose cache and earning power had continued to soar as he toured Europe with his sextet; he even found time to record and share the soundtrack for the film *The Hit* with fellow guitarist Eric Clapton.

A closer examination of Camarón's financial position in the eighties would reveal some surprising details, including the inability of the 'King of

Flamenco' to afford essential dental treatment. While Camarón was more worried about the state of his teeth and how their deterioration could affect his ability to sing and earn money, he hit out at his critics in the Spanish press.[6] In a thinly veiled attack on Antonio Mairena and the *Mairenistas*, Camarón questioned the whole concept of just copying the way things had been sung in the 'Golden Age'. Angry and isolated, with few friends, he was fortunate to have the support of the film star and singer Pepa Flores, better know as Marisol, who provided the substantial sum of two million pesetas to fund his dental work.[7] He would also have been heartened by the considerable respect he continued to receive from fellow gypsy musicians. Away from all his problems he was still perceived as a very successful gypsy and the highly successful group *Pata Negra* paid tribute with a track called *Camarón* on their new album.

If 1985 had been a black year for Camarón, 1986 was to be even worse, marked by two key events at the start and close of that year that he would never recover from. The death of his mother Juana Cruz Castro would severely upset him and he would be further troubled by a fatal road accident that would condemn him to a year's prison sentence. His mother had been his greatest inspiration and what footage exists of Camarón in her company illustrates his utter devotion and worship. For the singer, there would now be only memories of those legendary flamenco parties or *juergas*, where he and his mother would sing, surrounded by the elder gypsies who danced as Paco Cepero played the guitar. He could only look back to those halcyon days when, as an emerging star dressed in a jean jacket, he would give his mother a hug as she finished singing another inspired *bulerías al gurugú*. With these memories, prompted by this bereavement in February 1986, Camarón still agreed to a high profile interview. The publicity and spin for his new album *Te lo Dice Camarón* would result in his image gracing the cover of the influential and stylish weekly magazine supplement which accompanied the *El País* newspaper. Still in mourning, he had agreed to speak to Maite Contreras, whom he was eager to communicate his intention to work very hard for the next ten years so that his children would be provided for and so that he could retire. Aspects of the interview would be apocalyptic, as he would die in just over six years with the press running stories that his widow and four children were left with very little.

Contreras claims to have put in many calls which were never answered by Camarón, but the singer did eventually arrive on a Monday at the offices of *El País* on a publicity offensive which was no doubt masterminded by Humanes and Torrente. Camarón did not disappoint, as he was happy to accept that gypsies have always been hippies 'because Jesus Christ was the first to wander with a cart and a *burro* and with hair and a long beard'. Camarón was also happy to admit his affairs with women, but only as a seventeen-year-old teenager in those heady Madrid days when he 'was blond and cute'. He talked about his early life working in his father's forge at the age of twelve with a twenty-six pound hammer. But his answers, including not going to school like other children because he had to work at the forge, were clearly linked to the lyrics of his new album. Once again Camarón was asked to revisit the comments that the singer Manolo Caracol had made about his singing when Juan Vargas had tried to get him work in Madrid's *tablaos*. Memories of Caracol's dismissive attitude of Camarón's singing ability as a child were still fresh as he approached his thirty-seventh birthday, when he claimed that Cararcol went to his grave wanting him to appear at his club *Los Canasteros*. During the late sixties Caracol had visited the Torres Bermejas flamenco nightclub to hear Camarón sing. The singer fondly remembered being inhibited when Caracol turned up, but relaxed when the owner, Don Felipe, reminded Caracol that he used to get paid only 250 pesetas when he worked there. What emerged in this interview was the true character of the artist, his quiet unassuming demeanour and his unease at being considered a leader of a flamenco revolution. Camarón went on to freely admit to suffering from nerves before he performed. He even spoke of his body shaking and he confessed that he now suffered from vertigo. He was also very keen to explain that while he wanted to create new flamenco, it had to be untainted. It was not just the music that he wanted to remain pure but also the gypsy race; a race that would survive with its purity being maintained by forbidding marriage with non-gypsies.

The interview offered the reader a key insight into Camarón as victim, already on the road to destruction and his martyrdom. We were told that 'he leads a normal life' and he was presented as a family man living in La Línea de la Concepcíon in Cádiz province where you will usually find him, if he is not staying overnight in a Madrid hotel whilst cutting a new album. But how did this image square with Contreras' description of their encounter, where she thought:

> she was looking at Jesus Christ: ghostly, gaunt, black, tiny, longhaired, a cap, bearded and glasses. His tiny feet, encased in low-topped suede boots, also black, followed one after the other, carefully, as if each told the other when

it was its turn to move. He exudes elegance and style and he walks and has such class that, even if he wished to pass unnoticed, he could not. He radiates something magic, bordering on the realm of the occult. One derives pleasure from looking at him but also feels embarrassment even when he doesn't know he is being observed.[8]

More revelations followed with the news that three university professors had arrived with a dentist from Barcelona to undertake work dedicated to preserving Camarón's vital *embouchure*. It later emerged that Camarón was just hours away from facing his worst fear, the dentist's chair. Camarón was surprisingly candid, but laced his reply with irony when he was asked how does he 'show off' or enjoy himself, to which he replied laughing: 'To smoke a fat joint and get completely stoned. It's been a long time since I have done it, you know! I only show off for my children'. But tucked away in the body of the article was the real dynamite as his new agents, Antonio Humanes and Torrente, revealed their new plans for Camarón following his dental treatment. They clearly stated that the 'direction of work has undergone a radical change' and that he is now in the same league as Plácido Domingo. Any would-be promoter would have to pay the going rate and there would be no more listing his name on recital bills to boost ticket sales without contacting his agent. The subject of exploitation was now freely aired with the statement that Camarón now 'wants his place and is tired of being exploited'. His new management wanted the public to accept that Camarón was no longer just a flamenco artist but now a superstar and his concert fees from now on would reflect this.

Once again the geographical context of Camarón's birthplace: how he got his name and that he was the son of a blacksmith and a basket maker, were trotted out along with the customary platitudes for Antonio Mairena. Contreras was then ready to introduce the readers to what she considered the real story. Spain's middle classes were told how 'the morbid shadow of his supposed dependency on a drug called "horse" appeared on the street one dark day and, since then, the rumours have not ceased to be heard'. Vox pops and anecdotal evidence of his drug taking were also cited with comparisons of Camarón wowing the fans in Alcalá de Henares' football ground in 1984, but later failing to show at a theatre in the same town a year later. Apparently not all of the disappointed fans had been convinced by the excuse that his brother Juan Monje had died the previous day, while others realised he was being asked to do too much.

On its publication the magazine's cover would present a dark and serious brooding figure, while another photograph drew heavily on semiotic values that would communicate the gypsy stereotype. The public would also be introduced to a more relaxed Camarón reclining on a settee and looking very much the rock, and not flamenco, star. In another shot Camarón appeared wearing a beard in a striking *camisa gitana*, with a bracelet on his right hand, clutching a basket. The allusions were not subtle, as these images reinforced the cliché of the trade of gypsies, that of basket making. His mother's nickname was La Canastera, a reference to this profession, and here was her son holding a basket made from the *varetas*, special reeds that Camarón always sang about collecting from the banks of a river in another metaphor of love.

This interview would spawn hundreds of lines of copy regarding the notoriety of the singer and soon the myths surrounding his unhappy life would be further embellished. Ironically, only three days after the publication of this article, Camarón and his guitarist Tomatito performed in a Madrid sports hall in a concert that saw both artists in top form. This was also just the beginning of a saga where Camarón would often keep the promoters and the public waiting. On one occasion with only twenty minutes to curtain up in Madrid, Camarón was still in Cádiz province about to leave by road for Seville airport. His performance was characteristically short, but well received while Ángel Álavarez Caballero's review described Camarón as an enigma who despite his humble and introverted nature could attract thousands of people to a sports stadium.[9] Not even commenting on the actual songs performed, Álvarez Caballero, preferred to try and understand why the people who attended this venue in Madrid would only go to shows that featured Camarón as no other flamenco artist interested them. He also viewed a Camarón gig as a social event and recognised Camarón's ability to take a minority art form to the masses. Whilst accepting the artist as an all-time great, he did not have any answers as to why, despite retaining the purity of the *cante*, Camarón was unique in being able to communicate to such a wide public. Remarkably, this was not a Madrid 'public' of gypsies but of all classes from pensioners to lawyers.

The spring of 1986 saw the arrival in the shops of the new album from Camarón, whose title carried a thinly veiled message regarding his private life for his friends and enemies. Its lyrics were partly designed to reassure those among both his fans and the wider public who feared he was approaching the end of his life. Camarón would now address these concerns in his songs and tell everyone from Madrid journalists to presidents of flamenco clubs that he was a survivor. Within three years he would feel compelled to silence his critics with an even more direct message singing 'they say that my time is running out. They ask if I am alive or dead, and I say as long as my heart is boiling I will defeat my enemy'. His growing fan club had waited two years for *Te lo Dice Camarón* and those close to the singer were not surprised to see that the back of the striking white cover listed Tomatito as the guitarist. Having reunited with Paco de Lucía to record three albums between 1981 and 1984, this partnership, that had rewritten the flamenco rulebook, was again at breaking point with Camarón's health suffering from his drug habit. Their minor row in 1985 was to have significant consequences over the coming years.[10] There have, however, been claims that Paco de Lucía's presence on this recording was still anticipated as they entered the studios.[11]

If any album illustrated Camarón's claim that the only recording he ever prepared for was his first and the rest were improvised in the studios, it had to be his 'white album'.[12] But it was not just the selection of Tomatito as his chosen accompanist that sent out a message. Once again, Camarón's record company had issued an album without a new photograph of the artist gracing either the front or back cover. *Calle Real*, his 1984 release, had introduced his fans to a 'cool' Camarón with his face partially in shadow and his hair covered by a wide brimmed hat. *Viviré* in 1984, had on its front cover a portrait by the artist Máximo Moreno, but at least the reverse presented a contact strip of mug shots of Camarón singing. Yet there was not to be any new image of Camarón on *Te lo Dice Camarón*, only a reworking of one of the most charismatic photographs ever taken: Pepe Lamarca's stunning image from 1977. It was a return to a sensitive image of the artist dressed in a t-shirt that did not need any caption to tell you that Camarón was a gypsy. We can only speculate that Camarón's failing health led to the reworking of this iconic image from the late seventies, as a useable photograph could not be taken.

Camarón's new album did not receive an overwhelming thumbs-up from the critics who, on reviewing this recording, were undoubtedly influenced by reports elsewhere of his private life. Whilst praising some of the songs as 'truly exceptional', the eminent critic Ángel Álvarez Caballero went on to wield the knife in a brutal fashion.[13] Reviewing the album for the newspaper *El País* on 18 April, Álvarez Caballero stated that not only was Camarón's voice not at its best, but that he was not in 'the proper physical condition to be able to develop his work'. He had inside information that the recording of the album had been troubled and that the finished product was made up from various takes spliced together with the technicians having to work 'miracles' with their razor blades and sticky tape! The writer, José Manuel Gamboa, when reflecting on this album several years later, went even further describing the poor production as being 'full of blatant blunders, tonal changes in the mixing and poor sound quality in general'.[14] While Gamboa speculated that Camarón's circle of friends had become even smaller after this album, he overlooked its importance in later helping build Camarón's iconic status.

Álvarez Caballero was also keen to flag up the absence of the Lucías and the return of Tomatito, who was now seen as being joined to Camarón by an umbilical cord. But Camarón's decision to take over the musical direction was viewed in a positive light as it created a fresh approach to recording and a very different sound. The albums with the Lucías, while being of a phenomenal standard, were considered as almost manufactured factory products, with very little difference between any of the recordings. Camarón's instinct to improvise in the studios was crowned by his decision to sing the *soleá* and the *bulerías a palo seco* and *de colmao* unaccompanied, just marking the rhythm with knuckles on a table to give the songs an even greater gravity. Away from the lyrics and song arrangements of Pepe de Lucía and the guitar of Paco de Lucía, Camarón had made a very personal statement. A new influence on Camarón was emerging, Antonio Humanes, who would produce the album and co-write the songs that also now bore Camarón's name. Humanes had also been responsible for brokering a deal that would help Camarón's precarious financial situation. Camarón now had a contract to produce three albums, for which he was paid eleven million pesetas.[15] He was now free to sing a homage to his childhood hero, La Perla de Cádiz, and to pose political questions as to why the flamenco clubs did not have photographs on their walls of La Perla or El Chaqueta. He also felt liberated by singing about how, while the other children went to school, his childhood was spent at the family forge with the anvil, nail and blacksmith's hook. Camarón had left the sugary arrangements of Pepe de Lucía to rediscover his gypsy roots.

Much of Camarón's income came from his appearances at the outdoor flamenco festivals and those fans that saw him in the eighties would need considerable stamina as often the singer would not appear until three in the morning. They would pay their entrance money, pick up a fold–away chair and then face a long night ahead that would normally start with performances from the local talent. Getting a drink or something to eat at these events was always a challenge, as first you needed to go to a kiosk to exchange some money for *tikets*, which could then be exchanged at the bar. Having finally worked out how many *tikets* you required, and proudly obtained the right value of units for that beer and packet of crisps, the battle for refreshments was just in its early stages. There would be hundreds of other customers all calling for the attention of the *camarero* in a bun fight where Andalusian *machismo* rules apply. Observing the queue and simply waving *tikets* around would leave you very thirsty but when you finally did get that beer at a summer festival in Andalucía it was a very special kind of heaven. By midnight many of the men would be very drunk as they started using the ladies toilets and the level of chatter would now be drowning out the flamenco. The president of the local peña would then introduce every artist with their complete life story as he tried to milk his moment of the year for as long as possible. These are just some of the reasons why Camarón disliked doing these events, but money talked especially when you were the highest paid performer and could get away with doing just ten minutes!

What was the fascination of seeing Camarón at a live performance and what did he sing about? Many of his songs came from an established body of work that the aficionados would be very familiar with. They would be more interested in the style, excellence and execution of the interpretation. Camarón sang about many things including relationships with gypsy women, his family, and often his respect for Samara, the queen of the gypsy quarter. The academic, Mercedes García Plata, identified the key themes as love, family, adversity, death, religion, prison and the loss of freedom. His songs also contain much autobiographical detail and pride in his place of birth and the gypsy race. He also included bullfighting themes, verses about the land of Andalucía and her history combined with the laments of those who worked the mines in the Cartagena region.[16]

One of my favourite Camarón songs, which he would sing to the delight of the audience, is a perfect example of how he often used metaphors. He sang of sitting by the river under an old tree when he saw a bird that could not sing because it was hoarse. This made him take pity on the bird and give it some river water with mint leaves from his hand so that it would be refreshed. From this verse Camarón would on occasions develop the theme, which has undertones of love, to sing about sculpting a candlestick from a granite rock to give him light, but he did not want any more light because he lived in darkness and wished to remain a hermit. The Andalusians say that there is no language like flamenco song, but much of it does suffer in translation especially when it draws on their love of diminutives. A good example of this would be the line '*Mi cuerpesito lo tengo, moraito como un lirio*' which could be translated as 'my little body has become small, purple and has the colour of an iris'! But as Rancapino once said, 'flamenco should be sung with spelling errors'.

1987 was to be a year of great triumph, with Camarón's conquest of Paris where he gave performances over three days in the second week of May at the Cirque d'Hiver in Paris. These performances and his return in 1988 would be critical in helping to create the icon people so revere today. Camarón faced a bare stage in Paris, except for two wooden chairs and some monitors, but the atmosphere was electric. Dressed in a sharp dark suit with white shirt and cravat, he would find the Parisian audience far more respectful than the festival crowds of Andalucía. Gone were the matching white suits that the duo wore for concerts in the early eighties, as Camarón had shown his class whilst communicating to the packed audience with ease. Paris also witnessed Tomatito on fire, as he launched into a very difficult variation within minutes of being on stage. Camarón sang with great power, precision and intonation as he gazed intently at his guitarist, characteristically clapping time with *palmas sorderas*, or light flamenco clapping. The pair were at their best bringing the music of Cádiz to France in style. This was a different experience to their gigs in Spain where they would often turn up late and have to go on straight away. Camarón had explored Paris earlier and now, unusually, had time to rehearse his performance and test the sound system by singing some of his classic lines for *bulerías*. He had arrived at the venue early, dressed in cowboy boots and jeans, to do a full sound check and had been very particular about the balance that he was looking for between the voice and the guitar. He was a man on a mission and would only stop for the inevitable fag break as he produced endless packets of Winstons.

Later that evening he would sing a perfect introduction to the *taranta*, as he closed his eyes and his face became contorted with the strain of the concentration. As the verses flowed he would craft the sound and texture of every word as it left his lips, Tomatito accompanying him with a cigarette hanging out of his mouth. Then came the excitement of his *bulerías*, *Tiritiando de Frio*, as the pair really started cooking. The highlight of the performance finally arrived when Camarón sang his hit *Como el agua*, accompanying himself on a traditional peg-head guitar. The light had reflected off the gold rings on each of the fingers of his left hand while only the *menique* finger of his left hand displayed a ring. Under his shirt was even more gold jewellery that included a necklace of Christ carrying the cross on his way to Calvary.

Away from Paris, Camarón wanted his fans to believe that he was in good health. The reality had been very different and in 1987 he found himself in a house in Ronda facing up to his addiction amongst friends.[17] He had been advised to make an appointment with a doctor called Miguel Casas in Barcelona, who was so shocked at meeting 'an almost ruined man, both financially and physically' that he decided to treat him without any charges. His problems had been building for some time and had first manifested themselves in the disruption he had caused to the recording of Tomatito's first solo album *Rosas del Amor*. It is customary for solo guitar records to have a singer, at least on the first track, to assist with the promotion and they did not come much bigger than Camarón. Carlos Lencero, one of the singer's lyricists later revealed the effects Camarón's use of drugs like Rohypnol and Mogodon had during this period.[18] Having travelled to Madrid to record the title track, Camarón failed to turn up for the first and second days with his wife explaining that he had been asleep for over two days. This situation was to continue into a third day until Camarón finally showed up on the fourth day, recorded the song in one single take and then left immediately for his home in La Línea![19] When the album was released it featured a very young fresh-faced Tomatito on its front cover but the reverse of the sleeve told the real story. It featured images of the producer Ricardo Pachón and all the other featured musicians except Camarón.

It may well be for reasons of Camarón's declining health that a new studio album was not a possibility in 1987, and his record company opted for the release of some of his classic live performances when he braved the festival crowds with Tomatito. His producer, Ricardo Pachón, was forced to rummage in his archive of tapes recorded between 1977 and 1979 to find some classic appearances. Coming in a very attractively designed sleeve that cleverly reflected the artist's nickname, this collection was more than adequate to satisfy the increasing demands of the growing bands of *Camaroneros*. The new album, *Flamenco Vivo*, presented the inspired and passionate Camarón that fans knew from the festivals, but he would shortly undertake the most important studio recording session of his life.

6

Echoes of the White Towns, 1988–1989

Prawn shells and sawdust littered the floor, and sausages and hams hung over the counter. At the bar Don Ibrahim and La Niña drank in silence. On the radio Camarón was singing.
Arturo Pérez-Reverte, *The Seville Communion*

San Fernando's tourist brochures, which trade on the past artistry of the town's chosen son, omit to mention the day that the authorities humiliated Camarón by incarcerating him over a weekend in late August 1988. San Fernando is now proud of the statue of Camarón that was erected opposite the Venta de Vargas and the official Camarón trail. The town council encourages tourists to visit the house where he was born, his father's forge and the imposing mausoleum where he now rests. The Camarón trail does not, however, include the cell where Camarón spent a very stressful weekend after having a row with a municipal policeman. The trail should include the building where the singer lost his freedom over something as trivial as a parking offence, as it would later leave its mark on Camarón and further undermine his confidence. The event was made even more painful as it occurred at a time when he was considering returning to live in La Isla once again. Camarón would soon turn his back on San Fernando and deeply resent the publicity that occurred over a mundane parking incident.

The newspaper headlines claimed that Camarón had threatened to slash a policeman with a knife following an argument over the singer parking his car in a prohibited zone.[1] The contretemps occurred during a visit by Camarón and his family to the Campo Soto beach where, according to his minder José Candado, Camarón had wanted to park his car as close as possible. Camarón decided to leave his car next to some other vehicles when a policeman told him that he must move it. Once again Camarón's fame and being a gypsy were to work against him, as the policeman had apparently overlooked the other motorists who were parked in the prohibited zone. Not surprisingly, Camarón took this as an insult both to himself and his family and uncharacteristically lost his temper and threatened to kill the policeman with his knife. It later emerged that it was the policeman's action of waving a walkie-talkie in a threatening manner that provoked Camarón to retaliate. The policeman's aggression had caused Camarón's children to start crying; deeply upsetting the singer.[2] This incident would soon see the town of La Isla being linked to the singer for all the wrong reasons in Spain's newspapers. Camarón's arrest would also result in a very frosty relationship with the San Fernando Town Council over the coming years. The irony of this bizarre event seems forgotten today in a town where Camarón's statue and photograph are lovingly reproduced on the tourist maps.

As a result of this unsavoury incident, he found himself detained over the weekend until Monday morning when a judge was available to hear the charge and decide to release him. Although Camarón was allowed visits from his family and friends, Rancapino later recounted how these two days of being incarcerated made him very depressed. Once again Camarón had courted controversy, but the prisoner who had lost his freedom in that San Fernando cell had little in common with the canonised creation of 2007.

1988 had begun so well, with the artist's return to Paris in March alongside Tomatito and the dancer La Tati. The audience response had been even greater than on his previous visit, with nightly attendances of 2,000 people, but now he faced very lively and noisy crowds. The Parisians had heard reports of his appearances and were drawn by the attractive posters that went up around the city. Camarón was depicted in a classic flamenco pose with his hands outstretched as the passion of his singing contorted the features of his face. This black and white image, punctuated by splashes of vivid colour, was very successful in attracting full houses. Camarón's triumphs at these concerts even prompted the French newspaper *Liberation* to call him the 'Mick Jagger of flamenco' as they published a photograph of the singer deep in concentration, clapping his hands on their front page. This publicity was to lead to Camarón being introduced to luminaries of the rock world and ultimately Jagger himself. While Jagger would later give Camarón his linen jacket, he would also ask the singer for his underpants in the expectation that some of his magic might rub off on him![3]

In their dressing room the artists had warmed up with glasses of wine while some chose to drink something a little stronger. Camarón had emerged on stage wearing a dark pin-stripe suit and a loud red shirt but his hair, benefiting from that customary perm, appeared lighter than usual. Surrounded by the audience on all sides he began, as was his custom, with an *alegrías* from his hometown. The vociferous punters shouted for a *taranta*, which he ignored and nodded to Tomatito to play the faster *bulerías* that presented his guitarist with a quick opening key change. Soon he would be singing those familiar words about working at the forge while other children went to school. Tomatito had seamlessly included some licks from his solo album and the two had found some special chemistry on this occasion. Despite being in great form Camarón did not look well, but once again he had triumphed in Paris. Throughout 1988 he would excite audiences everywhere he sang; he began to emerge as an international artist who would visit cities from Río de Janeiro to Caracas. It may have been a difficult year, but he could look back on it with some satisfaction and he could also look forward to some landmark concerts in Madrid and New York.

During the spring of 1989, while concerns were being raised over his medical health, Camarón issued a public statement regarding his financial health. He had agreed to an interview with the journalist Fransciso Espínola that was to appear at the end of May. Camarón stated that he wanted to rehabilitate himself and fight his drug habit as it created a negative image for flamenco. He was also concerned about his influence on young gypsies who saw him as a role model. However, the real story regarding the state of his finances was buried at the foot of the page. After initially claiming that he was capable of undertaking more concerts per year he wanted the readers to know that he was now going to take life steadier.[4] It is questionable whether his body would have sustained more work at this time, but it is clear that these remarks were aimed at a wider public. Camarón then hit out at the *hacienda*, or exchequer (the equivalent of the Inland Revenue in the UK), whom he claimed wanted two years' back-tax and had sent him a bill for ten million pesetas. He talked about a ludicrous situation of tax inspectors sitting in comfortable armchairs whilst imposing large demands. They demanded half of his concert fees while he was out on the road risking his life. The writer Rodríquez Sánchez had seized on these revelations where, for the first time, Camarón had publicly expressed an interest in money.

The singer had admitted that the authorities were recovering unpaid tax by making deductions from his concert fees and he had confessed to not knowing how he would settle such a large demand. Rodríguez Sánchez had also highlighted that the minister in charge of the *hacienda* at the time was the well-known figure José Borrell. The inference being that as Borrell was a Catalan, he would pursue Camarón to the bitter end to obtain the back-tax!

May 1989 would also witness Camarón reaching the peak of his pioneering concerts in sports stadiums, when he returned to Madrid to face a remarkable audience of 15,000 people. He was now emerging as something much more than a flamenco singer, as the critic Manuel Rios Ruiz wrote:

> On finding oneself in a most inappropriate venue for the *cante* such as Madrid's *Palacio de Deportes*, crammed full of spectators (gypsy families, executives, artists, politicians, the jet set …), one has to admit that the event proves without a shadow of a doubt that, in terms of popular opinion, Camarón de la Isla is the greatest flamenco artist. For this huge audience, that only he is able to assemble, other artists would represent a poor substitute. Is he the *cante*?[5]

Seville, 15 July 1989

The guide books will tell you that July and August are not the best months to visit Andalucía, and in particular Seville, when temperatures sometimes approach 50°c. I had first arrived in this colonial city on a hot August night during the final years of Franco's dictatorship to be greeted by a grubby coach station in need of decoration. Its bar was impregnated with the overpowering smell of smoke from *Ducados*, those classic aromatic black tobacco cigarettes and fish frying in the finest olive oil.

I had first come to the capital of Andalucía in search of flamenco's greatest luminary, whose records I had constantly played as a child in a North London council flat. Two decades later I was back, unaware of what a momentous year 1989 was to be for a singer whom the Spanish press compared to the Beatles and the Rolling Stones out of respect for the remarkable way he had revolutionised such a traditional art. My childhood hero had only recently conquered audiences from Paris to Brazil and now this gypsy icon was entertaining the citizens of New York. The arrival of spring of 1989 had dispelled all the gossip of Camarón's illness and his inability to perform at the high standards he had set. He had recovered from a car accident that had left two people dead and threatened to finish his career.

He had also recovered from emphysema and claimed that his addiction to heroin was over. Camarón was about to embark on one of the most energetic phases of his career, headlining the summer festivals and recording an album that would become a best-seller; confirming his status and contributing to his inevitable martyrdom. Only those close to him knew that this remarkable artistic energy masked Camarón's ill health. Ten years as a resident of Madrid had taken its toll both physically and mentally. There had been many rumours about the state of his health which were further fuelled by his 1986 album, *Te lo dice Camarón*, featuring a photograph of the singer from 1977. Aficionados had also questioned why the cover of his previous record, *Viviré*, had used a painting of the artist and not an up-to-date image. The titles of these two records had indicated Camarón's own irritation at this gossip, and the comments of some critics, and he had wanted to convey a clear message. But this was the spring of 1989 and 'our José' had moved back to the south and was spending more time in Seville than Madrid.

When I arrived in Andalucía, eager to imbibe another season of flamenco's summer festivals, I was greeted by a very different Seville as it was not only Camarón who was about to re-establish himself. This former Arab capital of Spain, which had once boasted the most important inland port in the world, was also having a makeover. Seville, whose charm owes a lot to her architecture and gardens that survive from the 1929 Exposition, was getting ready to greet the world again. The city was in a frantic state, attempting to complete a mammoth modernisation plan that included new roads and bridges across the Guadalquivir. Soon, the development of the island of Cartuja would be completed for the opening of the Expo'92 where Prime Minister Felipe González would demonstrate just what southern Spain had to offer.

I wandered past the buses waiting in their bays at Seville coach station; as it was midday all the drivers were revving their engines, eager to travel to their destinations across Andalucía. I wandered under the towering arches past the colourful groups of animated passengers, some carrying caged birds and others with live chickens in their bags. I was looking for the stop for Los Palacios and VillaFranco, a small town that lies south of Seville just beyond the better-known urbanisation of Los Hermanas. I spotted the bay that was just beyond the *Comes* bus bound for Cádiz and the *Alsina Graels* about to head to Granada. It was a typical hot and busy Saturday and, like Camarón, I was heading to a town that was about to celebrate the talent of the twenty-four-year-old dancer El Mistela, who was the town's best-known flamenco artist. Camarón was to top the bill ahead of such distinguished artists as Chocolate, Paco Toronjo, and María Soleá, with Tomatito as one of the guitarists. As I alighted from the bus the searing heat hit me; I decided to head for the nearest bar where I could imbibe a *caña* and ask the directions to the Plaza Antiguo Molino Arrocero, where the outdoor event would be held.

Having passed several hours away in various bars where the sound of the *cante* competes with Spanish television programmes and the loudest one-armed bandits in the world, the moment had arrived. Earlier I had killed time at the local cinema watching a court drama starring Cher. The streets had been deserted all day, but as the evening approached hundreds of cars started to arrive. A crowd had gathered outside the window of a restaurant on the main drag where it was rumoured that Camarón and Tomatito were eating. By the early hours of the morning I was unaware that I was about to witness a unique moment: heralded by the tapping of microphones by a stout man holding a piece of paper. The president of the local flamenco club would, after a lengthy eulogy, introduce the artists including the aptly named gypsy singer Chocolate and the very entertaining and avuncular Paco Toronjo. Their role had been to warm up the audience for the eagerly anticipated appearance of a singer whose fame was now eclipsing the biggest names in bullfighting and football and sharing the headlines with rock stars. There were few wooden foldaway chairs left as the crowd roared with approval and excitement as the names of Camarón and his guitarist, Tomatito, were announced. In front of me a fringe group of local youths shouted abuse and looked eager to lob missiles and cause disruption. They say that Spain is *Un País Salvaje*, a wild country, and there is no better example than a flamenco festival in an Andalusian village on a steamy July night. These local kids had read all about Camarón's drug abuse and had heard all the stories about his failure to honour concert commitments. They were also aware of the mixed reviews Camarón had received in April whilst appearing in a major flamenco concert series in Seville. They appeared incensed that a gypsy drug addict from the salt flats of Cádiz could attract such a large crowd to their town and create news just by showing up.

As the applause faded, two smartly dressed artists took their seats on the traditional Andalusian chairs, distinguished by their upright backs and seats woven from reeds. Two proud and gifted gypsies were now dominating this dusty square, brought to life by a lively crowd drinking half bottles of ice-cold sherry. The artists were dressed in immaculate sharp suits, printed silk shirts and had, more importantly, shoulder-length permed hair which made them appear like proud lions. It also communicated an ethnicity whose roots could be traced back to North India. Flamenco, the music that was born in the dry land that lies between Cádiz and Seville, was about to be created in its birthplace. Although the night was a homage to the dancer, El Mistela, it was the singing known as the *cante* that had drawn the crowds.[6] As Camarón performed his customary cough to clear his throat I reflected on that well-known Andalusian phrase '*no hay lenguaje como el cante*' (there is no better form of expression than flamenco singing). People had only come for one thing, to hear Camarón sing the most exciting and creative form of the *cante*, the *bulerías*. They knew that he would recite love songs and speak about bad gypsy women with such creative metaphors as seeing a windmill by the light of his cigarette and then losing his way in the countryside when the fag was extinguished! The audience had heard all of the lyrics before, but it was all about Camarón's unique delivery: the sheer power, precision and quality of his voice and that extra ingredient, the gypsy guitar of Tomatito whose metronomic grasp of rhythm created the unique partnership that had taken Paris by storm. The aficionados had gathered beneath the stars to hear Camarón sing of hitting an old man in the street and then discovering a year later that it was his father. The *letras* or lyrics can appear trite when written down, but combined with the accompaniment of a flamenco guitar they become enriched with added meaning and poignancy. How else can you sum up a music that began as an intimate private art by which gypsies expressed themselves as they sang around the fires of the forge or maintained their spirits as they harvested crops. A music whose origins can also be traced back to the instrumentalist Ziryab, who travelled from Iraq to play the lute in the court of Abd al-Rahman II in ninth-century Córdoba. An art form that would also be enriched by the rhythms that were brought by the gypsies on their long journey from India, which finally ended when they entered Northern Spain in the fifteenth century.

During that hot summer of 1989, Camarón appeared back in control and the master of his art as he received many requests for appearances at the summer flamenco festivals. Business was not quite as good as during the early eighties, when the contracts would pile up in the office of his agent Jesús Antonio Pulpón, located just off the trendy Calle Sierpes where the latest fashion in clothes is to be found and close to houses where many of flamenco's earliest professionals used to live. It was an office where I had patiently waited in the early eighties, with an appointment to see this impresario with the intention of getting on his books as a jobbing guitarist. At this time Pulpón controlled virtually all flamenco activities and had been given the agency by Franco.

The release of Camarón's new record *Soy Gitano*, was just months away and it was an album that would confirm Camarón's status as the greatest flamenco artist. For the moment, there was the employment that Camarón hated the most, the Andalusian summer festivals where he would inevitably be expected to perform last, often in the early hours of the morning. The people would be restless, rowdy, often drunk and not prepared to pay the *cante* the respect it deserved. These nights, although enchanting and often magical, can become very tiresome when yet another president of the local flamenco club takes control of the microphone and proceeds to tell the audience the complete life story of each artist. Camarón, always nervous, would often be forced to ask the crowd to stop talking so others could hear him sing better, and then there would be the times when he would have to restart a *bulerías* or a *soleá* because of the constant chatter from the audience. This summer he was expected at the bullring in La Línea and then to top the bill ahead of the local star Fosforito, in Aguilar de la Frontera in Córdoba province. Later there would be a journey to Ojén in Málaga province to sing on the Patio del Colegio Los Llanos; with the leading singer Lebrijano's name appearing beneath Camarón's. It was in mid-August, at one of the flamenco calendar's major festivals in La Unión in Murcia province, that Camarón would receive another psychological blow. 1989 would mark the twenty-ninth consecutive staging year of this week-long festival to celebrate the songs of the region's miners and Camarón, as the star attraction, was to appear on the opening Monday 14 August. Here his presence was considered more important than the eminent guitarist Manolo Sanlúcar's performance of *Tauromaquia*, Utrera's leading flamenco sisters Fernanda and Bernarda, or the coolest act of the summer, the voice of El Pele accompanied by the guitar of Vicente Amigo.

The background to Camarón's most successful record, *Soy Gitano*, and its much hyped links to London's Abbey Road studios, were to add yet another chapter to the building of a myth. Camarón had never heard of Abbey Road but he understood that this new project would be recorded mainly in Seville, with some additional work in Madrid, and that London was only part of the equation because it was the home of the Royal Philharmonic Orchestra. Outside of the very insular world of flamenco he knew very little about rock stars, but had found inspiration in the music of that giant of jazz, Miles Davis. Camarón had never heard of the studios that had become synonymous with the work of the Beatles. After his triumphs in Paris in 1987 and 1988, where hacks first compared him with Mick Jagger, the lead singer of the *Rolling Stones*, the writer Paco Espínola revealed that this comparison meant little to Camarón as Jagger's name was unfamiliar to him: 'José had never heard of these celebrities and was baffled when people spoke to him about the admiration that Peter Gabriel, Frank Zappa, Miles Davis, Bono of U2 and David Byrne of the Talking Heads had shown for his singing. Once, when a journalist from *Liberation* informed him that Mick Jagger liked him as well and asked what he thought about the singer of the Rolling Stones, José returned the compliment saying Jagger was a great artist. A little while later he asked a friend: 'Mig Yagger? Who is that guy?'[7]

While Camarón was aware that some songs on his new album would be commercial, he was reported as saying that he could not understand why he needed to come to the North London location. My own enquiries to the bookings manager at Abbey Road were met with the response that there was not any record of the singer undertaking a studio session at the location. But Camarón did visit the building, best known for the pedestrian crossing that lies opposite. It was all part of a very creative marketing strategy for an artist whose international reputation had never been fully exploited. While the subsequent sales of *Soy Gitano* may not have rivalled the Gypsy Kings, the hype surrounding the name of Abbey Road and the choice of the Royal Philharmonic Orchestra went a good way to ensuring that 50,000 copies sold before the end of 1989.

Camarón's record company, Philips (part of the Polygram Ibérica group), had the number one flamenco artist on their books, but outside of Spain few had heard of the singer. They wanted to bring Camarón to the attention of a wider audience, both in Spain and further afield, and a newsworthy press release was issued. It informed journalists that Camarón would record his next album with the world famous Royal Philharmonic Orchestra in the equally celebrated Abbey Road studios. This was an ambitious gamble that paid off, with Camarón having his first hit record; he could now be rebranded as a superstar. The press release had worked, with the *El País* newspaper featuring Camarón on its front page on 27 July 1989 with news of Camarón's visit to Abbey Road. Now the Spanish people could see this flamenco hero sitting on the famous steps that led to the entrance of the studios.[8]

Most of the actual recording of Camarón's voice had taken place in the Panoleta Records' studios in Seville where, in the company of fellow musician Diego Carrasco, Camarón had drunk several litres of Seville's best-known beer *Cruzcampo*. John Kurlander, who had gained a formidable reputation in the rock world as a producer and had worked with the flamenco glam rock band *Carmen*, would later supervise the engineering of the master tape in London. Of far more importance was the publicity that Camarón would generate by being photographed outside the studios when he arrived from his hotel. Reflecting on the event fifteen years later, Camarón's lyricist, Carlos Lencero, commented on the level of intrusion from the press. The musicians of the Royal Philharmonic had become so frustrated with the photographers that they even downed tools and put their instruments away. Camarón was also unhappy on this London visit; he suffered from a stomach upset and he also found himself in a place he did not want to be with very little work to do in the studio. The writer José Manuel Gamboa, would later claim that the recording company faced a bill of one-million pesetas for a three-hour session![9]

The key to the success of this record would lie in how skillfully Camarón's voice could be mixed with the orchestral arrangements of Jesús Bola. Ricardo Pachón made several visits to London's Livingstone studios, in the less salubrious Wood Green, to achieve the perfect mix which, as Lencero recalled, received an unwelcome comment from a London taxi driver who just happened to be born in Málaga.[10] Pachón had been so keen to hear the results of the day's work at the Livingstone studios that he asked the driver to play the cassette while they drove to his hotel. The taxi driver had commented that the orchestra gave the impression that Camarón was singing flat and Pachón knew immediately, that he would not be returning to Spain the next day; the material would have to be reworked. Despite these initial setbacks the album *Soy Gitano*, which was launched on 2 December 1989, was to become a massive hit, selling 42,000 copies in its first week – an unthinkable quantity for a flamenco album – and it would earn Camarón a gold record.

While the singer was best known for the tattoo on his left hand, it was a paralysis in his right hand that was soon to become a major talking point in flamenco circles. The effect of the paralysis in the radial nerve was unpleasant enough but it would also have a psychological effect, further undermining a mental state already confused and influenced by the quantities of heroin and cocaine he had previously taken. The singer had experienced a similar paralysis in his hand three years before as a result of his excessive drug taking. This new affliction was to occur just before he was expected to take on El Pele in the festival of the miner's songs held in La Unión in August 1989. In the company of the guitarist Vicente Amigo, El Pele had been in top form that summer, working on some creative material that was to be released on the *Poeta de Esquinas Blandas* album the following year. They were very much part of the new wave of flamenco at this time and their image was enhanced by their spectacular sartorial elegance. El Pele had surprisingly given Camarón a bloody nose in a flamenco contest in Bilbao and this encounter in Murcia province would decide who the king of the *cante* really was.

While Camarón was regarded as a progressive flamenco artist, Vicente Amigo was using the exotic sounds of open tunings on his guitar, and El Pele's songs were more surreal than aficionados had been used to. Rather than sing about wild flowers in the countryside, El Pele preferred lyrics that talked of planting flowers in the asphalt outside his house or about buying his gypsy son a guitar only to discover that he preferred to play on his computer. On paper, Camarón looked to be up against it and his agent Pulpón, on learning of the paralysis in his hand, feared the worst and wanted the contest cancelled while La Chispa wanted him to perform. By half past ten o' clock in the evening El Pele was eager to start, but Camarón had failed to turn up. He finally made it by midnight, but then chose to further frustrate his opponent by saying he would have to shave and change first! A large audience were kept waiting, but Camarón rose to the challenge and delivered a stunning performance. El Pele's singing had suffered from a lack of concentration caused partly by the sound system playing up, but mainly due to the Camarón's supporters making lots of noise![11]

The paralysis was to convince Camarón of the need to seek confidential treatment again and a complete detox.[12] The help he had received over the past twelve months from the psychiatrist Marcelo Camus, who had even spent time with Camarón in his house in La Línea, had been successful up to a point, but now the artist was plunged into a fresh and engulfing crisis. Camus' success in treating Camarón had been demonstrated by his stunning performance in San Fernando's theatre, where he shared the stage with fellow artists Chano Lobato and La Susi. His performance of the *siguiriyas* demonstrated just how good he could be without drugs and with the backing of a dedicated psychiatrist.

Writing shortly after his death, the journalist Francisco Peregil felt that Camarón's cleansed state could not last. For Peregil, Camarón was surrounded by too many people who would invite him to parties and offer him vast quantities of drugs. By the start of the eighties, Camarón had been courted by rival factions who would compete to see who could give him the most drugs. His producer, Ricardo Pachón, remembered a situation after a performance in Barcelona, where a large soup bowl in a nightclub was filled with coke.[13] As a journalist, Peregil was keen to focus on this, the most difficult and controversial aspect of Camarón's life. His drug dependency had developed from the early days of smoking joints in studio toilets to laying out lines of cocaine. The older generation of flamenco artists, including Manolo Caracol and Porrina de Badajoz, had found alcohol adequate for stimulating the *cante* but those days were gone. Now there was a singer whose prominence did not appear to be diminished by the amount of drugs he took and, as Peregil noted, here was an artist singing with such purity, despite his body being so contaminated. The drugs may well have had a positive creative effect on the making of *La Leyenda del Tiempo*, but as Peregil correctly identified, the overall contribution of these hard drugs on flamenco artists would be disproportionate to the innovations they stimulated. This level of drug taking, particularly amongst gypsies, reached an alarming peak in the late eighties. It prompted a campaign with the slogan *contra la droga* that was to be very visible on banners to be seen announcing flamenco festivals.

Tomatito, Camarón's constant companion as they toured the outdoor festivals, has often been asked why he had not done more to try and encourage Camarón to give up drugs. His defence has always been the difficulty of telling a man, who was eight years older than him, and whom he worshipped, what he should do with his life. While not confronting the singer's drug habit, Tomatito feels that he played an important role by keeping their whole act together. Speaking in 2001 he recounted how it always fell to him to walk to the side of the stage, waste time tuning his guitar and look calm while the promoters were panicking over the whereabouts of Camarón. This was the philosophy of a gypsy guitarist who also said that he had only ever got drunk twice in his life. One of those occasions had been at Christmas when he had later suffered from a bad hangover. It was Tomatito, the accompanist for an artist who devoured drugs, who once stated that that he could spend a whole night at a flamenco party with just one gin and tonic![14]

Camarón openly showed his concern about the level of his drug-taking; he told Paco Espínola that 'you have to set an example for younger generations and you can't take drugs'.[15] The singer had been addicted to heroin for eight years but now he vowed to 'act in a responsible manner' having taken 'a lot of risks', but sadly it was too late and Camarón would enter the nineties as very damaged goods.

7

The Last Goodbye,
1990–1992

Not dead, merely resting
Vicente Amigo, *ABC*

Camarón's past really started to catch up with him during 1990, including the ongoing saga of his well-documented car accident of 1986. Finally, in March 1990, the demands of the prosecution lawyers who had asked for Camarón to be sent down for one year were satisfied. The provincial court of Cádiz had duly convicted him to a year in an open prison, taken away his driving licence and, more interestingly, had removed his right to vote and hold any public office.[1] The court was satisfied that Camarón had not been concentrating on his driving and he finally received his punishment. However, the story was not over as the sentence was suspended before the month was out as his lawyer lodged an appeal. The authorities were unaware of Camarón's previous form, which had seen him locked up in San Fernando; the threat and fear of another spell in prison would follow him to the grave. The Venta de Vargas remained one of the few places where he could find peace, as it reminded him of his childhood and all those late nights staying up singing for the punters. Away from the stage he could relax on the patio, dressed casually in jeans and espadrilles, surrounded by the exotic plants and the singing caged birds. He could reflect on finally erasing the bad memories of Manolo Caracol for whom he had sung at this very inn.

Every July the city of Granada hosts a major international festival of music and dance; in 1990 Camarón was one of the stars to be lined up. His booking and subsequent non-appearance was to provoke one of the few lighter moments in the last few years of his life. With a tight deadline and knowing that these flamenco concerts often continue into the small hours, a local journalist decided to write the review before the concert! Camarón was forced to issue a statement saying:

> hasty exits and late entrances is a black legend they have labelled me with. This is my case for example. Often I have problems because companies sign me without my consent, they call me up a day or two before to tell me 'you're going to Majorca, you've got to work'. How can I go … if I arrive there what I am I going to do? Make a hasty retreat. When I can't control myself I do it up there, on stage. I prefer to do it there and for people to say that I was bad, that I sang too little or whatever they want. But as I have confidence in myself, there I am.[2]

One date that was both agreed and in his diary was another visit to the United States in June, to give a recital in New York as part of the 'New Music Seminar'. While Camarón had hated the food in England, which had made him sick when he visited Abbey Road, New York's cuisine was also to disappoint him. Andalucía is often referred to as 'the land of the frying pan' and Camarón was to complain that in Manhattan, he could not find any fried fish to eat!

On Sunday 16 September, I was to discover one of the reasons why Camarón had not appeared in Granada; I was confronted with his physical decline as he appeared unannounced at the *Lope de Vega* theatre in Seville.[3] The critic, Manuel Martín Martín, reported that only 130 were present for Tomatito's appearance at Seville's prestigious flamenco jamboree, but those in the know were aware that a surprise guest was possible as Camarón was also expected at a party that night.[4] When Tomatito announced his name it sent the handful of Japanese fans scurrying for their bags as they furiously tried to find their cameras.

Aside from his health problems, the autumn of 1990 would be good for Camarón's stock, bringing the first signs of what would soon become a burgeoning industry. Although the Philips record company had issued a greatest hits compilation entitled *Disco de Oro* as early as 1976, a different type of collection was about to hit the shops. Now it would not matter if you had the first release of *Volando Voy* or *La Tarara* since, if you were a Camarón completist, you would have to buy *Autorretrato* to get the second version or even a third studio recording of *La Tarara*. The various takes from Camarón's most important studio album would now help create a volume of new mixes and previously unheard cuts.

Towards the end of the year Camarón, and in particular his now infamous concerts, were helping journalists fill the column inches; supplying scenarios that were custom-made for sensationalist headlines. Such was the notoriety of his concerts that they were now being used as venues for settling arguments between gypsy clans, whilst racially motivated violence between gypsies and non-gypsies would also occur. His concert in the sports pavilion in Barcelona in December 1987 had hit the headlines for all the wrong reasons, with reports of the crowd fighting with chairs and the venue being described as a battleground.[5] Camarón's pleas had failed to stop the fighting and he was to face similar scenes at many of his concerts around Spain, including Santander and Castellón, where gypsy families clashed while the singer escaped out through his dressing room window.[6] The worst clashes, according to the journalist Paco Espínola, were to occur in La Coruña where one person died and ninety-four were injured. While Camarón hated the lack of respect that he received at the outdoor festivals, these outbreaks of violence between his fellow gypsies proved even more difficult to cope with. On being asked how he felt about his concerts being overshadowed by these gypsy fights, his reply was characteristically philosophical: 'we have to prepare and educate a section of the audience who go to flamenco to make trouble and not to listen. We give them a good time and end up having to pay the consequence'.[7]

Camarón's performance in Murcia's bullring was to be overshadowed by a very ugly incident that occurred during the concert.[8] The newspaper *La Verdad* reported that local police had been wounded in a fight that resulted in the arrest of a gypsy woman. The scale of violence at Camarón's concerts was now at an unprecedented level, with the newspaper claiming that a gypsy woman had attacked a municipal policeman with a meat cleaver, wounding him in the head. While Camarón was singing, a fight had broken out between two groups of gypsies and the venue's lights had to be switched on as the police tried to restore order. It was during these violent scenes that the middle-aged gypsy woman attacked the policeman, whose head wound needed many stitches. Camarón's concerts away from Madrid would also attract hundreds of gypsies who worshipped their idol. The singer had become such an important figure and role model for the gypsies of Spain that they would treat his concerts as almost religious events, choosing to wear their best clothes.

After a quiet start to 1991, another landmark in Camarón's career was achieved, when in July he received international recognition from the Montreaux Jazz Festival. The twenty-fifth annual festival, organised by Quincy Jones, reportedly paid Camarón a fee of three million pesetas for his efforts.[9] It is widely believed that the impresario Pino Sagliocco played a key role in securing the opportunity to appear at this world-renowned festival not just for Camarón, but for other stars from the flamenco world. Sagliocco had met Camarón several years earlier, but only in 1991 did he spot his potential and recognise that his recording legacy was not being fully exploited. Sadly, it was a relationship whose days were numbered due to Camarón's illness; there is little doubt that under Sagliocco's management, Camarón would have become a star of the world's stages. After Camarón's death the Italian impresario added the flamenco dancer Joaquín Cortés to his stable of luminaries which included Madonna and Elton John.

Camarón was also finally receiving recognition closer to home, as in 1991 he laid the first stone for the *Peña Flamenca de Camarón*, which later became a living museum to his life and work. This prominent and imposing building, which now regularly hosts festivals, club performances and competitions, aims to introduce more people to the art of flamenco and is the last stop on the Camarón trail. There had been other clubs dedicated to Camarón, most notably in Cádiz, but the idea for a *pena* in his hometown of San Fernando became a reality with its official foundation in 1989. The building finally opened in 1995, with his widow cutting the ribbon surrounded by hundreds of well wishers. Fifteen years after his death the club now hosts flamenco evenings throughout the summer, live performances every Sunday and an important singing competition named after Camarón every autumn.

Camarón was now able to command a fee of $30,000, but as 1991 progressed there was further evidence of his increasing illness, when he spent time in Olopte in the Pyrenees at the chalet of the agent Pino Sagliocco.[10] Camarón enjoyed this break in Catalonia but with his health declining it was only a matter of time before he would give a poor performance at a major event and the critics could finally have their day. There had been few signs of his losing his magic and ability when he took on, and easily outclassed, the fifteen-year-old El Potito in a contest held in the Algeciras bullring. The moment finally came on a hot September night in Seville as the organisers of Expo '92 sought to promote and test out the newly built auditorium for the forthcoming world fair. The barbed pens of the scribes had overlooked Camarón's poor performance in Seville in 1990, but this time he was not to be so fortunate. The concert, which had been promoted with Camarón's name as the headline artist, was previewed by the *ABC* newspaper publishing a full-size photograph of the singer. Also on the bill were three home-grown talents: Calixto Sánchez, Naranjito de Triana and Aurora Vargas. When Camarón and Tomatito took their places on the two Andalusian straight-back chairs, which were marooned amid the large stage, they could not have anticipated the bad reviews that would follow.

The event was described as a failure with the fans leaving the auditorium in the early hours of Saturday morning. They were very unhappy with the choice of artists that entertained them as they sat on hard seats for this near five-hour marathon. While the reputations of Aurora Vargas and Calixto Sánchez would survive this disaster unscathed, Camarón bore the brunt of the criticism. It was his disappointing performance that had members of the audience constantly disrupting the night by leaving their seats. The review penned by José Antonio Blázquez could not have been worse.[11] For Blázquez, Camarón's programme lacked substance and his performance showed him to be repetitive, lost and unable to maintain the all-important timing of flamenco known as the *compás*. Citing the world of bullfighting, he compared Camarón's position to that of the rivalry between the two sets of fans that supported Curro Romero or Rafael de Paula. You either loved Camarón or hated him and Blázquez's feelings were frank. Camarón should have been given a warning, in the same way that the president of a bullfight indicates that a *torero* is not up to the job, by waving a green kerchief and allowing the bull to escape the *estocada*. Despite elevating the *cante* to a new level, Camarón had been responsible for scandals that had brought the art into disrepute. Now he was doing his familiar routine, but without the all-important *duende*; sadly Blázquez felt his performance passed unnoticed. He simply 'was not at his best'.

Camarón would have been more preoccupied with the birth of his second son Joséico than this vicious, if deserved, review. Joseico would now be the centre of attention as he joined his brother Luis and sisters Gema and Rocío in the Monje household. Camarón also had more pressing engagements, including recording a special *tangos* to promote Tomatito's second solo album. This time he would not let his friend down and *La voz del tiempo* would soon receive much airplay across the Spanish radio networks.

Camarón may have finally given up cocaine and heroin, but he could not cope without his preferred packet of Winston cigarettes. Smoking heroin in tin foil had not helped his lungs; they were now in a very poor condition and were soon to further deteriorate. In the Barrio de Santiago in Jerez, one of Andalucía's most flamenco areas, gypsies had seen him smoking a reefer in a bar and urged him to give up for the sake of his health and his children.[12] The gypsies were used to seeing him overcome by the effects of heroin, but despite his fear of death, no quantity of any drug ever seemed to completely satisfy Camarón. Away from his vices and the stage he remained ever popular and there were few who would not testify to what a good person he was and without any enemies.

His concerts in the year before he died continued to be remembered for two things; how short his performances had become and whether there had been any serious violence at them. Far from Andalucía, in the north of Spain, a Camarón concert would often be the appointed venue for two rival gypsy clans to settle a dispute. The newspaper *La Nueva España* chose, on 15 November 1991, not to review his prowess at singing the *bulerías* or *soleá*, but rather to report on an argument that had started after one gypsy leader used some offensive language when speaking to another gypsy family. This verbal dispute, which occurred after Camarón's concert, then developed into something more violent with twenty more gypsies turning to sticks and sharp objects to make their point. Once again Camarón found himself the innocent victim of what was now becoming a common event.

As he continued to receive recognition and tributes, his health began to fail. A fact best illustrated by his appearance in the Carlos Saura's film, *Sevillanas*, for whom he was filmed towards the end of 1991. His magnetic stage presence had not faded, but the pain in his heavily beaded face was clearly visible. His guitarists, Tomatito and Joaquín Amador also communicated the tension of the performance as they put a gypsy spin on this popular folk music from Seville. It was a stunning interpretation enhanced by the dancing of Manuela Carrasco who, as a close member of the family, was well aware of the singer's illness. During the shooting of this film his doctors were to diagnose his multiple health problems and the news would break that he was seriously ill. These images of Camarón, which bordered on those of religious icons, were also to be found in Saura's portrayal of the singer in the film short *Sevilla*, shot in March 1992 to publicise the Expo '92. On the giant Sony screen that dominated the Expo site a very ill Camarón would first appear as a flamenco Christ; bearded, stripped to the waist, suffering the effects of cancer and experiencing great pain.

Early in 1992, the presenter of Spanish television's *Primero Izquierda* asked Camaron if he intended to be involved in the opening ceremony of the Olympics to be staged in Barcelona in 1992. The interviewer had expressed the view that the organisers would want him there to sing at the opening ceremony. Camarón had merely replied that he did not know and gave the impression that the audience would have to wait and see. Writing in the June 1992 edition of the Madrid flamenco journal, *La Caña*, Ángel Álvarez Caballero chose to ignore the singer's ill health when he reported that; 'Camarón was to be originally present in the official opening ceremony, but then for some unknown reason he was scrapped from the games'. On *Primero Izquierda*, Camarón had appeared alongside the popular singer Rocío Jurado and his hero, the bullfighter Curro Romero; although he looked unwell, his singing was excellent as he interpreted the *bulerías* after a percussive introduction on the damped strings of Tomatito's Reyes guitar. While the power in his voice had clearly deserted him, his command of the rhythm or *compás* remained intact, but, interestingly Tomatito avoided playing a single *falseta* or variation on his guitar, preferring to stick to the basic chords to accompany the song. Camarón seemed distant and dazed when listening to Rocío Jurado sing some *alegrías* in homage to Curro Romero, but he was always shy and unassuming in public and this was primetime television.

Camarón had earlier recorded the songs for his last album, *Potro de Rabia y Miel*, which would reunite him for the last time with Paco de Lucía. Paco was to spend many months working on the final master of this important work, which would complete the singer's legacy. The production of this record, which had started in 1991, was a very stressful ordeal for both Camarón, who was suffering from back pain, and Paco de Lucía. Paco had been sympathetic to Camarón's severe back pain, but was also preoccupied by the demanding task of completing the album. In the studios Camarón had struggled to lay down a single take of the songs and Paco needed to spend months in production, editing various takes to produce a saleable master tape. Their time together now was in stark contrast to those sessions in Madrid during the seventies, when Paco could not wait to finish a solo tour and relax by making a new album with Camarón. These recordings were torturous, with Paco under considerable strain and smoking constantly while a thin Camarón, in a knitted sweater, suffered mostly in silence. Later Paco would call Camarón to reassure him what a good record it would be, whilst writing in his own diary that the singer's illness had weakened the quality of his voice on this recording.[13] Paco would also tell Camarón to stop worrying about the recording and that he should also look after himself and try not to smoke.[14]

Despite the increasing gravity of his illness Camarón, still occupied with issues of money and the future of his family, had concerts lined up from the opening month of the year; culminating in a spectacular that would feature his old friend, the bullfighter Curro Romero, in Seville. On 24 January he performed with the gypsy dancer and singer El Güito in the bullring of Nîmes, France. The following day he travelled to Madrid to perform in the *Festival Flamenco por Tarantas*. Few amongst the audience of the Colegio Mayor San Juan Evangelista realised they were witnessing his last public performance, but it was reported as one of his best. The reign of the prince of flamenco was coming to a close as Camarón finally succumbed to the inevitable results of a life of over-indulgence, exploitation and over exposure.

On 19 March he stayed in the Quirón clinic in Barcelona, where he was told of the seriousness of his condition and that he also had pneumonia.[15] Days later, his wife's concerns finally convinced him to travel to Minnesota, USA, in a desperate attempt to find a cure and he left the Catalan clinic on 26 March. It was also now confirmed that he had lung cancer and the medical staff had also found traces of the disease in his bones. His doctor, Rafael Rosell Costa, concluded that the singer had been in this state for many months, which accounted for Camarón's back pain. He went on to say that it was unlikely that the illness was treatable.[16]

It would later emerge in a telephone call to Tomatito that his guitarist Paco de Lucía would be prepared to pay all the costs of Camarón's treatment during his month-long stay in the United States. Speaking in a rare interview, published in April 2001, Tomatito revisited the turbulent scenes that occurred at Camarón's funeral and the accusations that were being levelled at Paco de Lucía over Camarón's royalties. Tomatito considered the people making these allegations to be ignorant of the facts, and that their anger was fuelled by stories claiming that Camarón's expensive treatment would leave him penniless.

On 8 April Camarón departed with his wife for the Mayo clinic, which is situated in the district of Rochester in the state of Minnesota. His treatment was expected to cost over two million pesetas.[17] Family photographs taken of Camarón during his stay in Rochester at the four-stars Khaler Grand Hotel, show a much happier and healthier person. He had clearly benefited from the treatment and diet, and looked considerably better in comparison to his appearance in the film *Sevillanas*.[18] They had chosen this hotel, which is ten miles from Rochester International Airport, because it adjoined the Mayo Clinic complex and Camarón could visit the doctors from his room without having to walk in the street. Yet Camarón was to walk the streets of Rochester, arm in arm with La Chispa, and later pose for photographs wearing a sea captain's hat whilst warmly embracing the now ever-present minder, José Candado. For a man so seriously ill he looked in great shape, sporting sunglasses and wearing a jean jacket over a bright waistcoat. He also remained in very good humour while staying at the hotel and was reported as saying that he was only eating soup, a lot of vegetables and a great deal of chicken broth. He even began pronouncing chicken as *chiquen*, but for the rest of his conversations in English he relied on the nun, Sister Dora![19]

As the doctors examined Camarón in Minnesota, his great gift continued to entertain the public as footage of him singing *Dicen de Mí* was played on the opening night of Expo '92 in Seville.[20] The *Sevillanos* were now aware that he had lung cancer, which would spread to his spinal chord, and that he had travelled to the United States for an 'emergency checkup'. The diagnosis of the Mayo clinic would also confirm that he had lung cancer with *metastasis cronica* and on 5 May he returned to Spain to be met by his lifelong friend Rancapino. The singer, who had driven to the airport in the company of Camarón's agent Jesús Antonio Pulpón and the legendary *torero*, Curro Romero, remembered reflecting on how well Camarón looked.[21] Rancapino thought Camarón looked so fit and strong that he exclaimed that he looked like a Marquis and a bullfighter. Sadly, Rancapino was to discover the reality of Camarón's situation when he visited him at his home in La Línea. By mid-May, Camarón was in constant pain and always complaining about his back. A press release from his record company Polygram Iberica had stated that he was winning his battle against drug addition and that during his stay in the United States he had put on twenty-two pounds.[22] This increase in weight had even attracted the attention of the magazine *Ya* which reported that he had put on ten kilos, but the newspaper *El Correo de Andalucía* went further by claiming that reports that he was suffering from lung cancer had made him and his wife very unhappy.[23] The story was leaking out despite the spin and confusion created by press releases that claimed that he simply had pneumonia or that there was a rift between his wife and his agent.

Jesús Antonio Pulpón had assured the public that Camarón's forthcoming concert in Barcelona in June would go ahead, whilst La Chispa had stated that all his concerts were cancelled.[24] It was the *Vanguardia* newspaper that went as far as saying that the singer still hoped to recover from his pneumonia and perform at Seville's Maestranza bullring in September with Curro Romero. The newspaper quoted Camarón as saying 'I've looked the wolf in the eyes' as he relaxed at his home in La Línea.[25] His poor health would prevent him being present at the launch of his last record, *Potro de Rabia y Miel*, whose cover would feature a painting of two bonking donkeys! The air of expectation and excitement that occurred at the presentation of his last record in December 1989 would not be repeated.

Camarón was to spend the last weeks of June in a house in Santa Coloma de Gramanet owned by his minder, José Candado, who would shortly be at his bedside in hospital watching him die. The pair had spent more and more time together as Camarón's illness took hold and they undertook several visits to Olopte where Camarón relaxed and enjoyed himself in the company of Manolo de Marsella, who had known the singer since his golden years. Camarón would not appear at Barcelona's Plaza Mayor del Poble Español on 19 June, for the VIII Festival of Flamenco, which was organised as part of the cultural activities of the Olympics. Neither would he fulfill his booking at Seville's Maestranza bullring organised by the town hall for the VII *Bienal de Arte Flamenco*, scheduled for 16 September.

When Camarón returned from spending that month in the United States clinic he gave a very revealing interview for Spanish television. He was interviewed at his home close to the Campo del Gibraltar, as he waited for the diagnosis of his disease and the fatal results of the last test that would come within a week. Relaxing with his wife, his brother El Pijote and Tomatito, he hardly looked like a man who was about to die. The television script was brutal describing how the 'drugs made the myth stagger' as Camarón's drug dependence had started with alcohol, gravitated to cocaine and finally heroin. Camarón had spoken about how God had given gypsies something special that they then return to the grave and that they possess the *duende* that *payos* simply do not have. Then his mood became darker as he spoke about learning of the first indications that he might be seriously ill and his wife's suggestion that they should go to the United States for treatment. In America Camarón was told the bad news, but he resented the doctors causing so much alarm to his wife and family. He remained more preoccupied with the upset to his family than the actual diagnosis itself.

The programme claimed that he was not interested in money, having made a lot, but stated that others may have made more at his expense. For the first time in his life, his illness had made him consider the future and the all-important recovery of his record rights. Camarón was very clear that he now faced two scares, his ill health, and the simple fact that he did not own his work despite his enormous contribution to the art of flamenco. The singer was also keen to talk about a gypsy woman who had come to him with a sick child and asked for a cure. Camarón had found this very difficult, not having the religious faith of his wife who was a devout follower of the Evangelical Church. He also found the belief that he had almost magical powers very difficult to cope with. Throughout his life he had been constantly asked by fellow gypsies to lay his hands on their children and bestow some of his spiritual powers. He recalled eventually saying to the woman, with tears in his eyes, how am I going to cure him? He had then kissed the child giving him all his love.

By the end of June 1992 Camarón knew that not even the religious fervour of his wife's Evangelical Church could save him as he decided to abandon faith and opt for a more scientific approach to his illness. A few weeks earlier he had appeared alongside La Chispa with a more positive attitude that he could overcome his illness, but she had later conceded that he was 'extremely afraid and has little faith in worship. That is why he has not been saved already'. Somewhat dramatically, considering his increasing weakness, it was claimed that Camarón went on foot to the nearest medical centre and admitted himself to the Germans Trias i Pujol hospital in Badalona, Catalonia.[26] Whilst he did admit himself, there are several anecdotal reports of his arrival in Barcelona which indicate that he could no longer walk in the street unaided.[27] It was later suggested that he should have been treated in hospital far earlier and that the faith of those around him – that only religious belief could restore his health – should have been ignored. Camarón, a man whose appearance was largely defined by the magnificence of his permed hair, was terrified by the thought of going bald due to the effects of chemotherapy, but he understood that conventional medicine offered the only answer. On 10 June he had arrived at the hospital in Badalona for a session of chemotherapy and was due back on 1 July. During the month of June he had very little appetite, surviving just on water and fruit juice, but he continued smoking a handful of cigarettes each day.[28] Tobacco was not the only drug he continued to consume to the bitter end as his doctor, with great sympathy for the pain he was suffering, would administer small quantities of cocaine to allow the singer to sleep in peace through the day.

Early in the morning on Thursday 2 July the life and energy began to fade from Camarón's body as he reached for the hand of his friend and minder José Candado. At his bedside were his wife, and his niece Juana. His last words would be repeated in headlines around the world as he asked 'oh mother, what is it that I've got?' But was it José Candado's or his uncle Ramón's hand that he pressed as he uttered these words? Other more chilling words, which would find their way into the columns of the world's newspapers, were uttered by the doctor who had come to know Camarón during his short stay. Speaking into a row of microphones alongside José Candado, the head of the oncology unit Dr Manuel Rossell emphasised how Camarón had been an exemplary patient with a great character. His illness had been too advanced for treatment and despite appearing well over the past three weeks, Camarón had arrived at the hospital in a very bad way and was completely exhausted and dehydrated having eaten little. The hospital had been successful in reviving him, but a day later he suffered kidney failure with other complications and could not be revived. La Chispa had called for assistance at seven o'clock in the morning and within ten minutes he was dead.[29]

The unthinkable had finally happened, with the most influential artist in the history of flamenco being pronounced dead, and soon his fellow artists and closest friends would be shocked and stunned. Rancapino simply said 'it's not possible, it's a lie, Camarón has not died', while another close friend, the dancer Manuela Carrasco was lost for words but later said 'what a stupid life'. His wife La Chispa, left the hospital totally distraught surrounded by friends and family and with only her sunglasses to hide her grief. An early death was the only outcome for an artist who had been pushed to the limits and became a drug addict whilst being left to cope with his vast fame, with very little counsel or guidance. With the absence of a role model, he was on a one-way journey from his father's blacksmith forge to San Fernando's cemetery via the bright lights of Madrid and some of the world's most prominent stages. The journalist Francisco Peregil bluntly summed up Camarón's approach to life and his narcotic addiction: 'He approached everything with equal strength and drugs were no exception. First hashish, then cocaine, then heroin, and for four years only cocaine'.[30]

Seville's magnificent bullring, the Maestranza, would not now resound to Camarón's voice singing to his hero, the bullfighter Curro Romero. It would be Cádiz's Manuel de Falla theatre that would become animated by the personality of Camarón, sadly this time as it staged a homage to his memory. The singers Rocío Jurado and El Lebrijano, accompanied by guitarist Tomatito, would lead the tribute attended by Camarón's widow and his four children. All 1,200 tickets had been sold within hours of the announcement of the concert, with the Cádiz theatre unable to satisfy the enormous demand. There would also be an important speech at this concert that would have repercussions and echoes for the following decades, despite the absence of an overt reference to Camarón's royalties. The president of the gypsy association that had organised the event said that Camarón's family needed money because the singer had lived day to day, spending what he earned, and that he had expected to live longer.[31] All the receipts from the night would go to Camarón's widow and his children. It proved to be a very intense evening, especially when Rocío Jurado sang with such emotion to a bust of Camarón on a tiled stand surrounded by bunches of roses. Camarón's fellow gypsies, El Lebrijano and the guitarist Moraíto also said goodbye in their own unique way. The first of many compilations, *Una leyenda flamenca*, would soon appear, allowing the public to own their part of Camarón's life and extensive discography.

While Camarón's early death would fuel rumours of a feud between Camarón's widow and Paco de Lucía, which would later be fiercely denied, his other guitarist, Tomatito, would face a very bleak future. The last months of Camarón's life had seen so many journalists ask Tomatito what Camarón had meant to him, causing him much anger. He would reply that 'after playing with this monster of monsters, for who do I now play the guitar?'[32] Tomatito had, as he described it, been in heaven during his years with Camarón, playing in front of thousands of people for the number one singer. His fee was paid separately from the two or three million pesetas that Camarón commanded and it was said that he, as Camarón's accompanist, was the highest paid guitar player, the so-called 'half a kilo guitarist'.[33] Camarón's sudden death was a massive blow to Tomatito who had worked with the singer for nearly twenty years. Gone was the artist with so much authority, leaving Tomatito without a job and a large family to care for. Speaking about this situation many years later he explained how, after Camarón's death, his telephone did not ring with any bookings with the exception of the singer Enrique Morente. Tomatito faced two very fundamental problems in finding work or a life after Camarón. Firstly, promoters presumed that his fee was prohibitive and secondly, if a singer did contact him, that could expose the singer to accusations that he considered himself to be the new Camarón. Tomatito was forced to reflect on this difficult time when he agreed to an interview in the summer of 2001 where he described being left as an 'orphan' by the departure of Camarón'.[34] 'It was the worst. No work, to start with and crying because I just played for him. *Cantaores* didn't want me, they used to say "he is just a spoilt kid" and I never played solo. I didn't know how to do it. It was such a challenge'. Despite those black years, Tomatito remained so proud of his years accompanying Camarón: 'the public loves me, they have wonderful memories of Camarón and I, they accept me, they forgive my mistakes, they value my things'. Tomatito has said on many occasions that the most important thing for him is to have been considered as Camarón's guitarist.

Fortunately for Tomatito, he did later receive help from the powerful agent Pino Sagliocco, who had earlier wanted to acquire Camarón's recording rights and become his manager. Sagliocco knew that flamenco was one of Spain's principal exports, as he demonstrated with the career of the dancer Joaquín Cortés, and was able to place Tomatito on bills alongside major world artists; his career was ultimately rescued.

After recovering his musical career and on the eve of the release of his record *Spain*, Tomatito was to finally break his silence and speak about Camarón's royalties. He was asked for his reaction to Camarón's family's complaint that the singer's death had left them short of money. This was in contrast to Tomatito's situation of having sufficient funds to buy a house in Aguadulce for thirty or forty million pesetas.[35] Tomatito reacted by stating that he was always careful with money and did not have vices or fancy ideas for spending it. More importantly he felt the behaviour of some of the mourners at Camarón's funeral and the accusations against Paco de Lucía over Camarón's royalties were simply absurd.

Camarón's widow would later shed more light on her financial situation when she agreed to an interview with the Spanish *Rolling Stone* magazine on the tenth anniversary of the singer's death. She was asked whether she had received what she was owed in respect of Camarón's legacy. La Chispa stated that what monies the family were getting at that time came mainly from royalties because the author's rights generated very little. The article went on to explain that on the eve of his death Camarón was aware that only 27 out of the 164 songs that he had recorded would generate royalties based on his authorship. Most of the work he had recorded with Paco de

Lucía was registered with the Society of Spanish Authors under the name of the father of Paco de Lucía, Antonio Sánchez Pecino; a few songs were registered in the name of Paco de Lucía and others in the name of his brother Pepe de Lucía. Camarón's estate also suffered from the common practice in flamenco of registering what were often traditional popular songs under the name of somebody who was not even interpreting them on the disc. La Chispa had explained that her husband, because he was aware that his life was slipping away, had been worried about the future of his family. He had even asked on the Spanish television programme *Informe Semanal*, to have a part of these rights assigned to him. The *Rolling Stone* interview had also made reference to the crowd at Camarón's funeral that had hurled abuse at Paco de Lucía over Camarón's royalties. It also mentioned Paco's intention, offered on several occasions, to give the rights to Camarón's family had done little to ameliorate the opinion of some *Camaroneros*. The magazine also claimed that Camarón's family had sent a letter to the newspapers, distancing themselves from the insults that had occurred during the burial and expressing their admiration for the de Lucía family.

For Paco de Lucía, Camarón's death had meant a year of mourning before he spoke to the press. Paco finally gave a very candid interview during the afternoon of 27 June 1993, as he travelled on Spain's high-speed train, the AVE, through Andalucía to Córdoba.[36] For Paco there was a 'sinister person' who had initiated this row over Camarón's royalties by misleading La Chispa and her family. Both parties had become victims and he was keen to point out that he had had a delightful conversation with Camarón's widow only a month ago, when the King of Spain presented the *Medalla de oro de Bellas Artes* in Valencia. Paco claimed that Camarón's widow had even asked for his forgiveness. He also spoke of a figure of 500,000 pesetas relating to his authorship, for which he had a certificate stamped by the Spanish Society of Authors. He was keen to point out that the first two records he made with Camarón sold 1,500 and 1,700 copies respectively and that when a friend put his name down as the author, he did not understand its significance at the time.

Camarón's death had left Paco de Lucía in a state of severe depression that would result in him not giving any concerts as he abandoned his guitar to watch television for months on end. Almost a year after Camarón's death, Paco was clearly still in mourning for the singer and very keen to put the record straight. He spoke of a very strong and unique relationship that he had not experienced with anyone else. Camarón's singing was something very special and now they would never see each other again or record another album. The accusations against him, that were to damage the good name of the Lucía brothers, were for Paco just like being stabbed in the back and left him feeling insecure without any hunger for the guitar. He took the decision after the funeral to say nothing, as he was not guilty of anything. Paco would give up anything just to record with Camarón, for whom he had so much respect. He said he wanted to be a singer while Camarón would have liked to be a guitarist. This was not quite accurate as Camarón had demonstrated his ability on the guitar and would have only swapped singing for the matador's cape. During the interview, Paco's manager asked him if he was going to stay on the train to Sevilla, where in the spring of 1992 he spent a month working on Camarón's last record *Potro de Rabia y Miel*. It was in that Andalusian capital that, due to Camarón's lung cancer, they had to spend so much time working on one of the jewels of this album, the *taranta*.

In an article published a year after the singers' death, the writer Balbino Gutiérrez would put the remarkable press coverage surrounding Camarón's death in 1992 under the microscope. Gutiérrez posed the fascinating concept of a flamencogist working in the year 2050, embarking on writing an article on Camarón who, had he lived, would be a centenarian. He had conducted his research with the cult of Camarón in its infancy and had wondered whether there would even be a market for such an article if Camarón had not died young. On examining the print media in the weeks after Camarón's death, Gutiérrez identified three key themes worthy of investigation. The first being the remarkable amount of column inches devoted to the gypsy singer in all of the newspapers. For Gutiérrez, the articles chose to either concentrate on merely reporting the eventful funeral or to make comments on Camarón's position in flamenco art; using glowing eulogies and extravagant language to sum up the pain and loss. His second theme was the observation that the praise was 'unanimous' with no dissenting voices as all the luminaries of flamenco paid tribute to Camarón in the days after his death. Gutiérrez had overlooked a few who were conspicuous by their silence. Even Camarón's great rival Enrique Morente had conceded that nobody had ever influenced flamenco in this manner and went as far as admitting to being influenced subconsciously by an artist who was irreplaceable. Paco de Lucía, with whom Camarón had experienced difficulties, now described working with the singer as easy because Camarón would always be happy to accept his way of doing things. But, as Gutiérrez was keen to stress, one key voice was not to be found in the column inches, the voice of the man who only wished to be remembered as Camarón's guitarist, Tomatito. Gutiérrez's third and most controversial finding was that 'someone had tried to create a legend around Camarón'. All the Spanish dailies had gone alone with this scheme and 'gone big' on this story, but would this manufactured image stand the test of time?

8

A Gigantic Creation of the Spanish People

No nacera otro como el
Enrique Morente, *El País*

The poet Federico García Lorca once described flamenco as one of the gigantic creations of the Spanish people, but how was this instantly recognisable form of Spanish music created? Was the short career of Camarón the culmination of 250 years of development and can his status as flamenco's greatest artist be justified? Some clues to the answers to these questions can be found by returning to a key landmark in flamenco's relatively short history. The decision to stage a singing competition in Granada in the summer of 1922 had been taken by a group of intellectuals who had the noble and idealistic aim of halting the decline in what they saw as the primitive and dignified art of Andalucía. These intellectuals believed that the roots of flamenco could be traced back to the Muslim Spain of the eighth century when southern Spain was ruled as a province from North Africa. They also considered that its origins were directly related to the arrival of the gypsy people from North India in the fifteenth century.

The idea of preserving and consigning to the museum a living and developing art form was, eighty years after Manuel de Falla's legendary competition, to have echoes in the debate that arose over *nuevo flamenco* and again in the post-nuevo flamenco era. During this period, purists and contributors to flamenco's journals began to question the authenticity of the whole concept of 'new or open flamenco' that had been inspired by Camarón's revolution.

In the 1920s, a similar group of Spanish intellectuals had become concerned over the dilution of the *cante* that was occurring in the rowdy cafés of Andalucía and Madrid, as artists performed purely for financial reward. Their attempt to halt this perceived decline was as unsuccessful as was the call for a written definition of flamenco in the twenty-first century by a group of academics who considered new flamenco to not be flamenco at all. This schism, between aficionados over what they consider to be the transgression and blurring of the musical boundaries by today's artists, had little effect on working flamenco musicians and neither did Falla's ambitious competition. Yet there are parallels to be found between Falla's concern that the *cante* of the 1920s was suffering from an Italian influence and the doubts over the validity of flamenco fusion voiced by some of today's critics. Many remain concerned over whether flamenco can continue to absorb the influences of other musical cultures with alien instruments and still retain its integrity. These same critics had been very troubled over Camarón's controversial 'La Leyenda del Tiempo' album, which crossed the boundaries between flamenco and rock in the late seventies.

It is unlikely that Camarón would have been tempted to enter such a politically motivated competition had he been active in 1922. Camarón had entered a contest held at the Montilla festival in 1962, where he found success, and later found greater recognition at the fourth *Festival de Cante Jondo*, staged in the village of Mairena del Alcor four years later. But would Camarón have travelled from Cádiz to Granada like the gypsy boy Manolo Caracol, to perform in front of the great and good of Andalucía? Would he have had the motivation of the competition's joint winner, who trekked those many miles from Puente Genil near Córdoba to Granada? The reward for the seventy-two year old Diego Bermúdez Cala, better known as El Tenazas, was to be later attacked and robbed of his 1,000 peseta prize on his way home. Had Camarón travelled to Granada, his chances of impressing the judges would have been slim as they would have been unlikely to be engaged by such a young, innovative and dynamic talent. To really under-stand whether the teenage Camarón would have entered this competition, which provoked such fierce debate at the time, one needs to revisit that moment when very heavy rain fell on the audience as they listened to El Tenazas in *La Plaza de los Aljibes* on 14 June 1922.

Camarón would not have shared the concerns of the poets, composers, writers, painters and musicians who felt that the *cante jondo*, the essence of flamenco song, had declined so much that it needed to be rescued from the clutches of the cafés and their boozy customers. Manuel de Falla, Spain's leading composer at the time, and Camarón were both born in the province of Cádiz. They would also both be buried there, although in Falla's case against his will as his body was brought to Cádiz Cathedral in one of Franco's warships. In terms of wealth, education and ethnicity there was a huge gulf between them, but Falla had also grown up hearing the *cante* in his cot as his family's Andalusian servants sang to him.

Granada, 5 May 1922

Manuel de Falla had been in a buoyant mood when he climbed a steep hill with a hamper under his arm in preparation for a relaxing picnic in the countryside of Granada. Ahead of him lay the ordeal of next month's flamenco competition, which would be reviewed and put under the microscope by the world's press including the celebrated British Hispanist, J.B. Trend. After all he was, as far as he was concerned, about to rescue the sacred flamenco song from the current trend of contaminated and affected interpretations of the *cante*. He would become enraged at even the thought of the flamenco songs being performed as mere entertainment for the customers in cafés and theatres. Falla's big idea was to stage a competition, which would foster interest in the real *cante* of his beloved Andalucía, and this project had also found a resonance with the young poet, Federico García Lorca. He could now relax in the knowledge that the young student Lorca would provide, through his extensive contacts, a strong field of singers worthy of such a contest.

Falla wanted to encourage gypsies to sing unadulterated 'traditional' flamenco, which was a romantic view of flamenco song that may have developed while he was studying in Paris. It is this theme of romanticism that would later express itself in a composition that is still widely performed today. Falla's most famous work, the ballet *El amor brujo*, had been completed during the outbreak of the First World War, but afterwards he was to experience a barren spell and would not, over a period of twenty years, even complete his other important work *La Atlántida*. His ballet *El amor brujo*, had drawn on the so-called rhythms of the gypsies and was to have a profound influence on the young poet from Granada, García Lorca. Lorca also shared Falla's obsession to save the *cante* and frequently went on a *recces* to the caves in Granada's Sacromonte district, where he listened to gypsies performing flamenco.[1] Falla had enlisted Lorca's help in order to raise the money needed to promote this ambitious event and he had been successful in getting a number of prominent intellectuals and composers, including Juan Ramón Jiménez and Joaquín Turina, to sign a petition. It was even suggested that leading composers of this age, including Ravel and Stravinksy, should be invited as Lorca and Falla began to assume that they were the only people that could stage such an event: casting their work in a epic light, Lorca later declared that no two people were better equipped for the task 'than a musician like Falla … and a poet like Lorca, a Gypsy, a *granadino*, black and green like a thoroughbred pharaoh.'[2] These two artists were both influenced by the modernist movement and shared the misguided belief that purifying the gypsy song was the best way to tackle the loss of moral and national pride that had been dented in 1898 as Spain was kicked out of Cuba.

Although Lorca was not present at the picnic, Falla would still enjoy himself as the guitarist Andrés Segovia, another fellow Andalusian from Linares, would play the guitar as they ate and drank some superb Jerez wine. Few amongst the picnickers had bothered to listen to Segovia, preferring to chatter as they dined. Segovia, while uneasy with the situation, did not object to being mere background noise as Falla had promised him the opportunity to perform as a professional at the forthcoming *concurso* and to be one of the judges.

Plaza de los Aljibes, Corpus Christi, 14 June 1922

As the strong summer rain fell on the audience they lifted their seats above their shoulders to cover their heads while clutching a curious unsigned leaflet entitled *EL CANTE JONDO*, with the politically charged subtitle of *Cante Primitivo Andaluz*.[3] Its pen and ink cover appealed to those who sought to uphold Spain's traditional values and the artist had also incorporated the names of two key lynchpins of the *cante jondo*, the *soleá* and the *seguiriya*. A clue to the possible author was to be found in the words printed below the drawing which spoke of the 'musical values and influence on European Musical Art' of the *cante jondo*. The heavy rain came at an unfortunate time when the eventual winner, the balding El Tenazas, was performing on stage. He leaned forward resting on his cane with his hands outstretched to engage the audience. Amongst the judges in the front row was Andrés Segovia, easily recognisable by his heavy black-rimmed glasses. Segovia did not cover his head but preferred to stand gazing at the singer's accompanist, the gypsy Ramón Montoya. As a guitarist in his twenties, Segovia grudgingly acknowledged the talent of the forty-two-year-old maestro who was in the process of creating the foundations of the modern flamenco guitar.

Segovia had, after all, started his musical career playing flamenco; an art he would later publicly distance himself from as he carved out a glittering career as a master of the classical guitar.

Historians and many eminent flamencologists have long debated the precise origins of flamenco and in particular the *cante*. Written documentary evidence of the gypsy songs did not appear until the 1850s when flamenco's so-called golden age was in full swing with the emergence of the *café cantantes*. This lack of information is hardly surprising for an art form dominated by illiterate artists, who were unable to preserve in written form the details of their lives, or the words they sang; the oldest written records can only be traced back as far as the 1780s.

Camarón had much in common with the pioneers from this early period in flamenco's relatively brief history. One such artist was the eccentric gypsy singer El Planeta who we know, like Camarón, found giving public performances a very lucrative way of earning a living. He also shared with Camarón an obsession with his appearance and would dress in a colourful bullfighting costume, with matching exotic headgear that resembled a clown's hat decorated with red pompoms. Beneath that hat was a loud red tie that complemented a clean white shirt, finished off with ruffles that had been embroidered with red stitching. Around his waist was a cummerbund of soft black velvet, giving him the image of both troubadour and matador.[4] Carefully folded around his neck was a small handkerchief, made from reeds, to ensure that his flamboyant hat with its narrow brim would sit well and remain in place. Under his arm there was always his treasured and well cared for peg-head guitar. El Planeta often played an instrument known as a vihuela which, although similar in shape to the early guitars, produced a richer sound. This instrument was so well finished that it acted as an additional prop and gave El Planeta an air of confidence as he carried it under his arm. His vihuela was built by a craftsman called Martínez from Málaga province and would have looked splendid with its neck curved back gracefully to reveal tuning pegs made of black *granadillo* wood.[5] The pegs were decorated with ivory from which he had hung red and white ribbons, some of which were tied in bunches and plaited like hair. While the instrument had a fret-board made from the finest dark ebony, it also had wide bouts that produced more volume, enabling El Planeta to project his music in the noisy cafés.

El Planeta shared with Camarón the ability to accompany himself on the guitar while singing flamenco. He had also worked as a blacksmith in

the forges of Triana, Seville's then rougher *barrio*, on the wrong side of the
Betis River. More detailed research has revealed that despite gravitating to
the forges of Triana, El Planeta was, like Camarón, born in Cádiz, the oldest home of flamenco. There is another fascinating link between these two
illustrious maestros, separated by over 150 years, which relates to the other
prizewinner at Granada's infamous 1922 singing competition, the thirteen-
year-old boy Manolo Caracol. Caracol was a direct descendent of El Planeta
who went on to not only dominate the *cante*, but also to snub the teenage
Camarón by initially overlooking his talent. Caracol's triumph in Granada
had arisen from a chance remark made over dinner by the eminent singer
who would be appointed as the chairman of the judges at the Granada
competition.[6] Don Antonio Chacón, a bald and very smartly dressed man
with a black moustache that curled up at the ends, had been a good friend
of Caracol's father and was often invited to dinner at his house in Seville.
Over dinner, Chacón had mentioned Falla's contest and how the organisers were looking for singers to enter. He also bemoaned the fact that there
were not any young singers in Seville good enough to enter, but if he knew
of any this was the perfect opportunity for them to make their mark. The
young and enterprising Manolo Caracol had heard these words and later
engineered a meeting with Chacón, who, on hearing him sing, had no hesi-
tation in taking him to Granada. This anecdote, which was told by Caracol
only forty years ago, illustrates that not all gypsies possess the gift to sing flamenco. The secrets of the art have always been held and developed amongst
a relatively small number of artists from elite families who have tended to
live in the large cities of Andalucía.

If we could return to the Seville of the mid-nineteenth century we would
find a city in which, due to the changing course of Guadalquivir River, the
Romans had been reluctant to build a bridge linking Triana to the city. For
centuries no bridge spanned the banks of Seville and Triana until the Puente
de Triana was erected in 1852. But by the time the Expo was staged in Seville
in 1992 there would be many bridges from which to cross the Guadalquivir.
In the early nineteenth century El Planeta faced a more treacherous crossing when he wanted to visit the cafés of Seville. On his return home, after
a long night of singing and drinking rough *anís*, he would cross the great
river using the services of the 'bridge-boat' and its skillful operators.[7] How
often he fell into the wide river we will never know, but his exploits are
still remembered and cherished today. At the time of El Planeta's birth in
1785, the *cante* was still an intimate art that blacksmiths shared around the

forge, beating out the rhythms with their hammers on their anvils. Soon the *soleá* and *seguiriyas* would cross to the other side of the river, away from the slums of Triana which were often hit by floods. Flamenco song would find a new home in the cafés of Seville that flourished around the Campana and the Plaza de Duque. The *cante*, or songs, of the gypsies would soon entertain well-heeled clients and come to the attention of the many international travellers who arrived in southern Spain looking for romance, including the future British Prime Minister, Disraeli.

What had started as a migration of the gypsies from North India would later foster a music that entertained all classes from smugglers to prostitutes. El Planeta brought the gypsy songs of this very personal and intimate art from the seaport of Cádiz to Triana. A Triana that, during the nineteenth century, was considered ungovernable; being dominated by the gypsy clans that owned its fourteen forges. Those gypsies who inherited this tradition of flamenco song could not foresee the fate that General Franco would finally mete out to them in the twentieth century.[8] In the 1950s, both the gypsies and the working class of Triana were ruthlessly evicted and re-housed in council flats on the outskirts of Seville in estates including Las Tres Mil Viviendas. This could be interpreted as a reprisal against a district that had heroically held out against General Franco's rebel army for a week, or was it simply part of city planners' quest for modernity? The rebuilding of this quarter is now accepted as a mistake and few can now remember the sound of the blacksmith forges, or are old enough to have smelled the burning of fuel made from the skins of grapes, which blackened and stained Triana's tall chimneys.[9] All that remains of the old Triana is the Santa Ana church built by Alfonso X; apartment blocks that would be more at home on the Costa del Sol now overlook this area. When Triana lost its gypsy heritage it became gentrified and the Los Remedios district is now one of the most fashionable places to live. The price of land rose to a level that prevented industry from competing with housing and the homes of the gypsy dynasties were bulldozed. Camarón's ancestors would no longer light the fires of the forges and the sound of the *cante* would be silenced only to return annually for *La Vela* and the outdoor festival staged in the Plaza del Altozano. Triana's patios, decorated by the pots of geraniums that greeted the seamen as they returned home, would soon disappear but they can still be found in Camarón's home in San Fernando.

Seville, *22 August 1975*

I had only been in Seville for a day when the guitarist Pepe Martínez wanted
to take me for a drink in the Alameda de Hércules district; once home to the
great maestros of flamenco in the early years of the twentieth century, and
now Seville's red light district. This was the area that Pepe had visited as a
child in the early 1930s, peering into doorways and through windows to hear
the *juergas* or impromptu flamenco sessions, which made this the liveliest part
of town. We had first driven through the old Jewish quarter of the Barrio de
Santa Cruz in Pepe's latest Renault car. Within minutes we had arrived in the
Alfafa quarter, where all manner of pets from African parrots to turtles were
being traded. Pepe enjoyed driving along the narrow streets at breakneck
speed whilst not bothering to watch for pedestrians as we screeched round
the sharp corners! He was only interested in sharing his passion for Seville;
pointing out every place of interest, with his small right hand covered in ash
from his smouldering Montecristo Havana cigar. This was, after all, the city
where its legendary singer, La Niña de los Peines, had requested that Pepe
accompany her on the occasion of her seventieth birthday.

We finally arrived in Pepe's favourite bar in the Alameda, within sight of a
road that reminds visitors of the two Roman emperors Trajano and Adriano,
who were both born in Seville. Everyone knew Pepe and within seconds
two *cañas* of ice-cold foaming *cruzcampo* had been slammed down in front
of us. This was Pepe's favourite beer because it was always fresh, having been
brewed only a few miles away in the factory next to Seville's prison, beyond
the Gran Plaza. It is not customary to drink beer on its own in Andalucía
and two saucers of *alcaparras*, those delicious large caper berries were soon
placed in front of us. We then had another beer, this time accompanied by a
pavía, a delicious small piece of fish, either cod or hake, fried in a golden yellow batter and served on a bed of shredded lettuce with a basket of *picos* or
mini bread sticks. If you were to ask for a *pavía* outside of Seville you would
receive puzzled looks as only the *Sevillanos* know that this tasty *tapa* takes its
name from the yellow horizontal buttons on the tunic of General Pavía, the
man who restored the Spanish monarchy in 1874. The bar, its floor littered
with chicken bones, peanut shells and discarded lottery coupons, was doing
a roaring trade with more people outside than in. Before I was able to finish
my second beer I was aware that Pepe was leaving. He called for the bill and
then slung a handful of *duros* across the bar's stainless steel top shouting '*bote
gracias*'. We then departed, with the waiter on all fours, picking up the coins
and looking for his tip!

Seville, May 1990

I had come to Seville in search of the origins of *café cantantes*, those unique flamenco establishments that had flourished in the mid and late-nineteenth century. The songs that brought those cafés to life had provided the inspiration for much of Camarón's repertoire. The café culture which had been driven by musical performances, had proved popular all over Europe; but would I find the ghosts of Camarón's ancestors performing in these crowded venues that once stank from the smell of the oil lamps that provided their dim lighting? The so-called Golden era of flamenco can be dated from the opening of the Café de los Lombardos in 1847 to the knocking down of the Café Novedades on 19 March 1923, as *ópera flamenca* finally killed off the cafés when flamenco artists first began performing in theatres, cinemas and bullrings.[10] It was the artists who performed in these lively cafés, where often the customers only had to buy food and drink rather than pay an admission charge that provided the prototypes of not just the songs Camarón would sing but also the model for how he would perform them.

I was conducting research for a BBC radio series on *cante gitano* or gypsy song and wanted to visit the locations of these legendary cafes that are known mainly from paintings like Sergeant's *El Jaleo* or Gustave Dore's varied drawings of nineteenth-century life in Seville. These paintings had captured the busy cafés full of bearded men gazing lustily at young gypsy dancing girls wearing bright colourful dresses. There was always a row of guitarists with *sombreros* covering their eyes that followed the dancer's footwork, deep in concentration. A dozen artists would occupy the stage while women accompanied the dance with tambourines and *palmas* as the more privileged amongst the audience looked on from balconies on two floors. Some of the cafés were elaborately decorated with lavish staging and plush balconies from which the wealthier clients could view the show. The surviving oil paintings present the cafés as dark, poorly lit places that were ideal for escaping the fierce sun of Andalucía. Their walls were much like London's Italian restaurants in the seventies, decorated with all sorts of tat from old broken guitars to chipped jugs. Much valuable space was taken up by far too many tables and chairs that surrounded the small stage and seated under vaulted arches were the customers. Many wore hats resembling the English bowler and they were drawn from the deckhands that operated the boats on the Guadalquivir to ceramic workers, bullfighters, army officers and prostitutes. The nineteenth-century travellers who came to Spain from Britain, France and Italy during the 'Romantic Period' would soon join them.

Like the artists, the audience sat on the traditional straight back Andalusian chairs with seats woven from reeds and wooden slats to support the back. Many of the men would lean backwards, tipping those chairs as they relaxed to the music and dance while smoking. Here, in these comfortable surroundings on whose walls hung paintings of celebrated buildings from Arabic Spain including La Giralda, the customers would spend their *céntimos* on bottles of wine and the occasional *carajillo* of coffee laced with brandy. They had previously been used to seeing flamenco artists perform at livestock fairs, but now comparable performances were available on tap seven days a week. Even better from the audience's point of view would be the inclusion of turns from stand-up comedians and displays from wild animals.

The names of these establishments, which really took off in the last twenty years of the nineteenth century, are well known from the *Café Filarmonico* to the *Kursaal*. The very first enterprise, the *Café de los Lombardos* is believed to have opened in 1847, right in the heart of Seville. The stars of these cafés were not just the singers, but increasingly dancers who began to wear elaborate costumes covered in lace shawls. As Camarón would discover to his cost, 150 years later in Madrid, flamenco had ceased to be a gypsy form of communication, and was now simply an entertainment and business. One such businessman, who ran an important *café cantante*, was Silverio Franconetti who had left Spain to work as a tailor in South America only to later return and become the first flamenco variety club magnate. Camarón, from his days in the Málaga and Madrid *tablaos*, would have been familiar with a boss like Franconetti who expected several performances daily from his artists, many of whom were gypsies.

While enjoying a coffee in Seville's Campana that lies just off the Calle Sierpes and is best known for the department store *El Corte Inglés*, it was hard to visualise this area in its heyday. Gone were the fine houses that once graced the *Plaza del Duque* only to be replaced by a monument to one-stop shopping that does not even honour the *siesta*. It was here, in the great houses whose walls were lined with decorative tiles bearing Arabic motifs, that artists including Manuel Vallejo and Manolo de Huelva, dressed in their best suits and waistcoats, would pose for the camera. In a few moments I would be heading for the *Calle Amor de Dios* which leads to the Alameda de Hércules, watched over by the tall columns bearing the statues of Julius Caesar and Hércules, to search for the home of the *Salón Filarmónico* which once made no.23 the noisiest building in the street. All I found was decaying buildings as Seville's Town Council had decided that the forth-coming Expo '92 was a higher priority than the area once considered the cradle of flamenco, and now a prostitute's paradise.

My historical search for Camarón would not have found him in the *ópera flamenca* age that was dominated by falsetto voices with non-gypsies often performing gypsy songs. The great Antonio Chacón would bridge the era between the *café cantantes* and *ópera flamenca* as a new genera-tion of stylistically very different artists took over. By the forties the voices dominating flamenco would have a higher pitch than Camarón with a sweetness and sentimentality that it would be inconceivable to hear him adopt. Yet Camarón would have identified with the queen of flamenco singing in this era, because much of her flamenco material was created in the record-ing studio, allowing Niña de los Peines to take her trademark *al gurugú* to a much bigger audience. The new commercial maestros of flamenco, Pepe Marchena and Juanito Valderama, were not gypsies and sang in a very different way; producing a type of 'white man's flamenco'. There was one prominent artist in the forties who would not only dominate flamenco, but also have a very big presence in the cinema: the gypsy Manolo Caracol, who went on to carve out a considerable career after his 1922 triumph in Granada.

The Spanish monarchy has historically been a keen supporter of flamenco and its artists, as have many of the country's politicians. The reigning mon-arch, King Juan Carlos I, and the former socialist Prime Minister, Felipe González, were both prominent admirers of Camarón and had sent letters of condolence to his family on hearing of his death. The King of Spain has always enjoyed the art of those two gypsy sisters, the late Fernanda de Utrera and her sister Bernarda, but close links between the monarchy and politicians with flamenco have a long history that can be traced back to the reign of Alfonso XII. The singer Juan Breva, who in the late nineteenth cen-tury had been the master of the *malagueña*, was even accompanied to *juergas*, the flamenco parties, by King Alfonso XII.[11] Such was the King's admira-tion for a performance given by Breva at the Royal Palace that he gave him a tie clip bearing the Royal crest and offered him a pension.[12] The pension failed to materialise, with Breva spending his last years in Málaga with very little to live on, despite having once been such a high earner in the Madrid tablaos. Fortunately this story did have a happy ending when Breva reminded the new King Alfonso XII of his father's promise and the pension was paid.

The first two decades of the twentieth century had seen many great artists, including Antonio Chacón, performing for not just for the monarch, but also aristocrats including the Count of Grisal who was reported to have given Chacón 25,000 pesetas for a night's work![13] During the dictatorship of Primo de Rivera, life for the flamencos had become very difficult because of a clampdown on bar opening hours which forced the flamenco parties to move to the *ventas*, the country roadside inns that the authorities would find harder to police. Despite imposing these restrictions, Primo de Rivera was a fan of flamenco and even went as far as organising festivals and sitting as a judge on festival committees.[14] The inauguration of the Second Republic, which followed this dictatorship, was to usher in even harder times for flamenco artists. While the members of the new parliament were keen to introduce reforms which would restrict the power of the church and tackle the issue of land reform, they were not concerned with the patronage of flamenco. The art's chief paymasters, the aristocracy who had held power for so long, had been ousted and their absence from the cafés in Madrid was to have serious economic consequences for the development of flamenco during the thirties. Flamenco artists now needed to band together and form companies that could tour theatres and bullrings. My own maestro, Pepe Martínez, would benefit greatly from this development after the Second World War, as he was valued for more than just his guitar-playing. His father's status in the banking world enabled Pepe to cash the cheques that were made out to the artists in these companies and he was later to find lucrative work with Juanito Valderama.

In 1935, Fernando el de Triana, published his *Arte y Artistas Flamencos*, an A to Z of all the professional artists of the day. This important publication was a true labour of love as Fernando had patiently photographed and written accompanying biographies of the leading artists. The female singers and dancers were photographed in classic poses against painted backdrops of Seville's classic buildings, smoking cigars or drinking *años*. This book, which was an inspired project for its time, suggested that flamenco was now becoming an accepted and more formalised art. The thirties would also see the guitar begin to develop in the hands of the gypsy Ramón Montoya, who would revolutionise the instrument introducing many new techniques including the *trémolo*. Paco de Lucía would later complete Montoya's pioneering work in the seventies, as the guitar with its new harmonies became the engine room of flamenco. Working mainly in recording studios, Paco would expand the vocabulary of this once dying art and introduce revolutionary ideas. He created *falsetas* that imitated flamenco song and injected the vital energy that would energize flamenco.

While the forties had been all about the supremacy of Manolo Caracol, the fifties would witness two key milestones in flamenco's history: the record houses releasing anthologies documenting all the various complexities of flamenco song and rhythm, and the birth of the summer festivals. The *Antología del Cante Flamenco*, issued by Hispavox in 1958, completed the journey of the gypsy song from the forges and the fields to the homes of the middle class enthusiasts who now owned boxed sets of ten-inch records to play on their newly acquired turntables. Gypsy artists like Rafael Romero had recorded many of the regional styles including 'country styles', 'dancing songs' and 'songs without guitar accompaniment', but a box set containing three albums and a book was indicative of the academic grip on flamenco that Camarón would ultimately have to overthrow. This scholarly approach to the art, which had as its basis the assumption that flamenco song had reached its peak many years ago, would also spawn chairs in flamencology at Spanish universities and create, in the person of the gypsy maestro Antonio Mairena, a single source who claimed to be the guardian of the past. This approach would naturally lead to a decline in creativity of the art, with even gypsies finding the *cante* dull and staid, until the revolution staged by Camarón and Paco de Lucía. Of far more importance than the numerous anthologies and 'in the field' recordings that began to flood the market was the emergence of the outdoor festivals. While producers, including Deben Bhattacharya, were still taking their tape recorders to Seville and Puente Genil in 1956 to record what they termed the *Living Tradition* of singers performing around the Easter processions, a new way of bringing flamenco to the public was emerging. It would prove to be far more influential than the albums, portraying flamenco sung at gypsy gatherings in San Maries de la Mer, which found their way into homes throughout Europe and the United States during the fifties. By 1958 flamenco had really come of age with the inception of an academic chair for the study of the art in Jerez and in 1969 a flamenco congress would sit for the first time. Every year since, representatives from all fields of flamenco from presidents of the clubs to academics and festival organisers have gathered to discuss how the art can be best developed and promoted.

In 1954, with the opening of the *Zambra* in Madrid and later the Torres Bermejas where Camarón would perform in the seventies, a new and more expensive style of *café cantante* would be born, known as the *tablao*.

While the Café de Chinitas in Málaga, which had been running since 1860, was to close amid the political upheavals of 1936, it was to be reborn as a *tablao* in 1970. These new nightclubs, where the cream of flamenco's artists could be heard, would flourish in the latter part of General Franco's dictatorship. Soon the academic centres for flamenco study based in Córdoba and Jerez would formalise singing competitions and further extend their study of the art by appointing dedicated professors; preparing the way for a new trend, the flamenco festival.

There is little doubt that the reign of General Franco affected the public performance of flamenco, because any gatherings after early evening that involved any sort of noise were not permitted. The power of the police during the dictatorship was immense, but it failed to deter the young Camarón and others from performing under age and out of hours. Despite these restrictions there were easier ways for artists to perform flamenco that involved appearing at *juergas*, or flamenco parties, held in the stately homes of the rich and powerful. Flamenco remained a symbol of the old Spain, representing traditional values and Franco's government, for these reasons alone, would frequently employ artists. But the *juerga* would in time become a rarity as the upper classes would, like everyone else, have to go to a nightclub or buy concert tickets if they wanted to hear and see the art. By the sixties the concept of paying flamenco artists to perform at a private party was dead: partly because singers and guitarists would no longer play for peanuts but also because flamenco had ceased to be fashionable for the moneyed classes. Soon artists would find work in the flamenco *peñas*, clubs that became shrines to flamenco artists, in every village and town with a dedicated membership buying a building where intimate performances could take place.

The first recognised festival was the *Potaje Gitano de Utrera* staged in June 1957 and organised by the religious brotherhoods of *Stmo. Cristo de la Buena Muerte y Ntra. Sra. de la Esperanza 'Los Gitanos'*. As the name suggests a meal was served to all who attended, consisting of a black bean stew containing generous amounts of *chorizo*. The tradition of the wooden spoon, green tablecloths and serviettes soon became established in Utrera. The first simple menu, printed on one side of a card, had stated that there would be just one item available: the bean stew which contained generous amounts of garlic, to be served from ten o'clock in the *caseta* Tiro el Plato. The greats of the time, including Antonio Mairena and Juan Talega, would all perform as a new flamenco trend was established. The theme of food and flamenco would soon find an echo in two other neighbouring towns of Seville province, where a very young Camarón would make an appearance.

In 1963, Morón de la Frontera would compliment the stew of Utrera by launching a festival accompanied by another Andalusian gastronomic delight, *El Primer Gazpacho Andaluz*. The town of Los Aruncitanos, with its legend of *El Gallo*, would put Antonio Mairena and all the greats from Diego del Gastor to Andorrano on a poster for a concert to raise money for charity on that first Friday in September. The area around the Círculo Mercantil would be full to witness the sisters from Utrera, Fernanda and Bernarda, who were rewarded with great applause and bouquets of flowers. Another annual flamenco festival had been established and six years later Camarón would receive the honour of being invited to sing at the *VII Gazpacho Andaluz* that was held in late August in 1969. The classic sixties poster, with a female flamenco dancer in flamboyant pose alongside the sponsor's sherry bottle and glasses, would announce the festival as a homage to Antonio Mairena as both Camarón and Enrique Morente were to make their debuts. The critic Miguel Acal would praise the smell and taste of that famous Andalusian cold soup made from liquidised tomatoes, green peppers, cucumber, onions and the all-important stale bread, wine vinegar and hint of chilli. He also praised the quality of the artists, including Camarón who he felt had some weaknesses due to his youth. Acal was astounded at Camarón's ability to sing *bulerías*, which he simply described as extraordinary. Accompanied by Juan del Gastor, Camarón had sung dressed in a white suit with a great smile on his face. He had been warmly welcomed by the Morón public and was rewarded with two further invitations to the *Gazpacho de Morón* before his death. Camarón was also a key participant in the *Caracolá* in Lebrija that completed the trilogy of outdoor gypsy festivals in flamenco's golden triangle. Snails were now the ideal accompaniment to the *cante*, as Camarón in the company of Lebrija's leading artists including El Lebrijano paid tribute to the late Juaniquí.

The festivals continued to expand until the nineties when they encountered financial difficulties but they remain exciting showcases where the Spanish public and tourists can see, beneath the stars, the best artists for a very reasonable price. Most towns and villages in Andalucía have an annual outdoor flamenco festival where proud mayors compete to promote leading artists alongside local talent. They also offer the chance to experience some of the worst portable loos in the world and while providing memorable moments they often deteriorate in the early hours of the morning as the alcohol consumption rises. Camarón had dominated these festivals in the late seventies and eighties

when his name was to be found at the top of every bill. But his ability
to attract large audiences and command substantial fees for relatively short
performances did not meet with the approval of everyone. Gerald Howson,
who had greatly admired Aurelio Sellés, the Cádiz singer who was popular
in the fifties, felt compelled to write:

> A few years ago, the late and famous young singer Camarón was asked to per-
> form at a festival in one of the small pueblos along the coast from Cádiz. A fee
> of 3 million pesetas was demanded and agreed to, which left almost nothing for
> the other artists due to appear. Moreover, whereas Aurelio had sung all night for
> his 1,400 pesetas, and, 'if it caught me well', had delivered some great art into
> the bargain, El Camarón sang for less than three-quarters of an hour before
> speeding off in his chauffeur-driven automobile. Where is the diversity?[15]

Others had complained much earlier in Camarón's career about the singer's
tendency to offer short performances, including Miguel Acal when he reviewed
the 1982 *Gazpacho* festival for the ABC newspaper. Acal, who would decades
later campaign against the move to recognise Camarón with flamenco's highest
honour, was concerned that the organisers allowed the singer to do only one
spot, unlike the other artists. The festival had been a financial failure but Acal did
accept that Camarón gave the audience a demonstration of how to sing, finishing his set on a high with the hit song *Como el Agua*. While Camarón could
certainly draw a crowd at a festival his fees were often exaggerated and his name
often appeared on a poster for which no contract existed.

The festivals had proved that this once private art was now for the masses,
but as they continued to grow in popularity, two other important developments were to occur that would further stimulate interest in flamenco outside
of Spain: the expansion of flamenco touring companies, some of them government backed, and the trilogy of films featuring flamenco artists from the
director Carlos Saura. *Cumbre Flamenca* would, as its name suggests, bring to
the world many of Spain's finest flamenco artists, as would the later *Corazón
flamenco*. During the same period, Carlos Saura directed three very influential
films: *Blood Wedding*, *Carmen* and *A Love Bewitched*. The dance companies of
Antonio and Rosario and José Greco had brought flamenco to an eager international audience, while Antonio Gades, Mario Maya and Cristina Hoyos
would follow them. An interest and appetite was created with an audience
generated that can now support the tours of the companies dominating today's
stages including Sara Baras, Javier Barón, Joaquín Cortés and Eva Yerbabuena.

Flamenco had always had an historic relationship with Spanish cinema that was firmly cemented in the forties and fifties by Manolo Caracol and Lola Flores appearing in *Un Caballero Famoso, Embrujo, Jack el Negro* and *La Niña de la Venta*. From the early thirties the singer Pepe Marchena had been starring in films and in 1935 he had appeared in *María del Carmen*. He left a strong body of work from *Paloma de mis Amores*, through *Martingala* released in 1940 to his best-known and last film, *La Reina Mora*, in 1954. This tradition of exploiting the genre of film as a vehicle for flamenco stars had started as early as 1936 when Carmen Amaya and Pastora Imperio appeared in *María de la O*, while the films featuring the high pitched voice of Josélito had long been classics. In 1953, with the release of *Duende y Misterio*, the director Edgar Neville would bring to a much wider audience the singing of Antonio Mairena and Fernanda de Utrera with Antonio dancing in a variety of exotic Spanish locations. By 1963 Carmen Amaya was back on the silver screen with *Los Tarantos* starring alongside the king of the male dance, Antonio Gades. Its director Rovira Beleta followed it up the next year with *El Amor brujo*, again starring Antonio Gades and a very young Camarón. Marisol would also make several films with a flamenco twist as a child star in the sixties, and later star as Pepa Flores in Saura's *Carmen*. Who can forget *Los Duendes de Andalucía* in which the feisty Paquera de Jerez starred alongside Porrina de Badajoz, best known for his dark glasses? Lola Flores was also to appear in the box office success of 1972, *Casa Flora*, which also gave a bit part to Camarón. In 1984 flamenco music broke out of the narrow genre of the Spanish cinema when Paco de Lucía wrote the music for the soundtrack of *The Hit*, starring John Hurt and Terence Stamp. By the nineties, directors were returning to the old classics for inspiration and *Los Tarantos* was remade as *Montoyas y Tarantos*, starring Cristina Hoyos, with a score by Paco de Lucía in 1990. Saura's success, particularly with *Carmen*, enabled him to make *Sevillañas* released in 1992 and *Flamenco* in 1995. This was quickly followed in 1996 by *Alma Gitana* which examined the lives of young gypsies against the backdrop of the music of *Ketama* and then came a surprise appearance by Tomatito and El Potito in *The Devil's Advocate*. These films became another part of flamenco's evolving history, as did *Flamenco Women* by the influential director Mike Figgis. By 2001 the filmmaker Tony Gatlif was able to make the far more ambitious flamenco film *Vengo* staring the dancer Antonio Canales. But flamenco had also found an admirer in the new giant of Spanish cinema, the director Pedro Almodóvar, who would undoubtedly have cast Camarón in one of his films had he lived. In 1993 his film *Kika* used the voice of Fernanda de Utrera to kick start

the story while *El Flor de mi Secreto*, released in 1995 drew on the emerging talent of the dancer Joaquín Cortés. Who can forget the emotion of the
bulerías from Vicente Amigo and El Pele that closed *Hable Con Ella* in 2002?
But his love affair with flamenco was also to find a place in what is now
regarded as one of Almodóvar's finest films. *Volver*, which was released in
2006, turned to the new female star of flamenco singing, Estrella Morente for
its inspiration as actress Penélope Cruz mimed the words of that *bulerías* from
the old school to perfection.

Away from this productive relationship with the silver screen cinema and
particularly the realism of Saura's films, a movement that came to be known
as 'new flamenco' was emerging, with its artists taking their inspiration from
Camarón's albums. Many consider that the origins of the so-called 'new flamenco' can be traced back to 1970 and in particular the group *Smash*, founded
by Gualberto who was later to play the sitar on Camarón's celebrated lullaby.
Others have even argued that some of the controversial treatment of flamenco's South American influenced rhythms by Pepe Marchena in the fifties
had first broken with tradition. Much later would come the groups *Triana*,
Alameda, *Crack*, *Guadalquivir*, *Galaxia* and *Mezquita*, but it was down to a
photographer who became a record producer, to foster a stable of artists who
radically changed the sound of flamenco. Mario Pacheco had first heard the
exotic sounds of flamenco on the radio as a child and his father had worked
on Manolo Caracol's films in the forties. When I met Mario in London in
1992 he had told me that 'when you get into recording pop music in Madrid
you've got to record flamenco'. In 1983 Pacheco's fledgling label, which had
at first flirted with post-punk bands, released a stunning solo guitar album
from Pepe Habichuela, *A Mandeli*. Rafael Riqueni's *Juego de Niños* followed
shortly, but Pacheco's most important work would be with the generation
influenced by Camarón. His label, *Nuevos Medios*, was to provide an outlet for
the gypsy bands *Pata Negra* and *Ketama* and a host of other artists who created
the new open flamenco in the early nineties.

Camarón had influenced many groups who have considerably advanced
flamenco music. The flamenco rock group *Carmen*, who toured with David
Bowie, are one such example and their 1973 album *Fandangos in Space*
remains a classic. The duo of *Lole y Manuel* should also be considered alongside the distinct albums that Lebrijano and Morente made in the seventies
and eighties. We should also include *La Barbería del Sur*, whose members
were drawn from the younger brothers of *Ketama*, and the daring band
from Madrid, *Los Chorbos*. Without Camarón, could *Navajita Plateá* and

Mártires del Compás have produced their revolutionary treatments of the *bulerías*? It is also unlikely that Pepe Habichuela would have recorded with the *Bollywood Orchestra*. Tino Di Geraldo and the bassist Carles Benevent with *Jazzpana* are two highly individual artists who have built on the tradition of Camarón to produce a new repertoire. Without Camarón's pioneering efforts, would we also be able to enjoy the sampling, reggae and rap found on Elena Andújar's flamenco records; Diego Carrasco's ability to draw on so many other musical genres but still remain flamenco; and then of course, there is Tomatito. Camarón's successful challenge to the flamenco establishment would also open the doors for groups like, *Radio Tarifa* and *Ojos de Brujo*, who have triumphed in the market place with a repertoire which largely draws on flamenco.

Flamenco music remains as strong and as vibrant as ever. It continues to evolve daily; not just in the hands of its leading performers, but in the people who live in the council flats on the outskirts of Seville or the gypsy quarter of Jerez. In the same way that the art was 'nationalised' by General Franco, so the politicians governing Andalucía, from Manolo Chaves to Teófilo Martínez, have also adopted it. Once the music of the gypsy forge, it is now studied in universities and has its own foundation situated in a former palace in Jerez. The music of a people who had arrived in Spain from India and would later be called Egyptians and persecuted, is now the height of fashion in bars from Madrid to London.

9

The New Che,
1993–2005

Con Camarón comienza el flamenco.
José Mercé, *El País*

With the prince of flamenco now dead and only a few years away from becoming a saint, the race was on to produce the first book about Camarón's extraordinary life. His record company had already issued *Camarón de la Isla – 1969-1992 – Una leyenda viva*, a two record set to mark his passing, but very little written material existed. Only the lavishly illustrated *Maestros del Flamenco*, which had boldly chosen Camarón's image for its introductory photograph three years before his death, had charted the singer's life. Andrés Rodríguez Sánchez, with the publication of *Camarón – Se rompió el quejío*, emerged as the first author to release a biography of the singer in the year of his death. Sánchez's book was soon followed by *Vida y muerte del cante* in which Enrique Montiel showed his uncritical respect for Camarón as an artist. These left a gap in the market for a hack to fully research and publish what could be discovered on everything from the singer's drug-taking to his precarious financial position.

On Friday 4 July 1993, to coincide with the first anniversary of his death, the young journalist Francisco Peregil appeared at a press conference in Madrid to publicise his book, *Camarón de la Isla, el Dolor de un Príncipe*. The title alone, with its reference to the pain of a prince, signalled Peregil's clear intentions, with the twenty-six-year-old writer from the province of Huelva not pulling any punches over his aim to produce a warts-and-all account. What made it even more attractive was the accompanying compact disc that would be available with the intial print run. If the first indications of Camarón's cult status could be identified by any single product it has to be this publication; while not the first, it would set the trend. Naturally I found myself in Seville during July 1993; trailing round the city's bookshops while my taxi driver waited patiently, having been told that I could not leave for the airport until I had found a copy of Peregil's book. My initial enquires were met with the usual puzzled expressions one receives when asking for any new product relating to flamenco in Spain, but I did eventually find a shop that had just received some copies and eagerly handed over 3,000 pesetas.

Peregil had announced that his main motive for writing the book was the deprivation he felt at not having seen, unlike his friends, any of Camarón's performances in his final years.[1] He was to produce the fourth and final book to be written about Camarón in the year after his death and it was also to prove the most controversial. This biography claimed to be very different to its predecessors; written either by authors who had known Camarón, or by music journalists, aiming to satisfy the demands of the market place. Peregil was a staff journalist with *El País*, who had started his research six months before Camarón had died and who had interviewed the singer shortly before his death. His friends had told him much about the enigma of Camarón and he intended to unravel all the mysteries, tell the real story and lift the lid on the world of flamenco.

Also Peregil would not side-step the delicate subject of the relationship between Camarón and Paco de Lucía regarding the authorship of the singer's royalties. He would accept the much-supported Paco explanation of the saga, recounting that Camarón had little interest in the fine print of contracts, but crucially his book would neither attack nor defend Paco de Lucía. Peregil would inform his readers of Paco's offer to finance Camarón's medical expenses that had placated the majority of Camarón's followers. Many *Camaroneros* continued to believe that Paco had a very good relationship with Camarón, his brothers Manuel and Pijote and his wife and children, when the singer was alive and in years that followed. They also felt that far too much has been made of the so-called 'feud' by journalists. Unlike the other biographies, Peregil would return to primary sources and base much of the book on face-to-face interviews with Camarón's friends. Using emotional language Peregil had been very eager to emphasise how he had sweated over this work that would not dodge the issue of the singer's drug habit or the complex arguments over Camarón's financial affairs that surrounded his death. Peregil's publishers *El País – Aguilar* had in addition negotiated a deal for a compact disc featuring twelve of Camarón's best songs to accompany the book. This was just one of the novelties that would, in these early years, accelerate the singer's rapid progress towards cult status.

Away from the book launch in Madrid, Camarón's widow La Chispa had received an honour on behalf of her husband that should have been bestowed while he was still alive. In front of a gathering of 200 people, the mayor of San Fernando, Antonio Moreno, had announced that Camarón was now the chosen son of his hometown as the dignitaries filled the square where the young Camarón had often gone at night to sing in the Venta de Vargas.[2] A monument, cast in bronze and designed by the sculptor Antonio Aparicio, had been erected opposite the inn representing two images of the singer. One showed Camarón as a mature man, seated in his characteristic pose and the other of the young Camarón in those untroubled times when he was frequently seen in this square. Despite this tribute there was also another key badge of recognition from the world of flamenco, which would take a further seven years to resolve, the sensitive issue of the *Llave de Oro*, flamenco's highest honour.

Camarón's last recording had been his *sevillanas* for Carlos Saura's film of the same name, with the soundtrack being released in 1992, but demand was growing for a posthumous Camarón album. During 1978 Ricardo Pachón, Camarón's producer in waiting, had taken his Nagra tape-recorder and Newman condenser mic to flamenco festivals all over Andalucía to record Camarón and Tomatito at their best. Now, two years after the singer's death, the double CD *Camarón Nuestro* would start a trend of releasing previously unissued material and repackaging all of Camarón's *Universal* catalogue. 1994 would also see the release of *A Camarón*, a very emotional tribute led by Camarón's cousin Parrita. Many other prominent gypsy artists, including Manzanita, appeared on this homage that had allusions to a *fiesta* in heaven. There were also contributions from his former lyricist Antonio Humanes and the guitarists Tomatito and Juan Manuel Cañizares. The bassist Carles Benavent would also unveil his remarkable re-working of Camarón's *Dicen a Mi*, in a duet with Paco de Lucía that imitated the cadences of that remarkable voice. Later in 1994, just in time for the festive season, Universal would release on CD his *Nochebuena Gitana*, a collection of *Villancicos* or flamenco songs for Christmas Eve recorded with Paco de Lucía in 1973. Employing similar marketing techniques to the world of rock, this CD now contained different versions to those found on the original seven-inch records, making it a 'must have' for the growing number of Camarón collectors and completists. However, this was insignificant in comparison to what the Spanish post office had planned on 14 June 1996, when letters were franked bearing a nineteen-peseta postage stamp featuring a photograph of a bearded Camarón. On that day in June a set of two stamps were issued, the other being a tribute to Lola Flores who Camarón had starred alongside in the film *Casa Flores*. Camarón was truly on his way to becoming an official Spanish product, as he appeared in the company of the King of Spain on a postage stamp, clapping his hands in the traditional flamenco manner. There were also the first indications that his legacy would be maintained by his eldest son Luis who was emerging as a competent flamenco guitar player and in 1998 was featured on the record *Melismas*.

Five years would pass before the release of the next Camarón CD, *Paris 1987*, which celebrated Camarón's triumph in the French capital by drawing on the original tapes, mastered and remixed by Ricardo Pachón. This album, which was released in 1999, was sold at the very competitive price of thirteen euros and not surprisingly entered the charts. It also contained the novelty of CD ROM images of Camarón walking in Paris as he sang his anthem *Como de Agua*. Such was Camarón's growing fame that other artists began paying their own tribute to Camarón by covering some of his most popular material. One such artist was María José Santiago Álvarez, who released *Flamenco Son: A Tribute to Camarón de la Isla* in 1999, which featured many of his commercial *tangos* and *rumbas*.

Towards the end of November 2000, with Camarón's iconic status steadily growing, the producer and renowned guitar collector Ricardo Pachón released an image that would reinforce the public's perception of the gypsy singer's profile as something well beyond mere cult status. Pachón commissioned an adaptation of Alberto Korda's world famous photograph of Che Guevara, taken in 1960 as the Cuban revolution entered its second year. The graphic artist Rafael Iglesias took his inspiration from the iconic poster of Che to produce a new image that would be very successful in selling even more Camarón merchandise.

While many Spanish people had already virtually canonised Camarón as gypsies had started the custom of kissing the ground of his birthplace, this new 'saint' was also to be portrayed as a revolutionary as Inglesias' artwork introduced a curious political dimension. The market had been hungry for another Camarón album and Pachón and the Universal company were happy to feed this demand by releasing *Antología Inédita*; a collection of unissued material recorded in the villages of Mairena del Alcor, Montilla and Umbrete, where Camarón had laid down a session with the group Dolores. While the material was of interest to *Camaroneros*, it was the sleeve design that received the most attention since it bore all the hallmarks of the political posters of the Russian Revolution. It presented Camarón as a universal hero for the masses by adopting the techniques, used by newspapers, of the photomechanical transfer; the cheap half-tone image that had transformed Korda's famous portrait of Che Guevara.[3] As the artist Gavin Turk, who created the *Death of Che* pointed out when posing as Che; 'You only need key elements of the photo – the beret, the long hair, the position of the eyes (as with classical icons, looking up and to the right), a bit of beard – to make it function as a symbol'.[4] This new portrait of Camarón contained several of these key elements of Korda's original including, most importantly, the beard and long hair, but unlike Che, Camarón's eyes gazed downwards. Crucially, Camarón's now subversive image was printed on a red background signifying links with revolutionary movements such as communism. While the portrait of Che Guevara depicted him as a defiant and uncompromising revolutionary, Camarón's downward gaze indicates that he was now also a religious figure akin to Jesús Christ. The print also had another small detail in common with Korda's original. Much of the success of the Che Guevara image was derived from the impact of his beret and in particular the star on the beret. Reproducing Camarón's well-known tattoo, featuring the Crescent Moon and Star of David, on the sleeve's bottom left-hand corner would now mirror this. Camarón's notoriety as a junkie, whose concerts attracted trouble, was now a distant memory, as this adaptation of the classic bedroom poster image would reinforce the impression that the now sanitised Camarón had died as a flamenco martyr. The cover design would soon be reproduced on everything from key rings to cushions, as backroom industries sought to exploit Camarón's image.

On Sunday 26 November 2000, the Spanish newspaper *El País* announced in a full-page article the release of the album *Antología Inédita*, which would feature previously unissued recordings of Camarón from 1967 to 1990. It would soon be followed by a compilation entitled *Una leyenda flamenca* with Alberto García Alix's most commonly found iconic image on its cover and another collection, *Antologia*, which also used the Madrid photographer's work. Yet the ultimate prize for any would-be *Camaronero*, a box-set entitled *Camarón Integral* containing twenty CDs and an informative book, would also soon be available. These latest releases were a distraction from the real story that was to be found at the foot of the page. The *El País* headline had simply said *La cuarta llave*, which was a reference to flamenco's highest and most prestigious award, the Golden Key of the *cante*. Pressure was building to honour Camarón by making him only the fourth singer in history to receive this award but many had questioned why he had not been recognised while he was alive. Why had it taken eight years since his death for him now to be considered for the honour? The answer would lie in the award's history and what is expected of the person who holds it. Of more significance would be identifying who are the dignitaries that ultimately decide which singer gets his or her hands on the so-called mythical golden key?

Prior to Camarón only three artists had been awarded the *Llave de Oro* and they had been charged with the responsibility of maintaining the purity of flamenco song by practical example. A posthumous award would clearly be at odds with this principal and not serve the fundamental purpose. When the third holder of the Golden Key, Antonio Mairena, died in 1983, his natural successor was Camarón although some aficionados had argued in favour of Fosforito or even José Menese. The award was by this time in the gift of Andalucía's regional parliament who appeared reluctant to bestow it on Camarón because, although he was considered the greatest of all eras, he was viewed as a drug addict and no longer a purist, which ruled him out as a suitable candidate.

The Golden Key of the *cante* had started life in the backroom of a nineteenth-century establishment for public flamenco performances, known as a *café cantante*. It was in these humble circumstances that a group of knowledgeable and enthusiastic aficionados had the idea of giving the first distinction to the singer Tomás el Nitri in 1862. Tomás el Nitri was a gypsy from Cádiz province who lived and breathed flamenco but he was not the most outstanding singer of his generation. By being portrayed with the key in his right hand, Tomás el Nitri was able to initiate a unique chapter of flamenco folklore that would have lasting consequences. Drawings captured him with his extraordinary bushy sideburns, seated in an armchair with a gold pocket watch and cigar to indicate his exulted position. He had received the award because flamenco was an important part of his daily life, and not an art form that sought to entertain an audience. The decision to award the next Golden Key in 1926 was even more arbitrary, as it is believed to have been bestowed on Manuel Vallejo to make up for his failure to win the *II Copa Pavón* flamenco singing competition. The manager of the Teatro Pavón in Madrid had decided to appease the arrogant Vallejo with the award by making sure he received the second Golden Key. Vallejo, who looked more like a factory boss than a flamenco singer, was delighted to be chosen above his rivals that included Antonio Chacón, Manuel Torre, Tomás Pavon and Aurelio Sellés. More importantly, he had got one over the young rising star Pepe Marchena and the Golden Key would give him much kudos with the public and enable him to increase his fees.

By the early 1960s, with university academics dominating flamenco art, it was decided that just awarding the Golden Key in smoky backrooms was not appropriate for the modern age and that it should be decided by a singing competition. Artists were invited to perform in front of judges at the third *Concurso de Córdoba*. This city was very much the academic centre of flamenco in the sixties and it was hardly surprising that the judges chose a like-minded artist when gypsy singer, Antonio Mairena, became the third holder of the Golden Key. Once again, this was not completely satisfactory as it could be argued that Mairena was a good friend of the organiser, the poet from Córdoba, Ricardo Molina. Although Mairena was a gypsy he was also part of a movement that took itself far too seriously; he would claim to know precisely how any particular flamenco song was performed in the late eighteenth and nineteenth centuries, a viewpoint and approach shared by the judges at this high profile competition. The panel had chosen to ignore the talents of Manolo Caracol and Pepe Marchena when they were faced with a decision of electing either Mairena or Fosforito. Their verdict led to Mairena subsequently exploiting every opportunity to be photographed with the outsized Golden Key that was now embellished with a coat of arms and decorated with a woven tassel. From the sixties onwards the Mairena brand would be synonymous with that Golden Key clutched in his left hand, his right hand outstretched to indicate his flamenco passion, and his trademark gold teeth. Mairena could now legitimately hold up any claims he made about the history of flamenco as fact and the key's power became part of Spanish folklore. On Mairena's death, Fosforito's name was considered the only possibility for the concession of a fourth key, but he had many years to wait before the issue of a fifth key.

Seventeen years after Antonio Mairena's death, rumours had started that those with the power to award a Golden Key within the Andalusian government were at last ready to honour Camarón in death, with what they were never prepared to concede when he was alive. The concept of a controversial posthumous award immediately prompted a negative reaction from many quarters that attempted to put pressure on Manuel Chaves, the president of the Andalusian Parliament and the Spanish Socialist Party. Middle-class members of flamenco clubs from Seville to Jaén wanted Chaves and Francisco Vallecillo, who held the remit for issuing the 'Golden Key', to ignore the constant demand for Camarón to be honoured. However, Chaves was a politician who understood the affection that many of his electorate had for Camarón and now the dead singer was a national treasure who just happened to be born in Andalucía. Chaves would later admit to not being a great fan of flamenco, but he recognised that he had to respect it. Despite only 'liking it a little bit' it was the music created in his government's region, the former Arabic Spain known colloquially as *La Nación*.[5]

Some of the strongest words of objection were to be written by Miguel Acal whose siren voice found similar echoes in the *Candil* flamenco journal based in Jaén.[6] For Acal, it was controversial just to float the possibility of giving Camarón the fourth key and to be in favour of it was very misguided. Acal sensed that Camarón's supporters wanted the award as a way of further enhancing his memory, but that was not its purpose. Those members who would take the decision had the power to create a considerable business and Acal was clearly concerned by the burgeoning Camarón industry and commodification of the singer. It was a decision that could either enhance or diminish the dignity of the world of flamenco and he openly warned of the dangers of granting the key to Camarón. Adding his name to that small group of people at the very pinnacle of flamenco, would be seized upon by those involved with the Camarón industry and used to promote more products. Acal had stressed that his objection was in no way a comment on the quality of Camarón's singing or his historical importance, it was based on the Golden Key being awarded posthumously, an act that would have been previously been unthinkable.

Acal had chosen to support his argument by reprinting some columns from the weekly *Sevilla Información*, which had stated that if the Golden Key is a symbol then it naturally follows that it cannot be given to someone who is unable to undertake the functions that this symbol requires. While the article grudgingly accepted that Camarón was a genius, that artistry ceased on his death rendering any posthumous award a perverse decision. The writer accepted that Camarón's name had always attracted much interest and emotion, but with that came the opportunity of financial gain.

Camarón's exploitation in life and death was also raised, but his death had ruled him out of holding the Golden Key because 'if the key became in the hands of Mairena, a symbol of controlling and safeguarding the quality of the *cante*, like the guarantee of origin on a bottle of fine wine, then the key cannot be held by anyone who is completely unable to defend these concepts'. The article went on to warn that the concession could have very dangerous consequences because it would honour the Camarón of mass appeal. The award had the potential to legitimise the popular flamenco movement, and the artists in this group who followed the singer. It would make the 'new flamenco' official and play into the hands of the multinationals that were only interested in the commercial flamenco that was easy to sell and only served to degrade the art. The artists that belonged to this popular flamenco movement were named in the weekly *Sevilla Información* as La Niña Pastori, Ketama, Omaita Ca, El Barrio, and José el Francés. This debate over the evolution of the art would resurface yet again in September 2006 on the eve of Seville's fourteenth Flamenco Biennal when its director Domingo González accepted that a 'revolution' was now occurring in flamenco dance. But it was the continuing development of the song and the blending of it with other musical forms that was to provoke comments from José María Segovia, who represented Seville's flamenco clubs. He complained that things had reached such a point that you could not be certain if you were listening to a *soleá* because many of the current artists were diluting the purity of flamenco song with their fusion projects.

Writing after the concession had been awarded, Acal was forced to admit that the words and pleas printed in *Sevilla Información* had fallen on deaf ears with the Consejería de Cultura deciding to award a fourth key. Acal was also keen to point out that some aficionados had suggested that Pepe Marchena should have been given the fourth key, but this suggestion was rejected outright on the grounds that flamenco needed a new *divo*. Ironically, the bid to elect Marchena had been turned down because he had died in 1976 and his fans had wisely given up on the idea. They understood that whoever the next holder would be he must, by definition, be a living person. For Acal, Mairena's tenure had given the Golden Key the importance it deserves because he wanted, could, and knew how to give it a dimension that nobody before was able to attain.

On November 18 2000 Alejandro Luque, *El País*'s Cádiz correspondent, announced that Camarón would finally be awarded *la Llave de Oro* on the very day that, had he survived, he would have been celebrating his fiftieth birthday. After all the bureauratic wrangling that had seen a head of steam build up behind the giving of flamenco's most prestigious decoration to Camarón, the authorities had finally caved in. On 5 December Camarón at last joined the ranks of Tomás el Nitri, Manuel Vallejo and Antonio Mairena as only the fourth singer to receive this award since its inception in 1862. Camarón's body of work had at last been officially recognised but, as his detractors were keen to point out, how could a dead gypsy inspire by example and guard the purity of the *cante*? The hotly contested dispute was finally settled when Carmen Calvo, a councillor from the Junta de Andalucía, announced to the press on 17 November at the launch of an exhibition celebrating Camarón's fiftieth birthday, that the Golden Key would finally go to San Fernando's chosen son. The industry that had grown up around Camarón now had the legitimacy it needed and soon it would be possible to buy even beach towels bearing the singer's image.

The proceeding months had seen considerable campaigning on behalf of the singer. Camarón's final elevation to the gang of three had received support from a group of twenty flamencos drawn from the great and the good that had gathered at the Venta de Vargas. In a highly visible publicity stunt, artists including José Merce, Manuela Carrasco, Sara Baras, Moraíto and Diego Carrasco had launched a manifesto calling for Camarón to get the award. The *El País* newspaper had also printed many letters from readers expressing the pros and cons of the concession. Juan Gallego Blanca, an aficionado from Huelva, had been dismayed by all the letters against Camarón receiving the *Llave de Oro* and had written in support. While accepting that Antonio Mairena was an exceptional artist, Blanca felt that Camarón had also scaled those heights and had sucessfully blended tradition with modernity and maintained the purity of the *cante*. Just the sheer volume of work he had recorded justified his position as an all-time great and Blanca rejected the notion that Camarón had bequeathed a negative heritage by claiming that he had opened his ears to flamenco art. Within five years people would wonder what all the fuss had been about when another golden key would finally be awarded to the singer Fosforito.

The anniversary of Camarón's fiftieth birthday in 2000 would be marked by more than the issue of a new album and the award of the Golden Key; plans were announced for an exhibition entitled *Encuentros Camarón*. Inside Cádiz's Palacio de la Diputación Provincial there would be lectures and debates on his life. Of more interest would be the personal objects that his widow,

La Chispa, allowed the writer Enrique Montiel to gather from her home. The star attraction was Camarón's Mercedes car that acted as a mobile home when he travelled to the festivals. Many unseen photographs would be on show, his complete discography and all the books that had been written about him since his death. Among the invited authors were Bernard Leblon, a specialist on gypsies in Cádiz and Mercedes García Plata, who had written a doctoral thesis on Camarón at Paris University. His producer Ricardo Pachón and biographer Enrique Montiel would also debate the theme of Camarón's fiftieth anniversary. On the eve of Camarón's birthday there was also a star-studded concert involving the Orquesta Manuel de Falla, a jazz band and the luminaries of the flamenco world including Montse Cortés, Farruquito and the guitarist Juan Manuel Cañizares. The following day was reserved for lively celebration with the staging of a *fiesta flamenca* involving all of Cádiz's artists led by Chano Lobato, Juan Villar, Niña Pastori and Sara Baras. Other gypsy singers including El Calli from Córdoba would also record new tributes to Camarón including a *tanguillo* to commemorate the fifteenth anniversary of his death. The City of Córdoba, far from Camarón's home in San Fernando, had also organised with the assistance of El Calli, a homage to the singer they described as unforgettable and irreplaceable

Camarón's fiftieth birthday had been marked and celebrated with even the politicians securing a satisfactory outcome. Manuel Chaves had fought hard to secure the Golden Key for Camarón's supporters, arguing that his legacy was undeniable and that he had created a special window on flamenco that thousands of people from the world of flamenco had looked through. He had inspired a whole generation of artists and the posthumous award was as much for his exceptional character as celebration of gypsy culture. Expressing these sentiments would lead to the Andalusian president being honoured himself when he visited the flamenco club in San Fernando devoted to the memory of Camarón. On 18 March 2001 Chaves received from the mayor of San Fernando the insignia of a *Camarón de Oro*. If the Golden Key had been flamenco's highest honour, then what value could you put on a solid gold bust of Camarón?

The tenth anniversary of his death, on 2 July 2002, presented another ideal marketing opportunity and the perfect peg with which to market more Camarón products. Camarón's producer, Ricardo Pachón, had been busy recording a tribute album which would also come with a DVD entitled *Por Camarón*, with participation from Diego Carrasco, Niña Pastori, Remedios Amaya, José el Frances, Chonchi Heredia and

Kepa Junkera. All of his best-known songs were covered, including *Rosa María* sung by Rosario and *Como el Agua* interpreted by the duo *Estopa*. Camarón's children Gema, Rocío and Luis Monje were also featured on a track named after and dedicated to their father by the group *Pata Negra* in 1987. Pachón had even engaged the Philharmonic Orchestra of Prague to record the *Nana del Caballo Grande*, which prompted a journalist to ask the producer if this choice of orchestra dishonoured the name of Camarón. The inference being that even making a new version of the *Nana* with a singer other than Camarón was bad enough, but replacing London's Royal Philharmonic Orchestra with a Czech outfit looked like penny pinching and a definite insult to Camarón. The album was to upset many of Camarón's fans who expressed their anger on the web forums. Despite this, *por Camarón* was a triumph of the recording studio that the producer Ricardo Pachón would later be congratulated for. This recording would be one of only three places where my search for Camarón would find any resonance. Ten years after Camarón's death *Estopa's* take on *Como el Agua* gave the song an almost eternal quality while Rosario breathed new life into *Rosa María*. Diego Carrasco had also created a fitting tribute, while Raimundo Amador turned to Camarón's first hit, *Detrás del tuyo se va*, for inspiration; it was an inspired decision to include the Municipal Band of Seville on *La Tarara*. Susi had also shown great courage in recording, with dignity, Camarón's haunting flamenco lullaby, the *Nana del Caballo Grande*.

With Camarón's widow and his producer Ricardo Pachón present at the launch, which was organised by the Universal record company in association with San Fernando Town Council, echoes of the row over the singer's royalties were to resurface. A journalist from the Spanish *Rolling Stone* magazine, Hector Márquez, had wanted to know why, as did many of Camarón's fans, Tomatito and Paco de Lucía did not appear on this tribute album. La Chispa had diplomatically side-stepped the question by saying that some artists were not able to appear and others simply did not want to. Márquez later caught up with the producer Pachón and asked him why Camarón's guitarists were absent, to which he replied that as musicians contracted to Universal, they had been made an offer by the company but did not respond. Tomatito had apparently gone as far as agreeing to record on 6 May, but then telephoned the day before to say that he had not finished writing his contribution. Pachón even confessed that Julio Iglesias had been at the top of his wish-list, as he had been very keen to sing *Volando Voy*, but he later became uncontactable. Pachón was asked why, as the producer, he did not join the other artists at the press launch. He claimed that he had not been invited and had come for the presentation of Mercedes García Plata's doctoral thesis on the work of Camarón!

La Chispa's comments to the Spanish rock magazine were to be even more revealing as they indicated that, even after a decade, the relationship between Camarón's family and that of Paco de Lucía remained minimal. Márquez wanted to know about La Chispa's financial situation as a widow surviving on the small income derived from the composer royalties and author's rights from her late husband's albums. Her response indicated that she was clearly unhappy with the situation of people profiting from the traditional songs that Camarón has sung. *Rolling Stone* magazine also flagged up, as have so many others, that Paco de Lucía had often expressed an interest in assigning the rights to the Monje family.

It remains difficult to assess whether the prolonged saga over the ownership of Camarón's royalties was a major issue, particularly after examining the sales of his albums a week after his death. For an artist of such stature the figures were exceptionally low and illustrate just how small sales of flamenco albums are in general. The combined sales of his first two albums were a mere 3,870 copies, while *La Leyenda del Tiempo*, the record that had revolutionised flamenco and rewritten the rule book, had only sold 5,470 units.[7] *Como el Agua*, Camarón's first commercial record had sold 7,541 with only albums like *Viviré* and *Flamenco Vivo* demonstrating more robust sales of over 30,000 copies. His most successful album *Soy Gitano* had sold over 80,000 copies while his last studio record, *Potro de Rabia y Miel*, had reached 50,000 and thousands more copies were bought in the months after his death.

Based on this evidence, these sales would not have yielded Camarón or his family much capital, so the argument really centres on the rights to his recordings. His guitarist Paco de Lucía has claimed that he had only received $10,000 in royalties for the entire twenty years of his professional career with Camarón.[8] Paco had also argued that it cost him $200,000 in lost revenue and concert cancellation fees because he spent so much time working on Camarón's last record. Paco's response to this issue in various interviews had demonstrated that he was deeply upset by allegations that he profited from Camarón's albums and there have been numerous occasions when he has sought to rectify the situation. The writer Paco Espínola had even spoken of Paco calling La Chispa, while he was on tour in the United States, with an offer of financial help when Camarón was still alive, only to be told that the family did not need any help. This offer has also been confirmed by Tomatito while Paco, with deep concern for Camarón on his return to Spain, was advised not to bother him.

Camarón's financial situation at the time of his death is also unclear, as there have been many contradictory statements. While his lyricist Carlos Lencero, painted a portrait of a gypsy who did not want to deal with paperwork the journalist Paco Espínola spoke of a far more financially savvy artist with a portfolio of properties. Writing shortly after his death in 1992, Espínola stated that Camarón had a flat on the Cádiz coast at Valdegrana, close to the highly gentrified and wealthy area of El Puerto de Santa María, two flats in San Fernando and a chalet in La Línea.[9] Espínola also mentioned that Camarón had opened four bank accounts each with a sum of $150,000. Shortly after the benefit concert headed by Rocío Jurado, a bullfight was arranged in Camarón's hometown of San Fernando, with the *toreros*, including Curro Romero, donating their services. A television company stumped up $80,000 for the broadcasting rights while $300,000 was taken on the gate. The bid to raise funds for Camarón's widow and family was further enhanced the next day with a flamenco festival in Madrid raising $70,000. Despite these considerable sums there remained those who were very concerned that Camarón had not been justly financially rewarded for his artistic efforts. Juan Toro Barea, from the flamenco journal *Sevilla Flamenca*, felt the only solution was a foundation to protect Camarón's financial interests and his reputation. For Toro Barea Camarón:

> was an artist who generated millions of pesetas, but whose family has been left with very little. But, in any case, we think that if he generated a lot of money while he was alive, now that he is dead he is likely to generate even more and speculators are liable to appear from all sides.

Camarón did indeed generate millions of pesetas, but he also liked spending and giving his family the best; even he could not foresee a situation where his image would sell thousands of unlicensed products.

With only a day to go before the tenth anniversary of his death, away from the ongoing saga over her husband's royalties La Chispa was understandably in an emotional state and had become very tearful when thanking her children in front of the press. Such was the power of her feelings that she had to be consoled by Niña Pastori and the mayor of

San Fernando. She revealed after the presentation that Ricardo Pachón had wanted her to sing on the album *por Camarón*, to which she had replied that she did not sing when Camarón was alive and was not about to start now.[10] Neither did she have any intention of remarrying but wished always to remain Camarón's wife, although she did accept that as an artist he belonged to the world. She later confessed, while talking to the press, that she always felt on her own without him and while she would like him to rest in peace it was not possible because he had become a myth loved by the people. She did not want praise, but preferred to dwell on those who say that behind a great man is always a great woman. Speaking alongside his mother, Camarón's son, the guitarist Luis Monje, announced that he would be recording his first album in September and the family tradition would continue with the involvement of his late father's close friend, Rancapino. It had been a very difficult day for Camarón's widow but she found some comfort in recalling the seventies, when the singer dressed like a rock star, and how over three decades his output had never dated and remained the blueprint for young singers. Ten years after her husband's death La Chispa was no longer spending the whole day looking at Camarón's mausoleum in that San Fernando cemetery, but the bond with her husband was as strong as ever.

Also speaking at the launch of the new album in the Palacio Consistorial was Niña Pastori who compared Camarón to Michael Jackson and said he was the greatest ever flamenco artist. Camarón had played an important role in her career when he introduced her on stage in the Teatro Andalucía de Cádiz when she was only eleven. In 1995 a photograph of this historic event was featured on her *Entre dos Puertos* album. After the speeches it was time for more celebrations as the Venta de Vargas would once again play host for a musical homage while a mass was celebrated in San Fernando's main church; then it was time for a fiesta from leading flamenco artists as Tomátito, Diego Carrasco and the Farruco family performed through the night. The artist Luis Saldana had an exhibition in the History museum of his oil paintings that had been inspired by Camarón, while another photographic exhibition was mounted entitled *Amigos de Camarón*, featuring José Luis Chillada's memories of his funeral. Once all the celebrations were over it was time, on the following Monday, for a more sober assessment of Camarón's achievements when the *Foro Libre*, a cultural organisation, met in a restaurant to consider the literary triumphs of the singer dubbed the 'Picasso of the Cante'. The president of the Diputación Provincial also launched the thesis on Camarón that had been written by Mercedes García Plata. There seemed no end to the events as on Tuesday a magnificent floral tribute was placed at his Pantheon while in the evening Antoni Ribas gave a lecture on the singer, illustrated by his documentary. The commemorations finally ended on Tuesday afternoon with a broadcast on Canal Sur Radio of a round table discussion in the Casa Consistorial, involving the presenter Manuel Curao and the singers Rancapino and Chato de la Isla.

2002 also witnessed Camarón receiving national publicity, as the drive to viewing him as a saint who had healing powers when he was alive, gathered momentum. The announcement of an *Encuentro Nacional*, with a weekend dedicated to Camarón, prompted the colour supplements to send their reporters to San Fernando to cover the growing sense of beautification that was happening spontaneously. Writing in *El Mundo*, Ana Bueno chose to draw on religious images when mentioning the locations that would soon be officially recognised as part of the Camarón trail.[11] Her article spoke of the Christ of the Medinacelli, which is displayed in San Fernando's main church, where people came to kiss his feet while outside gypsies travelled from all over Spain to kiss the soil where Camarón once walked. The singer had lived just two blocks away from this church that greatly influenced his life, while the collection of treasures held in the flamenco club constructed in the singer's honour were just as precious as the figure of Christ. Their glass cabinets held some of the detritus of Camarón's forty-one years, including his shoes, cigarette lighters and most interestingly his penknife. Was this the knife he threatened the municipal policeman with, or just the implement he needed, as his brother said 'for his things'? Even the shirt given to him by the Royal Philharmonic Orchestra was on display in the Venta de Vargas, where it would soon be auctioned to raise money for the building of a church in the San José district. More importantly the *El Mundo* article revealed that the public were no longer interested in whether Camarón had smoked pot or taken cocaine and heroin. For *Camaroneros* old and new, the singer's life was predetermined and he would have died on that fateful 2 July, however he had lived his life. Camarón's image was now moving away from that of a revolutionary to be based on a softer religious figure bordering on a martyr. In his well-known *Las Comparaciónes* column also published by *El Mundo*, Carlos Boyero would now compare Camarón to Billie Holiday as an all-time great.[12] Although Boyero confessed to not being amongst the militant aficionados of post-modernism and modernism who have discovered the grandeur of flamenco, he could feel Camarón's *quejío* or cry. He also greatly admired his ability to express very intimate thoughts that touch the heart to make it beat faster. This was a quality that only great artists possess.

With several of the earlier books on Camarón now out of print, two new titles were to appear in 2002, including the publication of another controversial volume charting the singer's life that claimed it would uncover 'the myths surrounding the man'. Penned by José Candado Calleja, Camarón's former minder during his last ten years, and the writer Luis Fernández Zaurín, *Camarón, Biografía de Un Mito* received considerable publicity for a tome about a flamenco artist and would later inspire the director Jaime Chavarri to make his biopic film. Candado had been at Camarón's side as he died and the press release promised that this would not be a sanitised account of his life and would not avoid the important question of Camarón's record royalties. Its intention was, through anecdotes and testimonies, to tell the full story of Camarón's rise to glory, charting his fame, illness and finally death. The book would also reveal much about Camarón's relationship with La Chispa and Candado had even secured the right to publish a photograph of Camarón's death certificate!

The journalist Teo Sánchez and the editor Antonio Pastor Bustamente had also been busy compiling an anthology of Camarón's lyrics that were now described as poetry. *Camarón, Anthología* featured almost 100 of the singer's songs, lovingly transcribed and labelled with their flamenco styles. The volume also included some of the traditional lyrics that Camarón had drawn on: the work of Federico García Lorca, Omar Khayyam and his own lyricist Kiko Veneno. 2002 also saw the release of the DVD *París Camarón* which included footage, from Miguel Vallecillo, of his performances in the French city in 1987 and 1988; a previously unissued interview; and photographic images from the Paris adventure. The head to head did not give much insight into the life of Camarón because the questions were not searching enough, but it was amusing to see how many times the singer could say his favourite phrase, 'you understand'. Sitting on a roof against a background of chimneystacks and clothes drying on a washing line, he spoke of his admiration for Manolo Caracol, his childhood spent singing in the Venta de Vargas and his journey to Madrid.

Camarón's memory had also been marked over the past few years by a flamenco competition named after him and at the end of July 2003 it was announced that a fourth competition would run on Saturdays from 20 September to the 29 November. Organised by the *peña camarón* in San Fernando and the Town Hall, its aim was not just to honour Camarón, but also to discover new talent. The president of the flamenco club, Antonio León, was proud to announce that, over the four years since its inception, the competition had grown to become one of the most prestigious in Spain, offering handsome prizes.

In 2003 his memory was to be further enhanced by another major work on his life and the creation of a tourist trail in San Fernando which included a guided visit to his first home and his mausoleum. The writers José Manuel Gamboa and Faustino Núñez had published a very weighty tome which as well as covering his life also analysed his songs in great detail, with the reader even being informed which key they were in. Late in 2003, the Spanish newspaper *El País* reported that the town council of San Fernando was to launch an official route where tourists could encounter the most important places in the life of Camarón and even receive a certificate to prove it.[13] The singer was about to officially become part of Spain's and Andalucía's tourist industry, with the guide books omitting to mention the weekend he spent in jail for threatening a police officer with a knife. On 25 November 2003, Francisco Romero announced to the press, gathered for flamenco's world fair in Seville, that San Fernando's chosen son would be officially recognised with a trail that would start from the bronze statue of Camarón in the Plaza Juan Vargas. This was the very spot where Camarón's remarkable voice was first heard by María Vargas and the illustrious singers La Niña de los Peines and Manolo Caracol, when he was just eight years old. The tourists who gathered outside that famous roadside inn, the Venta de Vargas, would just have to imagine how imposing it once was when it also served as Camarón's second home. Would they be able to imagine this building crammed with travellers seeking refreshment and aficionados who had come from Seville just to hear the young Camarón? Their imagination would have to overcome the fact that the main traffic into Cádiz no longer passes this venue, since a bridge was built linking the city to the mainland, and the inn is not as visible as it once was. The Venta de Vargas, which lies beyond a set of roundabouts at the end of the Calle Real, is now partially hidden behind all the buildings that have sprung up around it including the *Municipales de Electricidad*. It is still a very elegant two-storey building with its windows protected by the traditional *rejas* or iron grills and I can recommend the *papas aliñá*', a delicious potato tapa topped with the inn's special dressing.

The Camarón route, for which there would be no charge, would start on 8 November on the second and fourth Sunday of each month at half past eleven o' clock in the morning. The visitors could expect to visit the forge of Camarón's father where they would hear about Camarón's life from his brother Manuel Monje, then on to the house where the singer was born and the Carmen district of San Fernando where he grew up. The tourists would then go on to visit the town's cemetery where they could pay their respects at his mausoleum. Finally they would gather in the flamenco club, where so many photographs and momentos of Camarón can be seen. It is in the *peña* dedicated to the singer that the Camarón pilgrims would receive a glass of wine and a tapa, with a certificate to prove that they had completed the walk. It is also in the flamenco club that his music is played continuously over the sound system, making it the perfect venue in which to smoke a *Ducados* cigarette while drinking an *anís del mono*.

By the summer of 2004 the Camarón route had become more formalised, sharing space on tourist flyers with publicity for San Fernando's historical links with the Spanish Armada. But now, possibly because Camarón's brother Jesús El Pijote lived in the house where Camarón was born, the tours were only on Thursdays at eleven o'clock in the summer months and limited to just twenty people. The tours would still be free and visitors, courtesy of the Pedro Romero *bodega*, would still receive a glass of wine and a *tapa* while they toured the flamenco club. Stone monoliths were erected indicating the start of the Camarón trail, featuring elegant bronze reliefs of the singer in full flow with his left hand outstretched in characteristic manner. Plaques with information in both Spanish and English were also made for all the buildings on the trail, as Camarón's history and life became government property. The *Diario de Cádiz* sent the journalist Cristina Castro to follow a group of tourists on the Camarón trail and she reported that the assembled group had come from various parts of Spain including Barcelona, Valencia and Seville.[14] Most were flamenco fans to whom Camarón meant a lot and enough for one man from Seville to have a tattoo of Camarón's face on his back. Not surprisingly more than the twenty people permitted wished to go on the tour and were later reluctant to leave the first port of call, in the Venta de Vargas, because of the photographs that hung on the wall. Their next stop was the forge which had been reopened by Camarón's brother Manuel, who greeted the visitors and told them how eight children used to sleep in the tiny bedrooms, while having his photograph taken. The tourists were free to inspect the tidy forge that had a wide variety of implements including the various hammers and pincers neatly hanging on its white walls. Manuel Monje had lived in the forge for fifty years and now shared the building with his eight children.

Also on the walls were letters of condolence regarding Camarón's death sent by the great and the good including the King of Spain, Juan Carlos, and the former Prime Minister Felipe González.[15] Not deterred by the heat, the tourists were later marched to the church of El Carmen to be told that this was where Camarón married La Chispa; before leaving they were shown the *Cristo Nazareno* so worshipped by gypsies and Camarón.

The pilgrims then needed to stroll down the Calle Real and take the long walk up to the municipal cemetery where Camarón's remains rest close to his parents and his brothers Nano and Curro. At the cemetery the tourists must have found it hard to picture the scenes of Camarón's burial in 1992, but they would have noticed the abundance of flowers around his mauso-leum of black marble. Every day, for the past fifteen years, large quantities of fresh flowers have been laid at his resting place paid for by the sister-in-law of Camarón's brother Manuel. Interestingly, his brother regarded the water-ing of these flowers as an act of respect for Camarón's sainthood and prayers were now offered to the singer in the same way as they were to the *Cristo Nazareno*.[16] The pantheon has an elegant seated Camarón, serenely looking out through a rounded archway surrounded by a multitude of much smaller resting places of white marble. It is here that you will find his widow every fortnight.

The final stop was the *peña flamenca de Camarón* where, no doubt, the tourists marvelled at its sheer size; with his name announced from its roof dominating the local area of the calle collegio Naval Sacramento. Inside, the number of photographs of Camarón that the members of the club have managed to collect is staggering, ranging from rare shots of the singer bull-fighting to his early performances. There are even more framed photographs that adorn the tiled staircase that leads to the upper floor, but not that many with his guitarist Paco de Lucía. Camarón's voice dominates this vast build-ing, as a continuous looped tape plays songs from all his albums and on the stage there are four flags representing Spain, Andalucía, the Gypsy race and finally the flamenco club of Camarón. A scaled-down replica of the statue that stands outside the Venta de Vargas is also proudly displayed on the left of the stage. The club has a very haunting atmosphere created by the combina-tion of the lighting, the *cante* and being in the presence of so many artefacts that were once owned by the singer, including his clothes. It remains the one place where I felt that I really did discover the real Camarón and a visit to this club can provoke an almost spiritual experience. As the operating day for the trail has now changed to Wednesdays it is wise to check with the San Fernando tourist office to avoid disappointment if you are planning a visit.

The ever-growing bands of Camarón album completists were not neglected in 2004, with the release of *Camarón de la Isla, La leyenda* in January and *Alma y Corazón Flamencos* in the following month. *La Leyenda* contained four compact discs that were made to look like seven-inch vinyl records for the collector's market and they came with a scaled-down version of the book *Camarón, Vida y Obra*. The first disc was devoted to Camarón's hits, while the others covered all his work from 1969 to 1992 and the listener could read anecdotes about the singer while understanding his career 'within the social context of the time', which included a 'revolution of the record industry in Spain'. The publicity for this collection, which contained rarely seen photos, concert tickets and posters would, according to the publicity, 'become an object of fetishism for fans and an initiation pack for neophytes who need drawing up to the legend to be made easy for them'! *Alma y Corazón Flamencos*, which was released on 8 March, marked fifteen years since the appearance of *Soy Gitano* in 1989 and was significant because Camarón's son, Luis Monje, had directed the mixing in Madrid and the remastering at London's Abbey Road studios. Luis' name did appear on the credits, as did Ricardo Pachón, Antonio Sánchez Pecino and Pepe de Lucía because they had been responsible for the original versions. The remixing and remastering really did improve the sound of some of Camarón's vintage material and there was even a previously unheard Tomatito guitar lick for the purists. More importantly, fans were now offered the chance to hear Camarón's *bulerías, Samara* as he and Paco de Lucía originally intended. Within a few months Luis Monje, fresh from his exploits as a record producer, would make his live debut with his new band, *Buena Rama*, in front of his family and friends. The twenty-five-year-old son of the growing legend had to face the pressure of making his debut in Algeciras to publicise his first record *De buena rama, Familia Camarón* when he accompanied his brother-in-law Nene and his cousin Rodo.

On two consecutive Sundays in July Camarón's record company, Universal, took full-page advertisements to advertise all of his albums as part of the Spanish 'Day of Music' initiative. They offered not just his songs on CD; ring tones of *Como el Agua, Soy Gitano* and *Volando Voy* were now available. For just a few euros you could even buy the Camarón taster CD called *Pa' saber de Camarón*, as there seemed no end to the commodification of the gypsy singer. However, the true *Camaroneros*, including the singer

Diego Carrasco who had worked with Camarón, remained loyal to his memory. Carrasco's new album *Mi AND Flamenco* featured a track simply entitled *José Monge Cruz* that incorporated a reworked *Dicen a mí* to reflect Camarón's passing. Carrasco's words stated that Camarón was here with us, a gypsy and the fountain and tree from which the inspiration for flamenco came. In October 2004 another book on the life of Camarón arrived in the bookshops with *Sobre Camarón, La Leyenda del Cantaor Solitario*, offering the thoughts of someone who had known Camarón well. Carlos Lencero had written many of Camarón's lyrics, including the famous lines about Camarón singing as a silver moon shines over the port of Cádiz, and now wanted to contribute his memories. Lencero, in a reaction to the abundance of biographies and re-edited albums, felt he could offer a different perspective with the recording of *La Leyenda del Tiempo* at the heart of his book. On Saturday 4 December 2004, the eve of what would have been Camarón's fifty-second birthday, another award of the *Camarón de Oro* was made to those legendary gypsy sisters of the *cante*, Fernanda and Bernarda de Utrera, who could now join the elite group that included the Andalusian president Manuel Chaves.

During February 2005 it was announced that yet another Camarón record was about to be added to the catalogue, but this would be far more exciting than the endless 'best of' collections and the anthologies. *Camarón, Venta de Vargas*, despite all the hype surrounding the rediscovered tapes, would offer the purist a chance to hear exactly how advanced Camarón's singing was in 1967 before he left for Madrid. Ricardo Pachón was once again adding to the ever-growing Camarón industry as he directed this recording with the biographer of Camarón's early life, Enrique Montiel. More Camarón product was to be announced at the end of June with a reissue of the ultimate collection for any *Camaronero*, the limited edition box set entitled *Camarón Integral*. It contained twenty of Camarón's albums, including: all his studio recordings, his Paris concert and the new CD recorded in the Venta de Vargas. These CDs were now in a new digipack remastered format that had also appeared separately during 2005, with the added attraction of including the guitar chords. The box set also came with a booklet of photographs and articles by eminent flamencolgists.

Soon the *Camaroneros* would be able to buy, on bus station stalls, the paperback version of Candado's book, while the *Voz de Cádiz* newspaper would print Camarón's image on a full page to announce their special DVD offer of the series *Rito y Geografía del Cante*. The programme, devoted to his television appearances, would launch the series, while the quantity of books on the market about Camarón finally prompted a musician who had appeared as a musician on the album *La Leyenda del Tiempo* to speak out. The composer and songwriter Kiko Veneno told the *El País* Sunday supplement that he felt many of these works were written by people speaking without authority and he compared them to vultures who take the flesh while it is still warm.[17] Kiko had formed a team of determined specialists, named after his famous song *Volando Voy*, who were preparing *Camarón: los días y las horas*, a work of several volumes. Their account would tell the real story, unlike some of the other books which he considered simplistic and containing many errors, including inaccurate transcriptions of Camarón's lyrics in the booklets that accompany his CDs.

10

The Flamenco Christ,
2005–2006

El orgullo de los gitanos, ya se ha ido el mejor, era un gitanillo rubio en San Fernando nació. Camarón tu nombre llevamos - gitano, todo lo gitano en el corazón.
El Calli

Further evidence of the growing cult status of Camarón was to come with the announcement that the production company, Filmnova Invest, had signed a contract in 2005 with Monoria Films to make *Camarón, la Película*. Although having a budget of four million euros, the makers were keen to emphasise that the Junta de Andalucía had not contributed any finance, but there was support from Televisión Española and Telemadrid. Despite the lack of financial backing from Andalucía's regional government the highly visible president of the Junta de Andalucía, Manuel Chaves, would attend the film's premiere.

With memories of Camarón's death barely thirteen years old, a Spanish film director would accept the challenge to make this controversial biopic about the life of the singer. The ambitious feature film was to be directed by the Madrid-born Jaime Chavarri, who would also write the script with Álvaro del Amo. Buena Vista International had agreed to distribute the film in November 2005 to cinemas throughout Spain while Minoria Films, who produced the feature, announced that filming would start at the end of February. The intention was to be the first to bring to the screen 'the untold biography of the genius of flamenco music known as José Monje Cruz

"Camarón de la Isla"'.[1] The makers wanted it to be a film with Camarón at its heart, which would celebrate his flamenco revolution that had influenced a new generation of flamenco musicians. Minoria's press release even claimed that Camarón had broken down social and artistic barriers in Spain.

The film would tell his tragic story in three acts: from his discovery as an artist, through the recognition of his fame to his final farewell. Its audience would be introduced to his artistic involvement with his three of his guitarists: Paco Cepero, Paco de Lucía and finally Tomatito. His rise to international stardom would be charted along with the albums that had prompted a flamenco revolution and left such a rich legacy. And the film could not ignore the importance of his marriage to Dolores Montoya, La Chispa, which had been conducted according to gypsy tradition. Although the film was not a documentary it would reflect Camarón's early life, the influence of his mother, and his move from San Fernando to Madrid. There would also be references to his innovations, including the use of novel studio techniques that produced a fresh sound and had taken flamenco to a wider audience. These themes were expected, but tucked away in the last lines of the synopsis lay a more controversial storyline. The film would also tackle his dark side, including his love affairs, his flirting with drugs and 'his physical deterioration at an early age'. It was partly that deterioration that had contributed to Camarón's iconic status, but tackling this very sensitive subject in a feature film would be a great challenge for any director. Just how would the film's makers reflect his drug habit and decline?

Another statement, released in September for the film's premiere on a giant screen in the *Velodrome* at the fifty-third San Sebastián Film Festival, was even more revealing. It stated that, although not a documentary, the film would be 'based on real events and Camarón's family set three conditions when it came to shooting it: Camarón shouldn't appear in a wheelchair at the end of his life, he couldn't be shown taking drugs and at the end he shouldn't appear to be too emaciated'.[2] This sensitive request added to the hype and controversy surrounding the film and did not sit well with aspects of the synopsis issued by Minoria Films. Its purpose was to create more interest and make an eager audience at San Sebastián; curious as to how Camarón and his drug habit would be portrayed.

Jaime Chavarri, who had a considerable track record as a director since 1974, with films including *Las Cosas del Querer*, began shooting on Monday 28 February 2005 with the aim of completing all the filming by mid-May. The movie would be shot in many of the locations where

Camarón had lived and performed including Madrid, Paris and New York. There would also be time spent filming in the town of his birthplace, San Fernando, the cove of Bolonia and Conil de la Frontera. The delicate issue would rest on who dared, and more importantly could, play the role of the mature Camarón? Minoria Films had announced that the film had the support of Camarón's family and the leading lights in flamenco who had worked with him, including Paco de Lucía and Tomatito. My interview with Enrique Montiel after the film's release would cast some doubt over La Chispa's feelings regarding the portrayal of her husband in the film and whether the feature did have her full support. It is also unlikely that Paco de Lucía approved of the performance and interpretation from the looka-like actor, Raul Rocamora, who was chosen to play Paco during his golden years with Camarón in Madrid. Paco may have been relieved that the film largely avoided the issue of Camarón's royalties and the darker side of his relationship with Camarón's family and the so-called 'flamenco feud'.

To understand the background to this controversial interpretation of the singer's life and why it falls short of portraying the real Camarón, it is important to be aware of one of the sources where the producer Miguel Menéndez de Zubillaga found the inspiration for the project. During the summer of 2002, as the media again revisited the life of Camarón for the tenth anniversary of his death, another book appeared on the market. *Camarón, Biografía de un Mito* was written by a journalist, but this time with a key co-writer, Camarón's nurse, bodyguard and manager, José Candado Calleja. Candado had spent considerable time with Camarón during his final years and in particular his last days. Having read the various biographies and this new account, which had received wide-spread publicity, Miguel Menéndez decided to propose making a film on the life of Camarón. He had visited Jaime Chavarri and given him two books about Camarón's life including the one by José Candado. Chavarri, not surprisingly, had felt that the making of this type of film would be very difficult because it posed many problems. Menéndez would later call Chavarri and want to know whether they would proceed or not, and he received a positive reply. But there was another obstacle, Chavarri had already signed up to another project and if he was to be the director they would have to wait. Chavarri was the only name in the frame due to his experience and simply because he was also an aficio-nado of flamenco, and Camarón in particular. Having signed up Chavarri there would be a further two obstacles to this demanding project:

Camarón's recording company, and more crucially his widow and family. As this was to be a biopic in which the actor who played Camarón would be required to lip-sync to his famous recordings, including the famous *nana* or flamenco lullaby, the rights would have to be cleared with Universal Music of Spain. Many months of negotiations would also be needed with Camarón's family until their approval was finally given, apparently subject to those three conditions regarding the singer's portrayal.

Having obtained a director with a solid track record the team signed Álvaro de Amo, whose job was to study the life of Camarón and write a script for a 'fiction film based on a real person'.[3] The hardest job would be to find an actor who could convincingly play Camarón and while watching television Chavarri discovered the thirty-year-old Catalan actor Oscar Jaenada. If this film was going to work Jaenada, who was born in Barcelona, would need to spend a lot of time in San Fernando and Cádiz familiarising himself with the culture of Southern Andalucía. He would have to take lessons in flamenco song and dance and immerse himself in the character of Camarón. He would spend eight months studying the mannerisms of Camarón; he also visited the singer's widow in La Línea as well as meeting Camarón's oldest friend Rancapino and his guitarists Tomatito and Paco de Lucía. More importantly, in view of the interpretation that the film presents, he met with Camarón's minder, José Candado. He was to discover that Camarón was a man of few words and consequently studying his gestures and mannerisms would be far more important for this role. From the moment he got the part, Oscar Jaenada had listened to Camarón's *cante* every day, having earlier admitted to never having seen Camarón perform live. Jaenada now studied footage of Camarón to learn how he smoked a cigarette and to understand his breathing problems during his last few years.[4] Each day new material about the life of Camarón had arrived at the eager student's house. It was from studying these videos and talking to people who had known Camarón that Jaenada was able to successfully imitate the physical appearance of the artist and, in particular, his mannerisms when singing. The hard work would pay off as it was universally accepted that his interpretation of Camarón was a triumph, with the popular gypsy singer José Mercé, telling the press that Jaenada had mastered and captured the spirit of Camarón.

The more established actress Veronica Sánchez was later chosen to play the equally demanding role of Camarón's widow, although having been born in Seville, she would not face the difficulty of mastering the Andalusian accent.

Sánchez had met with La Chispa twice before she started filming and later claimed that Camarón's widow, on seeing the film, 'has liked it, so since then I can breathe in peace because it's so difficult to interpret someone who's still alive'. Martín Bello who took the role of Manuel, Camarón's brother, would also be vital to the authenticity of the film as he was born in San Fernando. When speaking about how supportive the people of San Fernando had been, Chavarri later paid homage to the work that Bello did with Jaenada on perfecting his accent. During the filming, members of the public would approach Chavarri and tell him that the lines uttered by Jaenada were too *payo* or not typical of a gypsy and that Camarón would not have spoken like this. Chavarri accepted and respected their judgement and did have the script adjusted with Bello's assistance.

On 20 April Chavarri and his crew had arrived in San Fernando to visit the key locations, including the municipal cemetery, the Plaza del Carmen and the entrance to the Capuchinas Convent that would appear in the film as Camarón's old school, El Colegio Liceo Sagrado Corazón. While the filming had necessitated closing some roads, the curious people that had gathered were disappointed not to see any of the major stars. It later fell to the father of the boy who would play Camarón aged seven, the singer El Arrebato, to sign autographs for the crowd![5] Parts of San Fernando had been reconstructed to resemble the sixties: with contemporary cars and rubbish bins being removed, walls repainted and period cars placed in the streets. Writing in the *Diario de Cádiz*, Fátima Díaz had been keen to inform her readers that although shooting the school scene took only thirty seconds, the crew has been preparing for five hours having started at nine o'clock in the morning. It was to be a scene that reflected the class divide of Camarón's childhood as the children entered the school by two doors, one for the well-off or fee payers and the other for the poor and gypsies. Soon the crew would be filming in Madrid, Paris and New York, but first there was the important matter of filming Camarón's mother's funeral at the local cemetery and then some shots close to the busy high street.

Within days of this early filming the world's media were again talking about Camarón and the anticipated biopic, but some journalists preferred to return to an old chestnut that had first surfaced in 1992. *The Guardian's* Madrid correspondent, Ben Sills, stated that Camarón's guitarist, Paco de Lucía would not be involved in the film and he was very clear about the reason; 'When Camarón died his wife, La Chispa, claimed that Lucía had cheated him of hundreds of thousands of pesetas in royalties from records'.[6] This allegation, according to Sills, had turned the gypsies against Paco de Lucía who they had verbally abused at the funeral. Once again it was not Camarón's music that was filling the column inches, but talk of his 'appetite for drugs' and how the 'film may end a flamenco feud'. Sills interestingly quoted Carlos Lencero, one of Camarón's lyricists, as saying that the feud was just the result of a misunderstanding that had come from Camarón not keeping a note of the lyrics he composed. However, Sills stated that Paco de Lucía did subsequently give up his own rights and their joint rights to the authorship of songs on Camarón's album, but had tended to avoid events where Camarón's family might be present. While commenting on the Camarón film Sills wrote that Jaime Chavarri had been chosen to direct it because he was not involved in this dispute. Once again, Sills turned to the thoughts of Lencero, who, only months earlier, had released his own biography of Camarón. Lencero saw the film as a way of finally settling the matter because 'the film will be from the family's point of view'.

By the last week of February, Jaime Chavarri and his crew had moved north to Madrid's flamenco nightclub, the Torres Bermejas, to film the story of Camarón's early career. The press would now be told that the intention of the film's director was, for 'this fictional film based on a real person, to reflect that inexplicable emotion Camarón used to make people feel when he used to sing'. Chavarri had also been mindful that he was working on a very sensitive project with memories of the singer still young when he said that 'the legend mixes with reality and the story is still very recent'. Whilst being reluctant to discuss the exact song repertoire that would be included in the film, Chavarri made a bizarre statement claiming that; '*cante jondo* doesn't work in cinema, but there are other kinds of song of his that are in everyone's subconscious and that will drive the narrative forward'. The cinema had been a very suitable venue for gypsy song before, so what lay behind these comments? Was Chavarri preparing the audience for a film that avoided including Camarón at his best, singing *seguiriyas* and *bulerías*, but instead went for a more commercial soundtrack including *Volando Voy* and *Soy Gitano*? Meanwhile a statement was issued informing the media that no date for the premiere could yet be determined because of the complexity of including the music in the post-production process.

Eventually, after shooting for over eleven weeks, the filming was completed on 13 May and it was decided that there would be a special screening before its premiere in Camarón's home of San Fernando on 20 October, and then general release throughout Spain on 4 November. There was also to be a special screening in the presence of Andalusian dignitaries in San Fernando on 20 November. Before that, the film would be screened at the prestigious San Sebastián Film Festival on 18 September with a press preview including English subtitles the previous day. The stars, Oscar Jaenada and Veronica Sánchez would accompany their director to the premiere as the film faced its first test of qualified opinion. After the screening Camarón's guitarist, Tomatito, was scheduled to give a recital to raise funds for the refugee children of the Sahara.

Camarón's name had attracted controversy throughout his life and now in death it would again be making headlines for the wrong reasons. The day before the film's screening in San Sebastián, the journalist, Luis Fernández Zaurín, who had worked on the book about Camarón with José Candado, announced his intention to sue the producers of the film for breach of contract.[7] Zaurín demanded 4,086 euros from Miguel Menéndez and Juan Riva for providing the synopsis and initial version of the script. Zaurín had received a contract in October 2002 for 18,030 euros to write a script for the film because of his knowledge of Camarón gained while co-writing the book with the singer's former nurse Candado. The film's producers had also bought the rights to this book. Zaurín now claimed that he had given the producers a document of 150 pages, including previously unpublished material and personal anecdotes about Camarón. He also claimed that he had started work on both the synopsis and the script, under the supervision of Menéndez who had approved his work.

There had been personnel changes as early as November 2004 when Jaime Chavarri took over as director and the script became the responsibility of Álvaro del Amo. Zaurín went on to claim, according to a news release, that he had received a letter from Menéndez telling him he was off the project because the widow of Camarón had not authorised his biography. Zaurín had responded by saying that Candado, his co-writer, was a friend of Camarón's widow and many passages in the book were based on stories told to them by the family. His final repost was to claim that he had not received a single euro for his work and that the producers had breached the agreed contract. If it transpired that the film did contain scenes based on the script he gave Menéndez, he may take further legal action, as the option to adapt the film from his book had expired a year ago.

Away from this caustic litigation, the film of Camarón's life had begun showing to a wider audience. It had received a surprisingly warm reaction mainly due to the ability of Oscar Jaenada to convincingly play Camarón, a fact that was openly acknowledged by the critics. Chavarri had conceded before the film's release that the work would be a very personal biography that would struggle to match the high standards of a legend and would not please everyone. The film did have its detractors who felt it followed the rather tired and clichéd pattern of the biopic, concentrating on the classic downfall of the artist. Other critics had praised the great technical and artistic efforts that Chavarri had clearly made, but felt he had omitted some of the key things that made Camarón famous. They would have liked to see a clearer interpretation of what Camarón meant to his followers and the inclusion of much more of his music. They had been happy with the film's treatment in relation to Camarón as a person which they felt gave the film great dignity. However, much of his life was taken for granted and the film did not furnish someone who had not heard of Camarón with enough information to really understand who he was. The director, taking for granted that the story of Camarón's life was so well known, had omitted important facts. Apart from assuming knowledge, some of the essential parts of Camarón's story were missing; including the extraordinary scenes that occurred at his funeral. Some critics described the film as being an uncomfortable journey for the audience as the pace and rhythm was overwhelming and the treatment bordering on the claustrophobic. Overall it was too busy and cluttered, with just too many anecdotes about Camarón's life. Most importantly, one critic, who had applied the rigors of journalism to his review of the film, was concerned about authenticity. The single sources of information for some of the scenes did not stand up because the stories could not be corroborated.

The film did take liberties with the chronology of Camarón's life to assist the telling of the story and also used some composite characters to represent aspects of his relationship with Rancapino and José Candado. There was little to reflect the influence of his producer Ricardo Pachón and a good opportunity to use more gypsy actors was not taken. While Camarón was not seen taking drugs, this controversial area was touched on by the appearance of a Colombian dealer and the depiction of drug taking on the tour bus and in a club. The exploitation of Camarón by Paco de Lucía's father was another sensitive subject that the film's script chose to confuse by giving the impression that he also pushed his own son to extreme levels in the recording studio. The film did seek to reflect the ethnic conflicts between gypsies and non-gypsies but once again gypsies were portrayed as primitives who wash from a bucket. An unnecessary amount of time was spent on the singer's illness to the detriment of covering many of his achievements, but the film's makers are to be congratulated for scripting the word *pisha*, that most popular of greetings to be heard on Cádiz's streets.

But few could dispute that it had been a successful dramatised documentary that would, at least, bring to the attention of a wider audience the life of this exceptional singer. The real winner was undoubtedly Oscar Jaenada, who superbly interpreted the dark and complex shades of Camarón and his contradictions. For the critics, Jaenada had become Camarón, with the audience soon forgetting that he was an actor and believing that Camarón had been reborn. While there had been misgivings about how the story was told the staging was also praised, as was the magnificent velvet texture of Gonzalo Berrido's photography which enriched the drama's darker moments. The use of Camarón and Paco de Lucía 's original tracks for the score was also viewed as a masterstroke. As one critic put it: 'Camarón is not terrible but it could have aimed higher'. Most controversially Chavarri had dared to flag up Camarón's Madrid fling with a middle-class woman whose consequences would remain secret until 1992, but on a lighter note it introduced to its audience the human side of an artist who was portrayed as being obsessed with collecting tape recorders! The film went on to win three *Goyas*, although not in major categories, but more importantly, it represented a major concession to the gypsies' contribution to flamenco.

With the *Camarón, la Película* being screened across Spain, the opportunity to add to the growing Camarón portfolio presented itself and the soundtrack was duly released; with the added bonus of a DVD that included the film's trailer, a scene from the film where Camarón sings *Soy Gitano* and images of all his albums. The publishers of *Camarón, Biografía de un Mito* also took advantage of the film's publicity to bring out the account of Camarón's personal nurse, José Candado, in paperback. The public could now read the so-called 'gospel according to Candado' for fewer than seven euros. Within a month of the film's release the newspaper *La Voz de Cádiz*, would also be using Camarón's image to boost their Sunday circulation. Readers would be able to buy, at a reduced price, the much-prized television series *Rito y Geografía del Cante* and the DVD devoted to Camarón would naturally be the first in the set. But could the considerable industry that had grown up around Camarón sustain itself in 2006, or was the market-nearing saturation point? The answer came in May with news of the release of *El Ángel* and in particular the first part, entitled *El Territorio Flamenco*, in which Camarón had appeared; it would be an image of him playing the guitar that would be used to promote the DVD set. Ricardo Pachón's television film, shot in the province of Seville, would soon be available for the domestic market.

Just as Spanish audiences were recovering from one controversial film about Camarón another, borrowing its title from his groundbreaking album *La Leyenda del Tiempo*, was released on 2 June 2006. This feature had been entered for the Rotterdam Film Festival where it was shown on 3 February 2006 and would soon be available to a wider audience. The film's publicity described it as a 'fictional documentary' through which the thirty-six-year-old Catalan director, Isaki Lacuesta sought to pay homage to Camarón. It is questionable whether it worked as a documentary and was met with tepid enthusiasm from the critics. Lacuesta had visited San Fernando and claimed that all he could find of Camarón 'were the remains of a legend, a presence both subtle and physical'.[8] Despite his failed search for Camarón, the landscape of San Fernando and its people did convince him to go ahead with the film.

The actors were allowed to play themselves with much scope for spontaneity as the film told two stories using 'the voice of Isra' and the 'voice of Makiko'. Both accounts would be linked by the overwhelming spirit of Camarón and set in the town of his birthplace. The plot was based on a thirteen year old gypsy boy Isra who was born into the world of the *cante*, but despite being an admirer of Camarón had abandoned singing flamenco after the death of his father and wanted to leave San Fernando. His voice was about to break anyway and he was now more interested in getting a girlfriend and his relationship with his brother after the passing of his father. The other character, a Japanese nurse called Makiko had travelled to Spain on a quest to learn to sing like Camarón. She wanted to immerse herself in the *cante* and the Andalusian way of life as a way of coping with her father's illness. Her Japanese background had prohibited her from showing any emotion over her father's plight, but maybe flamenco song was a suitable vehicle with which to express it. Camarón's brother Jesús Monje would play Makiko's teacher instructing her in the secrets of flamenco song. In the film she finds herself a very long way from Japan, experiencing an alien culture in southern Spain. At the heart of this story of two characters, which do not stumble across each other, is the fascinating power of flamenco to attract interest from non-Spaniards.

While Lacuesta had made a stunning debut with his film *Cravan vs Cravan* this ambitious film, whose poster for extras I had first seen in a Cádiz bar, did not receive universal approval. The critics felt the choice of subject was audacious and that the film said more about revolutionary approaches to film making than the presence of Camarón. Some may have wondered about the relevance of the Japanese fisherman and how all this related to Camarón. They were also unhappy at the imbalance between the duration of the two stories, with such intensity given to Isra's story and just a sketch of Makiko's journey. It was also clear that the mixing of genre between documentary and fiction was not successful but, as with the first Camarón film, the performances of the two actors were highly praised. The soundtrack which included music from Joan Albert Amargós who was responsible for many of Camarón's albums in the eighties, was also very moving. While the film borrowed much from other sources it did give its audience the opportunity to appreciate the unique countryside that Camarón grew up in, courtesy of the photography from Diego Dussuel. Lacuesta had shot considerable hours of footage in San Fernando and was then faced with some very difficult editing decisions.

Israel Gómez Romero, who had played himself, had been chosen by the director from over 300 other boys and the critics had enjoyed the interplay between him and his brother Cheíto. They also recognised, in the acting of Makiko Matsumura, a valid representation of the many girls who abandon their lives in Japan to study flamenco in Andalucía. The critic Nuria Vidal felt the film's narrative flowed well, but that it was not possible to classify it as it was neither documentary nor fiction but wondered if it was '*docuficción*'.[9] Vidal thought it approached neo-realism, with the desire of the director to discover and understand the land where Camarón was born lying at the heart of its story. Lacuesta had been happy to just film and listen to his actors and to let the film breathe; Vidal was impressed with the film's intensity, which attracts its viewer by its simplicity and poetry. However, it would be very wrong to consider this film as a documentary about Camarón. Not surprisingly, because it reflected their homeland, the people of Cádiz gave it five stars to the relief of the director at its premiere on the 1 June. But the film was to suffer from being released so soon after Chavarri's *Camarón, la Película* and made little impact.

11

The Long Journey

Soy gitano.
José Monje, José Fernández and Vicente Amigo

Those gypsies who reside in southern Spain appear to be very different to their brothers in other parts of Europe, but they do share the same history of persecution, prejudice and racism. Their long journey to Europe had started in Northwest India and was to end for some, when they finally entered Spain from the North. The rest would travel much further south and finally settle in the land that lies between Cádiz and Seville, where they would eventually develop flamenco music. While the gypsy trades of ironwork and the forge have all but disappeared from Andalucía, there are still gypsies in India who practice these trades and there are many groups of gypsy musicians who continue play traditional instruments. While Camarón is seen by Spanish gypsies as a deity, how representative was he of this little-understood nation without a country? Camarón had more in common with the Dhoad dynasty, from the North Western Indian province of Rajasthan, than the majority of now invisible gypsies in both Spain and Europe. He shared with them a liking for openly displaying his race and shared their taste for wearing distinct clothes fashioned in vivid colours.

Even more remarkable than Camarón's transformation from sinner into saint, has been the interpretation and mediation of his ethnicity in the Spain of the twenty-first century, where racism is openly expressed and endemic in its population. It is perfectly possible for those who revere and enjoy

Camarón's music to be comfortable with negative ideas about gypsies and their customs. Of more significance, is what he now symbolises for other members of his race. He is remembered as the epitome of what it means to be a gypsy, including all the values that accompany that identity; his song *Soy Gitano* would be recognised as a very important statement of belonging, not merely the title of an album.

Before examining the experiences of the gypsies who settled in Spain and the harsh laws they would face under the Spanish monarchs of Ferdinand and Isabella, it is important to understand the concept of visibility in relation to the gypsy people in Andalucía. Camarón was proud to be a visible gypsy and in the context of contemporary Spain had all the characteristics of the archetypal stereotype. His heritage had been the traditional gypsy trade of the forge and the production of ironwork which flourished in the nineteenth century. His mother's artistic name of La Canastera was a direct reference to that other gypsy trade of basket weaving, and in common with most gypsies Camarón had left school at an early age. His childhood would consist of working in the forge and hanging around bars to sing for the upper classes. He was proud to be recognised as a gypsy and chose to wear *camisas gitanas* or gypsy shirts adorned with gold chains. He was also proud of the tattoo on his hand, his expensive watches and his trademark gold teeth. Later, in common with many gypsies in the eighties, he would succumb to hard drugs but without these traits would the citizens of Paris have taken him to their hearts and would he have achieved his current iconic status in Spain today?

My own encounters with gypsies have come through performing flamenco. I have met and played the guitar with gypsies all over Andalucía and in particular in Jaén, Cádiz, Seville and Jimena de la Frontera. It was in Jimena that I experienced some of my most satisfying flamenco experiences with the gypsies that lived in the lower town. There were memorable late night sessions in the then *Bar Torres* and later in the new flamenco club with the town's best singer, Gabriel who had worshiped Camarón and his mastery of the *bulerías*. There had also been many sessions in the flamenco club in Jaén that had occurred after several drinks accompanied by free *tapas* of deep fried aubergine and smoked salmon. And one particular session, I was asked to play the guitar for a group of gypsies as they had taken on some *payos* in an impromptu *mano a mano*. Needless to say we won, treating them to the latest style of *bulerías* as they left in defeat.

Written evidence suggests that the first gypsy tribes arrived in Spain and specifically in Zaragoza during 1425.[1] Initially the gypsies had been well treated with King Alfonso V of Aragon going as far as calling for the *Egipcianos* to be assisted on their travels. For the next seventy-five years, life in Spain was reasonably pleasant for gypsies, with wealthy benefactors even giving them food and clothes, but from 1539 life for this race would change dramatically. In that year, Carlos I had signed a document called *La Pragmática del Medina del Campo* which condemned all nomad gypsies to become galley slaves and row his ships.[2] The origins of the law went back to 1499 and the edicts of the Aragón monarchy, but from the mid-sixteenth century gypsies were expected to have both a job and a master. They were given two months notice in which to comply and then, if found without work, they were given 100 lashes and kicked out of the Kingdom of Castile. A second offence would result in their ears being cut off, and a two-month jail sentence, while a further offence would bring life imprisonment. The authorities in England had also been tackling the problem of gypsies by accusing them of either theft or poisoning cattle. These false accusations had led to their extermination with the gibbets of England 'groaning and creaking under the weight of gypsy corpses'.[3] During the reign of Philip II of Spain, the Spanish parliament had also debated in 1594, the separation of male and female gypsies in a bid to eliminate the race.[4] Five centuries later in 1963, Jean-Paul Clébert published one of the best overviews on the history and customs of gypsies. Clebert had explained that after a history of repression, the gypsies had found a freedom in Spain which they only shared with their brothers in Britain and the United States, and that they had become integrated amongst the Spanish population.[5] With the possible exception of Jerez, sadly this level of integration has not been achieved.

Within two years of Camarón's death, Seville played host to the First European Congress against Racism and Xenophobia, sponsored by the European Commission and the Junta de Andalucía in May 1994. To mark the importance of this event the Queen of Spain was invited to open the congress and the Spanish Prime Minister, Felipe González to close it. The congress had examined some worrying statistics about the world's estimated twelve-and-a-half million gypsies, of whom three million lived in Europe.[6] Over half a million of these gypsies were resident in Spain, with 300,000 choosing to live in flamenco's home of Andalucía. The congress had addressed racism and illiteracy, the two key areas that were affecting the well-being of the gypsy people. Juan de Dios Ramírez, as a gypsy member of the European Parliament, had wanted to know why he was treated very differently by airport security when he travelled with 'whites' as compared with flying with fellow gypsies. He also wanted to know whether this was because the police believed that gypsies preferred to travel by bus or was it that they disliked the long hair and sideburns?

Despite passing several resolutions and being covered by both the BBC and CNN, the Congress was to have little impact as a decade later Spain was still witnessing headlines like 'Night of terror in Cortegana'. This incident had seen local residents not only turn on the gypsy population, but also beat up their animals as pure racism was unleashed on a Sunday night in January 2004.[7] It had been claimed that three gypsies had killed Mateo Vásquez, who had learning difficulties. This rumour had been enough to provoke 2,000 of the village's 5,000 inhabitants to become violent and seek revenge. The doors of the houses of the village's gypsies were kicked in, their windows smashed and afterwards the mob set about their cars and animals. Such was the level or hatred and racism in Cortegana, a small Andalusian village in Huelva province, that the crowd had burnt the animal's straw and then attacked the gypsies' mules. The gypsies responded by stating that the innocent were paying for the crimes of others, but next time they would defend themselves and there was a local cemetery waiting for whoever got killed.

Two months later, Luis Aragonés, the football coach of the Spanish national team, had made racist remarks that were broadcast on Spanish television and subsequently heard around the world.[8] Aragones had described the Arsenal football player, Thierry Henry, as that 'black shit' and then, on refusing to apologise explained that the comments had been designed to motivate another player, José Reyes, who he referred to as a 'gypsy' with the inference that he was lazy. By late August 2005 the flamenco dancer Farruquito, who had been charged in connection with a car accident in which a person was killed, was also becoming the subject of the racism against gypsies. The magazine *Muyer Hoy* had asked in a web survey whether its surfers agreed 'with the sentence that Farruquito received'?[9] The response was not surprising, with ninety-five per cent saying no. The magazine went on to state that almost 100 per cent believed that it was totally unfair that Farruquito had been give a minimum sentence because he had eluded justice. The remaining small percentage was happy with the sentence handed down against the dancer.

In January 2006 an article appeared in *El País* regarding a headline which had stated that a gypsy girl had 'received a beating from her classmates'.[10]

The item went on to say that the mother of the girl had filed a complaint to the police, stating that her daughter had received a beating from six boys and two girls which had resulted in a cracked rib, bruises and scratches. She had claimed that they bullied her daughter because she was both 'gypsy' and 'fat', while the head teacher had said she was not aware of the incident and did not accept that the school had a problem with racism. The writer had felt it was wrong to omit from the headline the words gypsy and fat because these had been the excuses given by the perpetrators to justify their attack. He went on to ask whether the newspaper would have printed 'a girl receives a beating from gypsy classmates', had it been the other way round. The article had concluded with a comment from Juan de Dios Ramírez-Heredia, the president of the gypsy union, on a recent murder in Seville where gypsies had been the suspects. He had reacted by stating that communities do not commit crimes and the biggest injustice is to make innocent people pay for the crimes that others have committed.

One of the best examples of the institutional racism that continues to exist in Spain came with the publication of a new dictionary in June 2006 from the Spanish Royal Academy. The dictionary's definition of the word 'gypsy' clearly indicated the country's overt racism. It was remarkable that such an august institution could have defined a gypsy as 'a person who acts with purpose of committing fraud by deceiving'. Not surprisingly gypsies, including Pilar Heredia the president of the gypsy women's association *Yerbabuena*, had found this very offensive.[11] Pilar had considered it embarrassing that such a definition could appear in an official work, but for her it proved that the word *gitano* remained a pejorative term that suggested inferiority. She had demanded that this entry should be removed because it could encourage xenophobic and racist attitudes. The response that came from the academic and lexicographer, José Antonio Pascual, was even more alarming. For Pascual, this was how the word gypsy is interpreted in the street and changing the dictionary's entry would not affect the social reality. For him these complaints had been a matter of political correctness being taken to excess, with people appearing to have lost their sense of humour and being unable to laugh at themselves. Pascual was also worried by this demand for the uniformity of language that could result in the loss of irony.

If the compilers of a dictionary could hold such views it was hardly surprising that the Spanish police continued to display prejudice when dealing with gypsies. The Losadas, a well-respected family of flamenco musicians living in Madrid, were to experience the prejudice that is influenced by the police having a clichéd image of gypsies.[12] Two robbers had broken into Tito Losada's home and shot his son as he defended himself. The police had been called, but spent fewer than two minutes at the house as they could see from Losada's features that he was a gypsy and concluded that the incident must be a revenge attack. His face had influenced their investigations as they had ignored that he was middle class, qualified, spoke other languages and was part of an established family of musicians. The police were not interested that the family had their own flamenco dance company that was about to tour the United States. For them, he was the son of a gypsy and so they suspected him, his family and his property.

In March 2006 the newspaper *El País* reported that recent crimes associated with gypsies had highlighted concerns over the failure of Spain's integration policies and reflected the negative perceptions that the rest of Spanish society held about gypsies. The newspaper's headline claimed that middle class gypsies were now in the majority amongst the race, but how much did the gypsy at the centre of their story have in common with the life of Camarón? Life for gypsies in the Spain of 2006 was changing with many of them apparently becoming bourgeois. The newspaper's readers had been presented with a portrait of the seventy year old gypsy El Tío Paco, who had moved to the city of Valencia over thirty years ago to live in a smart brick house surrounded by orchards on the outskirts of the city. Many other gypsies had also moved there and Paco had even bought a horse, but sadly his daughter died of leukaemia and then other family deaths occurred disrupting his hope of a happier and healthier life. Over the years Paco had tackled a variety of jobs from being a truck driver to a shop assistant. But of greater significance was his pride in the gypsy nation, a theme that he shared with Camarón. To emphasise this pride El Tío Paco had chosen to quote another high profile gypsy and flamenco artist, the dancer Joaquín Cortés. Cortés had recently said, when talking to the celebrated interviewer Jesús Quintero on Spanish television, that he was a gypsy before he was Spanish. This was a sentiment that El Tío Paco could identify with as he felt he was firstly a gypsy, secondly Spanish and thirdly Valencian. This portrait, and other interviews, would be used to illustrate that gypsy life was changing and would be very different in the future.

Although gypsies in Spain have been sedentary for countless years many people are only aware of being around gypsies when attending a flamenco festival, going to a late night flamenco bar in Madrid, or passing a *chabola* or gypsy shantytown on the outskirts of a large city. The newspaper's survey had discovered, not surprisingly, that forty per cent of those interviewed were uncomfortable with having a gypsy neighbour. The reality of life for gypsies in Spain had been painstakingly documented by a university professor from the UAB, Teresa San Román, who claimed that eighty per cent of Spain's gypsies were not visible.[13] She had also explained, that to come to terms and understand this simple fact, people need to look beyond their prejudices. Her findings had suggested that approximately 650,000 Spanish gypsies do not share the background of Camarón or other visible gypsies, as they neither possess the ability to sing flamenco nor do they do live in shantytowns. They are more likely to work as shop assistants and aspire to a middle class life by owning a house in a good part of town. José Manuel Flórez, a representative of the *Secretaria de la communidad gitana en Andalucía*, had summed up this misconception of the public when he stated that the gypsy stereotype is to be found mainly in the flamenco show or on the margins of society. For Flórez, statistics demonstrate that eighty to ninety per cent of gypsies do not fall into either of these categories. On this interpretation it would appear that Camarón was part of the twenty per cent that represented visible gypsies; the same group of gypsies that continue to be labelled with the stereotype of practicing anti-social behaviour, selling drugs and living in ghettos.

In Spain there remains one part of gypsy life that contrasts greatly with the customs practiced by non-gypsies. The rituals associated with a gypsy wedding and specifically the breaking of the bride's hymen to produce three blood stains on a white handkerchief as a proof of virginity are still common in modern Spain. In the late 1990s, Paloma Gay y Blasco conducted some in-depth research into the lives of gypsies living around Madrid, which included a valuable insight into the ritual of the gypsy wedding and the role that the female body plays in it. She had graphically described an elder gypsy woman explaining what must occur before a gypsy woman can be married. The woman had laid out three yellow stained handkerchiefs that related to her three daughters-in-law. Two had what she described as 'three roses' and the other only one rose and blood which meant, for the gypsy woman, that the girl was too 'closed' and the ritual was stopped. Forty years earlier a gypsy had explained this process and the subsequent rituals to the writer Donn Pohren in more blunt terms:

The test of the girl's virtue is in effect the marriage ceremony; the white silk
handkerchief is inserted, and, if it becomes stained with the blood of the girl,
the ritual of celebration begins. The girl is covered in a deluge of flowers from
all directions, and then the adoration of the bride is effected by the parents of
the couple falling on their knees around the girl and dancing a dance of the
upper torso and arms.[14]

Many other customs are followed including the singing of the flamenco
wedding songs known as *alboreás* and then the real drinking and celebrating
can start. The bride will have been through the ordeal of being examined
by a 'professional' in a room filled with married women, before she can
proudly show off the proof of her virginity.

Gay y Blanco had rightly emphasised that 'from classical times onwards,
throughout Southern Europe the breaking of the hymen has been considered the sign of loss of female virginity' but she found gypsy women in
Jarana who used other methods of proof as well.[15] Her research revealed
that elder gypsies were able to deduce whether a girl was a virgin from her
genitals and 'for a woman to be considered truly untouched she has to have
rosy, tight external genitals'. Despite this the gypsies in Jarana believe that
the *honra* is the real test of a woman's virginity. They had told Gay y Blanco
'that inside the body of a virgin woman there is an *uva* (grape), a white or
greyish hard grain the size of a chick-pea which contains her *honra*'. If a
gypsy girl were to have sex before marriage, then the yellow fluid known
as the *honra*, would be lost.[16] In contrast with the customs in Andalucía the
gypsies of Jarana did not see the stain of blood on the handkerchief at a
gypsy wedding necessarily as a sign of virginity. They also found the idea
that some non-gypsies keep their virginity until they are married impos-
sible to believe!

Before analysing the situation of gypsies, as opposed to their customs, it
is important to understand some basic figures and statistics relating to the
race in Spain. It is generally accepted that they arrived from North India in
the fifteenth century and that nearly half of them live in the heartland of
flamenco country, the province of Andalucía. A statistic not lost on George
Borrow who, writing in the 1840s was keen to point out that 'of all the
provinces of Spain, Andalucía was the most frequented by the Gitano race,
and in Andalucía they most abound at the present day, though no longer
as restless independent wanderers of the fields and hills, but as residents in
villages and towns, especially in Seville'. Borrow, who was a remarkable

linguist able to speak *caló* (the language of the gypsies), estimated that the gypsy population at the beginning of the nineteenth century was 60,000 and had declined to only 40,000 when he arrived eager to sell his bibles.

While other European countries had faced the problems people associated with travelling gypsies, this was not an issue in Spain because for many years her gypsy population had lived in the poorer districts and laws had prohibited their movements anyway. As the civil servant Angus Fraser discovered when undertaking research into gypsy communities in the 1980s, the main problem in Spain was the vast difference in wages paid to gypsies and non-gypsies. In Camarón's birthplace of Andalucía this would be even more acute because of the importance of agriculture. Fraser had revealed that in 1989 a male agricultural worker in Murcia was paid 300 pesetas an hour, while women received 250 pesetas and gypsies only 200 pesetas.[17]

Over half of today's Spanish gypsies are under sixteen years of age and up to seventy per cent do not attend school, while out of a university population of 1.5 million only 1,000 students are gypsies.[18] In common with Camarón they continue to leave school early, with thirty per cent leaving before finishing the ESO and not even one per cent finishing their secondary education. The statistics relating to education and gypsies have improved, including the lowering of those playing truant that once accounted for half of all gypsy children and now the majority attend. The level of literacy has also improved with sixty per cent of gypsies now able to read. A survey in 1977 had shown that eighty per cent of gypsies could not read or write. Despite this, over half of gypsies in employment do not have stable or even regular employment and eighty per cent are still involved with the *venta ambulante* or street trade. These statistics would seem to question *El País'* claim that the majority of gypsies are now middle class.

Gypsies are frequently described by an ignorant public as being lazy and not wanting to work, while they continue to be excluded from many sectors of the job market. A recent survey conducted in 2006 by the *Fundación Secretariado Gitano*, revealed some interesting statistics.[19] Of those gypsies in work, seventy-one per cent have a temporary contract compared with thirty-one per cent of the rest of the Spanish population while fifty per cent of employed gypsies work with just a verbal contract. Remarkably, seventy-two per cent of gypsies are illiterate compared with five per cent in the rest of the population and women make up seventy per cent of the unemployed gypsy population. Fortunately these worrying statistics are being addressed with the *Consejo Estatal del Pueblo Gitano* being awarded 34 million euros for the period 2006–2010. This body will use this money to promote measures that will accelerate the pace on integration. However it will have to combat the high level of discrimination that prevents gypsies from getting jobs in the fields of police, law, education, housing, and health services.

Where do all these stereotypes of gypsies, and in particular Spanish gypsies, come from? One of the richest sources is from an extraordinary man who had grey hair by the time he was twenty and who had travelled to Spain in the mid 1830s to sell bibles. George Borrow was also a tall and fit man and a superb linguist. These qualities, combined with his outgoing personality, enabled him to mix and talk to the gypsies in Andalucía. Such was his force of will and lack of fear, it is possible that if he had been born in the twentieth century, he may well have criticised Camarón for his drug abuse and sold him a bible into the bargain!

In his *The Zincali or an account of the gypsies in Spain*, published in 1846, Borrow first painted a romantic picture of gypsies smoking cigars around their fires on winter nights. But soon they were described as having 'their ears pierced, from which depended a ring of silver; their hair was black and crispy, and their women were sorceresses who told fortunes' and even worse they had their own language and spoke Spanish with a strange accent! They were master thieves who had no respect for the law, while their women were all prostitutes with the ability to cast spells. Borrow had gladly retold the tale of the lone traveller who would be robbed and then found the next morning as 'a naked corpse, besmeared with brains and blood'. But he had confirmed their expertise in forging iron and deriving a living from trading in horses and mules. Borrow, even knowing it to be untrue, went as far as recounting the tale of the bookseller of Logroño who, having been captured by gypsies, later befriended them and ended up marrying the daughter of the clan's leader. The bookseller eventually became the gypsies' leader, on the death of his wife's father, but it all went very wrong when he fell out with his wife and was sold to the Moors in Africa. Meanwhile, in Logroño, the gypsies had poisoned the population: their bodies swelling up and turning blue with crimson spots! The bookseller later spied on the gypsies who had brought the town to its knees and ultimately brought about their defeat. He painted a graphic picture of their bodies lying in the streets: 'there lay grim men more black than mulattos, with fury and rage in their stiffened features; wild women in extraordinary dresses, their hair black and long as the tail of a horse, spread all dishevelled upon the ground; and gaunt naked children grasping knives and daggers in their tiny hand'.

For Borrow these gypsies had entered Spain from France, crossing the Pyrenees, but on discovering the rich land of Andalucía had decided to settle specifically in the kingdoms of Granada, Jaén and Seville. Their ability to roam freely had been curtailed by the laws passed at Medina del Campo by the monarchs of Aragón, Ferdinand II and Isabella in 1499. Years later in 1586, Philip II had passed more laws forbidding the movement of gypsies and prohibited them from selling goods at fairs. By 1619 Philip III had decreed, without much success, that all gypsies were to leave Spain; leaving Carlos II to finally address the issue in 1692. He had ruled that gypsies could no longer live in towns with fewer than 1,000 families and they were also banned from wearing gypsy clothes, speaking their language and were not allowed to take up a trade except for working the land. How could gypsies survive without practicing the cannibalism that Borrow, although rejecting this ridiculous claim, could not resist including in his account? The gypsies, according to Borrow, 'live in filth and misery' in *gitanerías* and specialise in telling fortunes and disguising stolen animals! These *gitanerías* or gypsy ghettos were soon to be discouraged as they offered gypsies the opportunity to discuss their affairs and even intermarry. But Borrow had discovered that the *gitanerías* also provided a good service of entertainment at nightfall for the nobility who could afford it, a tradition that was to continue into Camarón's childhood:

> This was generally the time of mirth and festival, and the Gitanos, male and female, danced and sang in the Gypsy fashion beneath the smile of the moon. The gypsy women and girls were the principal attractions to these visitors; wild and singular as these females are in appearance, there can be no doubt, for the fact has been frequently proved, that they are capable of exciting passion of the most ardent description, particularly in the bosoms of those who are not of their race.

Borrow had also discovered the historic flamenco quarter of Triana, which he portrayed as the capital of crime because of its gypsy population. It had been a district dominated by the sound of the blacksmith's hammer and the smell of roasting chestnuts that the gypsies were preparing to take to Seville to sell. That was when they were not banging on doors in a bid to sell contraband goods brought from the English in Gibraltar!

In more recent times the writer Laurie Lee painted a more sympathetic portrait of the gypsies in Andalucía when he described seeing the daughter

of Manolo Caracol perform in Algeciras. On returning to Spain in the fifties he had remained fascinated by gypsies, but also saw them as people with
distinguishing features and the all-important ability to perform flamenco.
Lee was hypnotised by the 'controlled sexuality' that gypsies brought to
flamenco:

> After the girls came the star, Luisa Ortega, with her dark beautiful Indian face
> and anguished mobile mouth, to sing a series of songs she had written herself
> – songs of love, pain, the Virgin and 'mi Granada'. Her glittering eyes were like
> black fruits, juicy with tears, and in the negroid curls of her hair white roses
> hung like sheep's wool caught on thorns. The words of her songs, perhaps,
> were not so distinguished, but her passion clothed them in such fires that
> they spread like pentecostal flames over the audience and reduced the men to
> throaty, gasping cheers. Her voice was curious; hard metallic, yet fluent as the
> iron-work of Seville. But at the climax an explosive heat of sentiment seemed
> to fuse it into a wild orgasm of phrasing, so that she fled each time from the
> stage to a storm of compássionate cries.[20]

Ten years later Gerald Howson presented a contrasting negative portrait
of the gypsies in Cádiz when he was told a story of a horse that had been
killed at a bullfight. The carcass had been dragged into the street, presenting
a few unguarded moments that were ideal for the gypsies with their ability
for 'knocking things off'.[21] Such was their skill that:

> the police had to 'break the jaws' of half a dozen gitanos, on whom the
> immediate and obvious suspicion fell, before they retrieved what was left of
> the horse. The head was in one village, the legs in Sevilla, the guts in Morón
> de la Frontera, the hoofs if Jerez. 'Can you imagine disposing of a whole horse
> in two minutes?'

In 1995 the dancer Joaquín Cortés, a very prominent gypsy artist, appeared
in a film directed by Pedro Almodóvar which opens with a rich middle-class
author concerned that one of her earrings is missing. As her gypsy maid
searches for the missing item of jewellery, the common theme and cliché
of the *gitano* as thief was about to be revisited. In *la flor de mi secreto*, the
maid's talented son played by Cortés had needed money to promote his new
dance show and later confesses to stealing jewellery from the author's house.
140 years after Borrow's account of gypsies in Spain, this negative portrayal

of gypsies still persists. The film maker, Dominique Abel, has more recently sought to concentrate on the visible gypsy or flamenco performer without providing much explanation that these musicians are not typical gypsies and form an elite that live in the golden triangle of Seville, Cádiz and Morón. Her atmospheric and sentimental film, *Agujetas Cantaor*, painted a portrait of an eccentric singer from Jerez as he wandered through the parched land of Andalucía singing flamenco. It was reminiscent of the BBC Arena programme *An Andalusian Journey*, where the guitarist Moraíto is filmed strolling down the streets of Jerez carrying his guitar under the burning midday sun. Gypsy flamenco musicians do not, unless they are being filmed and paid for it, burst into song in the middle of the countryside or carry guitar cases around while thumbing for lifts. The producer and director of the 1988 BBC Arena programme even went as far as asking some of the most famous gypsy artists whether they were gypsies. This repeated question gave the film a touch of hilarity when it was put to Fernanda de Utrera, whose features alone would confirm to even the most ignorant that she is a gypsy. Fernanda, with a good sense of irony, fiercely denied being a gypsy, while the late Chocolate remarked that he certainly was not a fox terrier! Despite being at the height of his fame when this film was made, Camarón was not featured, as the director preferred to listen to the advice of a newspaper seller in Cádiz who, no doubt for a friendly price, could introduce her to the real stars of the art!

The travel writer Michael Jacobs once visited the Tres Mil Viviendas district of Seville where he was met with some hostility by the residents and advised to leave.[22] He described the district as one of the worst in Seville, where the typical journalist in search of a sensationalist story based on drugs or violence might venture. This area, which borders a railway line, continues to be a flamenco stronghold with its older, mainly gypsy, residents, still able to remember those halcyon days when Triana resounded daily to the sound of flamenco. Government plans forced these residents out as the bulldozers moved in and blocks of flats including Las Tres Mil Viviendas were constructed to rehouse them. Camarón's record producer, Ricardo Pachón, spent his childhood in Triana where he discovered flamenco on every corner until this important centre was lost in the sixties. Dominique Abel was to encounter a more friendly welcome than Jacobs when she shot another film, *Polígono Sur*, which had a flamenco theme based on the lives of the district's residents and a forthcoming tribute concert for a local poet. We can only presume that the fees she paid to the artists and residents would have helped to oil the wheels and create a friendly atmosphere.

The film remains an important record despite projecting a constructed image of visible gypsies and their lifestyle in this *barrio* and it offers many moments of inspired flamenco art. The film presented scenes of a donkey that we are to believe lives on the first floor of one of the apartments, while throughout the film we encounter a half-naked man dressed as a Native American Indian. The residents of the *barrio*, including both gypsies and *payos*, are constantly portrayed singing flamenco songs as they wander off to the local bar; while the district is shown as a place where violence does occur with people lighting random fires. These images also contrast greatly, and sit uneasily, with the concept posed by *El País* of an emerging gypsy middle class.

The film had much to say about the gypsies who live in this district and more importantly how important a role model and icon Camarón was to them. The influence of Camarón was to be found everywhere: from a poster that adorned the wall in the flat of Rafael Amador to the flamenco performed in the home of Juana la del Revuelo, her husband Martín and son Chico Martín. Not living in the historic district of Triana has had little effect on the culture and lifestyle of these gypsies, as illustrated by the young girls who sang some flamenco songs. These children will do more than just maintain the tradition; they will create new trends, as Las Tres Mil Viviendas was the community from where the ground-breaking music of the gypsy rock band *Pata Negra* had emerged in the seventies. At the heart of the film was the unassuming and humble guitarist Emilio Caracafé who summed up in his composition how important Camarón was and how his memory will never fade. He had gone to the remarkable trouble of arranging Camarón's most popular hit, *Soy Gitano*, for the solo guitar in the difficult key of E flat. In the film he performs this piece with such dignity and pride that one can immediately sense what Camarón's success as a gypsy meant to the people who live in one of Seville's less desirable areas; he was simply a god.

12

Fifteen Years Without 'Our José'

El Más Grande
Popular

Before embarking on my initial journey in search of Camarón I had
wanted to discover more about the reality of Camarón the revolutionary and martyr, as the fifteenth anniversary of his death approached.
An artist like Camarón would always fuel the debate over whether gypsies
possess qualities that non-gypsies do not have when it came to flamenco
singing. The tension between *gitanos* and *payos* had always existed in the
world of flamenco and was to be played out during Camarón's professional relationship with Paco de Lucía. As issues of race and ethnicity were
important to Camarón, I had decided to interview two important witnesses
to his life, one a gypsy and the other a *payo*. I wanted to meet the gypsy
singer Rancapino, who had known Camarón since he was seven years old
and who had been something of a brother and father figure to him. While,
from the *payo* tradition I contacted Enrique Montiel, who had often seen
Camarón as a child and had published a biography of the singer within a
year of his death.

I had many important questions to ask these two contemporaries of
Camarón and the answers were to provide a rich insight into how their
perception of Camarón has changed during his canonisation by the Spanish
public. I wanted to understand their thoughts on a number of key issues,
including why Camarón's fame had grown with the passing of time, why he
is now portrayed as a new Che Guevara and was he exploited financially?

There were also other issues, including his importance to Europe's gypsies, his long relationship with the guitarist Paco de Lucía, his portrayal in the film *Camarón* and finally his drug addiction.

Enrique Montiel could tell me about growing up in the town of San Fernando alongside the emerging maestro while Rancapino could talk about the golden years he had spent in the company of Camarón. The singer had expressed his worries about his family's financial future while speaking on Spanish television shortly before he died:

> On top of the big scare that myself and my family have suffered, it turns out that the work is not mine, so if it is true that I have made some contribution to flamenco, then I want something left, at least half of it, for my children and my family.[1]

Enrique Montiel would tell me that 'Camarón always had money' and Rancapino would inform me that Camarón left a considerable inheritance. My interviews would also provoke interesting comments about Camarón's widow and her input for the feature film based on his life. It was the biopic, *Camarón, la Película* that surfaced as an issue on which Rancapino and Enrique Montiel were unanimous in their unease at the representation of Camarón.

Enrique Montiel had invited me to his local government office, based in the Instituto de Formento, which now occupies Cádiz's splendidly restored tobacco factory. For decades I had been used to being greeted by the ruins of this once important building as I emerged from Cádiz's railway station, never thinking I would enter its refurbished interior to interview an important official. After being shown up to Señor Montiel's office I was granted a very friendly and revealing interview by a middle-class man who seemed an unlikely author of a book about a dead gypsy. I wanted to know how he might revise his book with new information, but our conversation was to touch on more sensitive areas surrounding the life of Camarón.

By contrast, my meeting with Rancapino, had started with a telephone conversation telling me that I was to come to his home in Chiclana de la Frontera. It was to end with a boozy and lively flamenco session in Cádiz's *La Última Carta* bar, situated opposite the imposing cathedral. Rancapino, a master of the *bulerías* had changed his mind and fancied a trip into Cádiz; I was to wait in the shadow of Cádiz's imposing town hall. As the hours passed I had attracted the attention of the bouncers who were minding a society wedding. They wanted to know whom I was waiting for, the reply of Rancapino enough to reassure them as they said what a great artist he was and when was he due?

On Rancapino's arrival we had exchanged hugs beneath Cádiz's famous town hall clock that chimes flamenco song on the hour. He had wanted to eat before we discussed anything about Camarón, but then quickly disappeared to return with pocket calendars, with the image of Camarón on their reverse. It had been a warm Saturday afternoon and as we had strolled through the streets, everyone in Cádiz seemed to recognise him and want to say hello. His favourite restaurant had been fully booked so we had started talking about Camarón as he tucked into a *tapa* at the bar. He had chosen fresh anchovies covered in virgin olive oil, the finest sherry vinegar from neighbouring Jerez and of course, plenty of garlic.

Flamenco always attracts trouble; sometimes violence, but usually just idiots who see a flamenco artist and are attracted like wasps to a sticky ice-lolly wrapper. They have usually had a little too much alcohol that convinces them they can sing flamenco and gives them the confidence to demonstrate their ability in front of a maestro. We were to be interrupted by one such customer who wanted to talk to Rancapino and show him how he could sing. After a good lunch and some brandy Rancapino demonstrated the real art of flamenco song and the restaurant erupted, with the diners showing their appreciation for his impromptu performance. But it was time to talk about Camarón:

Marcos: You've seen the film about Camarón's life, what's your opinion?

Rancapino: Well, there are things that are okay, but it doesn't portray the real Camarón. Camarón was completely different to that.

M: In what way?

R: Because Camarón had different ways, different customs and he was very timid. There is an expression that Camarón says in the film, '*mi mamá, mi papá*'. This is incorrect, Camarón never used these words. He never called his mother this. He used to call them *oma* and *opa*, but never *mamá* and *papá*. There are many things that don't ring true. They've shown the least important aspects of Camarón.

M: So, you're not happy with the film's representation of Camarón?

R: Of course not! If one makes a film about Camarón it should be based on the real Camarón. They should have looked for the people that lived with him. There are many, many things that don't feature in the film. Not bad things but traits like his interest in bullfighting, when he used to be involved in this activity. We both used to go bullfighting in the tentaderos in La Línea before he met La Chispa whom I had introduced to him.

M: What are your first memories of Camarón?

R: My first memories are when we were teenagers. When Camarón was fourteen and I was nineteen I used to take him to La Venta de Vargas and María and Juan Vargas used to say to me 'please don't bring him here because you are going to get the *La Venta* closed down' and I would say 'okay, I'll take him away in a minute' and we used to go to parties and people used to love him when they heard him singing, he was a genius, and from there we would wander into Cádiz. We used to visit *el Burladero*, a bar owned by gypsies who were butchers and relatives of Manolo Caracol. In those days Aurelio Sellés used to frequent *el Burladero*, and Pericón, and Uncle Agustín who was the bar owner and he would say 'come on nephews, sing me a *fandanguito*'. We would sing a *fandango* for Tío Aurelio and his friends and they would give us a peseta and we would have our photograph taken.

M: Some writers have said that you used to sing for money with Camarón on the Cádiz trams?

R: No, that's not true. Camarón never sang on any trams or trains. He never begged for any money either. That story is a lie. Perhaps, if I knew the people, they would ask us to sing and they would give us some money for it, but this was in the bars and parties and in *Cuevas Pájaro Sur* and in the Venta de Vargas.

*M: W*hy is Camarón's image continuing to grow as time passes and as we approach fifteen years since his death?

R: Well Camarón was a genius. He was a unique singer. Camarón had a musicality unlike any other singer. He didn't sound like any other singer. He was a complete individual.

M: Why is he portrayed as a new Che Guevara?

R: Well, because he was a genius, because Camarón used to improvise when he sang and because he had a totally different musicality to singers from the last, present and future century.

M: Do you think that Camarón was ever exploited?

R: Yes. He was exploited by many people.

M: What about the economic situation of his widow La Chispa?

R: Camarón left her some money, I know that. But other people are always looking for an opportunity to make money whether it's a book or recordings that haven't been released.

M: What memories does Camarón's funeral provoke?

R: That was a big shock for me because Camarón and I were always together during our lives and later with La Chispa. I was the one who used to take him to La Línea aged twelve, when he was still wearing shorts and we went everywhere together. In Madrid we used to stay at a *palmero's* son's house, the house of Bambino, where Fernanda, La Bernarda, Pansequito, Turronero, also used to stay. We paid fifty pesetas each to eat a watery *puchero* stew, they used to serve us and Camarón was working at the Torre Bermeja *tablao* at the time and I worked in the *cuadro* where Camarón was the main singer. There a woman called Mari Paz who fell in love with him and she had a daughter by him. Later Mari Paz, Camarón and myself moved to Dr Fleming street where he was offered a part in the film *Casa Flora* working with Máximo Valverde, Lola Flores, Paquita Rico, Conchita Piquer and a wide range of artists. Between 1966–9 Camarón and myself were performing at the Torres Bermejas flamenco *tablao* in Madrid and Ricardo Pachón used to come and see him and Camarón would say 'oh no, not him again'. Ricardo persisted again and again and tried many ways of persuading Camarón to go with him.

M: What's do you think about the artistic relationship between Camarón and Paco de Lucía?

R: Well they were two geniuses of flamenco. Paco was a genius at the guitar, one of the most advanced guitarists ever in the same way that Camarón was the greatest singer ever in this age. The Lucías helped Camarón and Camarón helped the Lucías.

M: Do you think Camarón has done much to improve the image of the gypsy people?

R: A lot. Camarón gave much to flamenco and the gypsy people worship Camarón because he sang so well. You won't find any gypsy children who haven't got a record of Camarón.

M: What's the truth about Camarón and drugs?

R: Camarón was a genius and like Elvis Presley and John Lennon he had to stimulate himself for inspiration like all geniuses, like all big artists.

M: But you're an artist as well.

R: No, no, no. Drugs are a bad thing. Camarón, when he was a little boy, used to wander the streets of San Fernando and Cádiz and a little boy at that age is offered all sorts of things. They gave him everything. It was the only thing that he couldn't deal with because it's very difficult to give it up and he couldn't. He was too much into drugs, but an artist of his calibre had to stimulate himself to get to where he got.

We then headed off to the 'Last card bar' for a flamenco session that was to include many songs inspired by Camarón including a popular local favourite the *tangos*, *Turú Turai* by Remedios Amaya. The next day I caught up with Enrique Montiel in Cádiz's old tobacco factory.

Marcos: Have you seen the film *Camarón* and what are your feelings about it?

Enrique Montiel: I didn't like it at all because it doesn't show the truth. It's a totally unbalanced film where there appears to be a division between the slut *paya* and the gypsy virgin. The *paya* in the film, called Isabel, represents a lot of *payas*, but in reality Camarón had a relationship, as I mentioned in my book, with Mari Paz with whom he had a daughter called Juana who lives in Barcelona. Out of respect for Mari Paz and her daughter, I think this part of the film is really awful. The film doesn't go into detail regarding the inner figure of Camarón. He was an exceptional artist and all exceptional artists have a great inner wealth, which is not portrayed in the film at all. I also think they have treated the issue of drugs with a dimension that shouldn't be there. When we talk about Camarón, are we talking about a drug addict or about a musician, a great musician?

And then there are several things that upset me a lot, for example the portrayal of Paco de Lucía as an effeminate camp guy with long hair, and to be honest I don't like the actor's treatment at all. Paco is a very mild person but he's also a person of extraordinary strength. The film doesn't feature Ricardo Pachón who was an influential person during Camarón's life. Pachón produced *La Leyenda del Tiempo* and *Soy Gitano* and he participated in Camarón's most ground breaking and original phase.

There are parts of the film where Camarón's life is reflected well and I think this due to the script being apparently based on information provided by José Candado. Candado knows about the final part of Camarón's life as he went on the journey to the United States and was also with him in Santa Coloma and this provided great input for the film. I think the script has also been fashioned by his widow. I think it was a great mistake to allow her to influence the script. She had called me but I didn't fully understand our conversation and she had also called me a few months earlier.

M: Have you spoken to the director?

EM: No, no. Chavarri didn't call me and unless he telephoned me I wouldn't call him either. But Camarón's widow did call me. La Chispa had rung to tell me that she didn't like the script but she didn't mention that it was a script by Candado and his friends. No, no, no, she said she didn't like it at all and said she had rejected it. Afterwards I found out that there were problems over the script, with the scriptwriter and with Chavarri. I was told that La Chispa had probably called me to ask me to participate in the script, but I can tell you something for sure, if I had written the script, I wouldn't have written the script they did. So they gave La Chispa the script and she said 'I rejected it because I didn't like it' but she didn't ask me to write it. I didn't say anything because I didn't really understand what she wanted. If she had said, I want you to write the script, but she didn't ask me. The bottom line is that I didn't like the film at all.

M: What are your first memories of Camarón?

EM: I am the same age as Camarón. He was born in December 1950 and I was born in May 1951. We were born in the same town, we went to the same school but I carried on studying at University. My first memory of Camarón is of a child who sang in a bar.

M: In La Venta de Vargas?

EM: No, not in La Venta de Vargas. No he sang in what's known in slang as *Güichi*, which was a very small bar that was at the castle.

M: How old was Camarón?

EM: Camarón would have been six. I was wandering down the street, because at that time children used to swim in the waters beneath the Zuazo Bridge and we used to pass this way. There used to be cockfights in the castle that attracted the children so I went to see a cockfight with some other people and I heard some noise coming from the *Güichi*. In the small bar I saw a child stood on a table singing and I stopped staring at the boy because I was a child as well. I may have been six, seven or eight, but when the boy became known as Camarón not many years later, I thought that was the child I saw singing. So this is the first memory I have of Camarón and after this I was very involved with Camarón until his death, obviously.

M: So why has Camarón's image grown with time?

EM: Well some of us have already talked about this. I said, many years ago, that Camarón sings better and better each day. I was the producer of Camarón's last CD, *La Venta de Vargas*. This album was recorded on a four-track tape recorder by Juan Vargas but the production of this album was done by Ricardo Pachón and myself.

M: Why is Camarón portrayed as the Che Guevara of flamenco?

EM: Well that was Ricardo Pachón's idea when he asked a graphic designer to produce the Che style face on the *Antología Inédita* album that he released in 2000.

M: What does Camarón mean to the gypsy people?

EM: Well Camarón was a God for the gypsy people, that's to say Camarón was the king of the gypsies, but not like Che, because gypsies do not have a great political awareness. They have an ethnic awareness but not a political awareness. Gypsy people don't trust politicians and they have good reasons not to. The politicians have always persecuted them and this is why they don't have a political consciousness. They are only aware that they need to keep a long way away from power.

M: Do you think that Camarón was ever financially exploited?

EM: I don't think so. Camarón always had money since he was very young as he was such a genius. He sang wherever he wanted and in addition to this he was a very humble person. He didn't mind eating a bowl of *puchero* or a bowl of lentils and he wouldn't want anything else. He never acquired properties or saved a lot of money. He wanted to live life, have a laugh and be happy as was reflected in his songs. Much of his work was autobiographical, particulary when he sang about living, dreaming and searching for his freedom.

M: What do you remember about his funeral?

EM: It was very impressive. I was there by the grave and I was totally overwhelmed. It was really hot and the light was typical of La Isla for midday in July. The light reflected off the white walls of the cemetery and I saw how they lowered the coffin into the grave and I saw a gypsy man with a torn shirt yelling 'Don't go Camarón, don't go'. I witnessed the family's pain, his brothers Pijote, Manuel and Remedios, Isabel and El Metepata.

M: Did you see the look of fear on the face of Paco de Lucía?

EM: No, not at all. It was the look of pain and probably of frustration too, because a few idiots made fun of him. They paid him a grave injustice.

M: What's your opinion about the artistic relationship between Paco de Lucía and Camarón?

EM: Well, thanks to that relationship, Flamenco advanced a thousand years and the relationship between Paco and Camarón was a miracle for flamenco.

M: What has Camarón done to improve the image of the gypsy people?

EM: I don't understand the question. What is the image of gypsy people? You have to be careful when you link a community with an image. What is the image of the English people, have they only got one image that is bad? One day I asked Camarón, because he was a good friend of the *payos* or non-gypsies, 'José, what would you think if one of your daughters married a *payo*'? And he replied, 'what do you mean about one of my girls marring a *payo*'. He couldn't contemplate the concept of one of his daughters marrying a *payo* and do you understand his joke? How on earth would one of his daughters marry a *payo*, how dare you I even suggest such a thing? He told me that his daughter must marry a pure gypsy, but regarding the image of the gypsy people one must consider that there are lots of different types of gypsies in the same way as there are different types of *payos*.

M: Since you wrote your book about the life of Camarón, over thirteen years ago, several other works have been published. Is there anything you would like to add to your work?

EM: There have been some interesting books published and one in particular by the authors Gamboa and Núñez. They have filled an important gap because they are musicologists and have analysed all the records released by Camarón, examining every track.

M: They have published a highly specialised and academic work.

EM: It's a very important book and there is another work which is very well written and that I really like, by Lencero.

M: What's in this book that you don't cover?

EM: I wrote things about the Camarón that nobody knew about and I talked about Camarón's childhood because I knew more about this than anyone. I also talked about the birth of his secret daughter. I was the person who wrote about Camarón's first twenty years and his last twenty years.

M: What about Camarón and drugs. How reliable are all the stories of his drug habit?

EM: Well this is a very complicated matter and there is much to talk about because in some ways Camarón was a very ignorant person as were many others in the sixties. Camarón used to smoke cigarettes and it was smoking that killed him. He used to smoke three to four packets of *Winstons* each day.

M: So you're saying his death wasn't related to drugs?

EM: No not at all and this can be proved by the medical report. In those days many people involved in the arts smoked marihuana or hashish, everyone did. Then one day somebody, and I know who this is but I am not going to name the person, said to him 'try this, this is better than *jamón*'.

M: Are you referring to high-quality hashish?

EM: Yes this is better than *jamón* so then Camarón tried cocaine. He started taking cocaine, which was amazing, but I would like you to name an artist of that era who didn't take cocaine because remember, we're talking about the seventies. A flamenco person might go without sleep for two days, singing and going to parties. But the drug of flamenco was *aguardiente* and Camarón liked *aguardiente*.

M: *Anís del mono?*

EM: No not *del mono* but *aguadiente* from Huelva. *Anís* is sweet, *aguardiente* is stronger and that is the one that Camarón liked. So this was the progression until someone offered him heroin another day and he smoked it. He never injected himself. Never, ever. He always smoked it. So he started smoking heroin and one day he found out that he was paying the price for it and from this moment Camarón's life was a battle against the effects of these drugs. So, as this battle was a decent one, I don't find it appropriate to refer to it. When you talk about Camarón and drugs you should always refer to it as his battle against addiction. That's how he referred to it out of respect for his own children and all the gypsy people. He could see the number of gypsies who were dying from drug addition.

M: Finally, tell me about Camarón's visit to the Abbey Road studios.

EM: Camarón had gone to London with Ricardo Pachón to record *Soy Gitano* and I remember that the orchestra was all ready to record with the Universal Company paying the bill. Camarón arrived late and so Universal had to pay the orcheer day. This was typical of Camarón, he was a genial artist but he was also a rebel but he did go to those studios and he did record.

I left Cádiz's former tobacco factory pondering Camarón's drug addiction after what Enrique Montiel had told me. I preferred to reflect on a more positive representation of the singer and I turned to my memories of Camarón's visits to the *Rocío*. That spectacular pilgrimage to the village of Almonte which occurs at Whitsun is undertaken by thousands of Andalusians riding on horses or in wagons pulled by oxen. This pilgrimage to the site of the 'Virgin of the dew' dates from the fifteenth century and while being a deeply religious occasion, it also involves flamenco partying twenty-four hours a day. They say you do not go to El Rocío to sleep, as the communal food and booze flows to the constant sound of flamenco. In May 2006 Camarón's presence at El Rocío had been as strong as ever with stalls selling DVDs, flags and elegant framed photographs of the singer. It seemed only recently that Camarón was last at this event, drinking bottles of *cruzcampo* beer as his guitarist Paco de Lucía, rode past on his horse. They had both gone dressed in the traditional Andalusian outfits of felt broad-brimmed *Córdoba* hats, brightly coloured cravats, herringbone tweed trousers covered by riding chaps and those ubiquitous Andalusian braces.

Reflecting on these images I returned to San Fernando for the last time, before completing this account, during a very hot July in 2006 and accepted that my search had been inconclusive. The real Camarón could not be found in Madrid but the city's gypsies still sang his songs in the nightspots of the Soleá and the Triana. His spirit was also still to be found in the sprawling outskirts of the now over-developed Seville, but few there were convinced by the portrayal of Camarón in the eponymous film. In the cool dark shade of the flamenco club dedicated to his memory, I felt closer to him than when he had been just a few feet away from me in Los Palacios. For the Cádiz aficionado Juan, he would always be much more than a mere memory. What did he mean to the teenage boy I saw buying the Camarón twenty-CD box set in Seville before I caught my flight? His presence continued to pervade every corner of the *Bar Manteca* in Cádiz, which doubles as a museum to the art of flamenco and bullfighting, while his tradition will be passed to another generation by the singers El Duquende and Montse Cortés. As I prepared to depart I bought the new album released by the coolest *Camaronero* El Potito, which paid tribute to the forge of his 'uncle Monje' and I knew that when I returned in December there would be a new winner of the Camarón singing prize. I saw Rancapino's son, Rancapino Cuico, proudly singing on television in the presence of Curro Romero, his father's *tangos, en la calle nueva,* but now Camarón was mentioned in the lyrics. As 2007 approached I was certain that documentaries of his life and the work of his producer Ricardo Pachón would still be appearing on Spanish afternoon television and yet another new album would be announced soon.

The stone obelisk, which marks the Camarón trail outside the flamenco club that bears his name, had just been vandalised, as had Camarón's bust. Using a paint aerosol someone had written the words 'without God you are without the master' but was this a reference to Camarón or an overzealous believer? Inside the *peña,* as I gazed at one of his jackets in a glass cabinet, his voice rang out from the speakers and I knew that the flamenco Christ would soon celebrate his fifty-sixth birthday.

Notes

1: *Hasta Siempre Camarón.*

1   San Sebastián Film Festival (18 September 2005) Velodrome: Camarón
    http://sansebastian.mister-i.com

2   Blázquez, J.A. (1991) Naranjito, Aurora Vargas, Manolo Franco, Enrique
    Paredes y Javier Barón triufaron en el Auditorio. *ABC.* (22 September 1991)

3   Castilla, A. (1992) 'Camarón fue enterrado en La Isla entre el llanto y las
    quejas de su gente.' *El País.* (5 July 1992)

4   Castilla, A. (1992) 'Un cigarrito para calentar la voz.' *El País.* (5 July 1992)

5   Howson, G. (1965) *The Flamencos of Cádiz Bay.* London, Hutchinson & Co.

6   Castilla, A. (1992) 'Un cigarrito para calentar la voz.' *El País.* (5 July 1992)

7   Llewellyn, H. (1990) split personality: 'Camarón de la Isla, the modern face
    of flamenco.' *Lookout.* (May 1990)

8   Márquez, H. (2002) 'Otra chispa de Camarón.' *Rolling Stone.* (Spain). No.34
    (August 2002)

9   Marcos. (1992) Script for 'Camarón de la Isla'. BBC Radio 3. (11 August
    1992)

10 Gamboa, J.M. & Núñez, F. (2003) *Camarón vida y obra.* Madrid, Sociedad
    General de Autores y Editores.

11 Lencero, C. (2004) *Sobre Camarón. La Leyenda del cantaor solitario.* Barcelona,
    Alba Editorial.

12 Gamboa, J.M. & Núñez, F. (2003) *Camarón vida y obra.* Madrid, Sociedad
    General de Autores y Editores.

13   Castilla, A. (1992) 'Camarón fue enterrado en La Isla entre el llanto y las
      quejas de su gente.' *El País*. (5 July 1992)

14   *ibid.*

15   Stills, B. (2005)' Film may end in a flamenco feud.' *The Guardian*. (25
      February 2005)

16   *ibid.*

17   Ortiz Nuevo, J.L. (1992) 'Toda la noche se oyeron pasar lamentos.' *El País*.
      (5 July 1992)

18   Grande, F. (1992) 'Aullidos negros.' *El País*. (3 July 1992)

19   Castilla, A. (1992) 'Camarón fue enterrado en La Isla entre el llanto y las
      quejas de su gente.' *El País*. (5 July 1992)

20   Ortiz Nuevo, J.L. (1992) 'Toda la noche se oyeron pasar lamentos.' *El País*.
      (5 July 1992)

21   Sevilla, P. (1995) Paco *de Lucía. A new tradition for the flamenco guitar.* San
      Diego, Sevilla Press.

22   Sánchez Ortega, P., Soler Guevara, L. & Soler Díaz, R. (1992) 'Camarón
      abandono su Isla.' *El Candil*. No. 1.057 (July/August 1992)

23   Salazar, G. (1992) A Special tribute to Flamenco singer, Camarón de
      la Isla (trascription of English Language Service of Spanish National
      Radio programme) *¡Flamenco! The Journal of Flamenco Artistry.* Vol.1, No.8.
      (October 1992)

24   Rodríguez Sánchez, A. (1998) Camarón and Tomatito cartoon by Ricardo
      y Nacho reproduced in *Camarón. Se rompió el quejío.* Madrid, Nuer
      Ediciónes.

25   Grande, F. (1992) 'Aullidos negros.' *El País*. (3 July 1992)

2: *A Gypsy of Cadiz Bay, 1950–1967*

1   Montiel, E. (2005) Personal communication. (November 2005)

2   Luque, A. (2005) 'La leyenda de Camarón se enriquece con una grabacion
     inédita.' *El País*. (18 February 2005)

3   Huélamo, L. & Santander, F. (1992) 'Llanto por un gitano.' *Panorama*. (6 July
     1992)

4   Flamenco World/S.C. (March 2005) 'Camarón in the Venta de Vargas.'
     www.flamenco-world.com

5   Lencero, C. (2004) *Sobre Camarón. La Leyenda del cantaor solitario.* Barcelona,
     Alba Editorial.

6   Luque, A. (2005) 'La leyenda de Camarón se enriquece con una grabación inédita.' *El País*. (18 February 2005)

7   *ibid*.

8   Molina, M./EFE. (2005) 'Renace el Camarón más joven y valiente.' *El País*. (27 February 2005)

9   Flamenco World/S.C. (March 2005) 'Camarón in the Venta de Vargas.' www.flamenco-world.com

10   Molina, M./EFE. (2005) 'Renace el Camarón más joven y valiente.' *El País*. (27 February 2005)

11   *ibid*.

12   Pohren, D.E. (1992) *Paco de Lucía and Family: The Master Plan*. Madrid, Society of Spanish Studies.

13   Huélamo, L. & Santander, F. (1992) 'Llanto por un gitano.' *Panorama*. (6 July 1992)

14   *ibid*.

15   TVE1 (1992) Homenaje a Camarón.

16   *ibid*.

17   Howson, G. (1965) *The Flamencos of Cádiz Bay*. London, Hutchinson & Co.

18   *ibid*.

19   Gamboa, J.M. & Núñez, F. (2003) *Camarón vida y obra*. Madrid, Sociedad General de Autores y Editores.

20   Howson, G. (1965) *The Flamencos of Cádiz Bay*. London, Hutchinson & Co.

21   *ibid*.

22   Lalaguna, J. (1990) *A Traveller's History of Spain*. Gloucestershire, The Windrush Press.

23   Fernández Zaurín, L. & Candado Calleja, J. (2002) *Camarón, biografía de un mito*. Barcelona, RBA Libros.

24   Blas Vega, J. & Ríos Ruiz, M. (1988) *Maestros del Flamenco*. Barcelona, Planeta de Agostini.

25   Salazar, G. (1992) A Special tribute to Flamenco singer, Camarón de la Isla (trascription of English Language Service of Spanish National Radio programme) *¡Flamenco! The Journal of Flamenco Artistry*. Vol.1, No.8. (October 1992)

26   *ibid*.

27   *ibid*.

28   Lalaguna, J. (1990) *A Traveller's History of Spain*. Gloucestershire, The Windrush Press.

29   *ibid.*

30   *ibid.*

31   *ibid.*

32   Salazar, G. (1992) A Special tribute to Flamenco singer, Camarón de la Isla (trascription of English Language Service of Spanish National Radio programme) *¡Flamenco! The Journal of Flamenco Artistry*.Vol.1, No.8. (October 1992)

33   Montiel, E. (1993) 'De la Isla a la eternidad.' *La Caña*. No.6 (Verano 1993)

34   Fernández Zaurín, L. & Candado Calleja, J. (2002) *Camarón, biografía de un mito*. Barcelona, RBA Libros.

35   Lencero, C. (2004) *Sobre Camarón. La Leyenda del cantaor solitario*. Barcelona, Alba Editorial.

36   Salazar, G. (1992) A Special tribute to Flamenco singer, Camarón de la Isla (trascription of English Language Service of Spanish National Radio programme) *¡Flamenco! The Journal of Flamenco Artistry*.Vol.1, No.8. (October 1992)

37   Núñez, F. (1998) *Todo el flamenco. Camarón de la Isla. La esencia del cante*. Spain, EDILIBRO/ Club Internacional del Libro.

38   Fernández Zaurín, L. & Candado Calleja, J. (2002) *Camarón, biografía de un mito*. Barcelona, RBA Libros.

39   Montiel, E. (1993) 'De la Isla a la eternidad.' *La Caña*. No.6 (Verano 1993)

40   *ibid.*

41   Fernández Zaurín, L. & Candado Calleja, J. (2002) *Camarón, biografía de un mito*. Barcelona, RBA Libros.

42   Marcos. (1993) 'Rincón Flamenco: Gerald Howson.' *Classical Guitar*. (August–September 1993)

43   Howson, G. (1965) *The Flamencos of Cádiz Bay*. London, Hutchinson & Co.

44   Preston, P. (1986) *The Spanish Civil War. An Illustrated Chronicle 1936–39*. New York, Grove Press.

45   Broué, P. & Témime, E. (1970) *The Revolution and the Civil War in Spain*. London, Faber and Faber.

46   *ibid.*

47   Preston, P. (1986) *The Spanish Civil War. An Illustrated Chronicle 1936–39*. New York, Grove Press.

48   Thomas, H. (1961) *The Spanish Civil War*. London, Penguin.

49   Sody de Rivas, A. (1992) *El eco de unos toques. Diego del Gastor*. Morón de la Frontera, Gráficas Olympia.

50   Thomas, H. (1961) *The Spanish Civil War*. London, Penguin.

51 Sody de Rivas, A. (1992) *El eco de unos toques. Diego del Gastor.* Morón de la Frontera, Gráficas Olympia.

52 Luque, A. (2005) 'La leyenda y el cante de Camarón crecen diez años después de su muerte.' *El País.* (2 June 2002)

53 Broué, P. & Témime, E. (1970) *The Revolution and the Civil War in Spain.* London, Faber and Faber.

54 *ibid.*

55 Sody de Rivas, A. (1992) *El eco de unos toques. Diego del Gastor.* Morón de la Frontera, Gráficas Olympia.

56 *ibid.*

57 *ibid.*

58 Sevilla, P. (1999) *Queen of the gypsies. The Life and Legend of Carmen Amaya.* San Diego, Sevilla Press.

59 *ibid.*

60 *ibid.*

61 Graham, H. (2005) *The Spanish Civil War. A Very Short Introduction.* Oxford, OUP.

62 Jacobs, M. (1990) *A Guide to Andalusia.* London, Viking.

63 Lee, L. (1955) *A Rose for Winter.* Middlesex, Penguin.

3: Castles of Sand, 1968–1978.

1 Salazar, G. (1992) A Special tribute to Flamenco singer, Camarón de la Isla (trascription of English Language Service of Spanish National Radio programme) *¡Flamenco! The Journal of Flamenco Artistry.* Vol. 1, No. 8. (October 1992)

2 de Lucía, P. (1993) 'Te recuerdo como eras en el último otoño.' *La Caña: Revista de Flamenco.* No. 6 (Verano 1993)

3 *ibid.*

4 *ibid.*

5 Case, G. (1994) An interview with Paco de Lucía. *¡Flamenco! The Journal of Flamenco Artistry.* Vol. 2, No. 5. (Fall/Winter 1994)

6 de Lucía, P. (1993) 'Te recuerdo como eras en el último otoño.' *La Caña: Revista de Flamenco.* No. 6 (Verano 1993)

7 Salazar, G. (1992) A Special tribute to Flamenco singer, Camarón de la Isla (trascription of English Language Service of Spanish National Radio programme) *¡Flamenco! The Journal of Flamenco Artistry.* Vol. 1, No. 8. (October 1992)

8   Gamboa, J.M. & Núñez, F. (2003) Camarón vida y obra. Madrid, Sociedad General de Autores y Editores.

9   *ibid.*

10 *ibid.*

11 *ibid.*

12 Sevilla, P. (1995) *Paco de Lucía. A new tradition for the flamenco guitar.* San Diego, Sevilla Press.

13 Marcos (2006) Personal communication with Mario Basilisco. (February 2006)

14 Pohren, D.E. (1992) *Paco de Lucía and Family: The Master Plan.* Madrid, Society of Spanish Studies.

15 Manrique, D.A. (2001) 'Tomatito, el toque perfecto de Camarón.' *El País Semanal.* (6 April 2001)

16 Fernández Zaurín, L. & Candado Calleja, J. (2002) *Camarón, biografía de un mito.* Barcelona, RBA Libros.

17 *ibid.*

18 *ibid.*

19 *ibid.*

20 Marcos. (1989) 'Flamenco Maestros. Paco de Lucía.' *Guitar International.* (August 1989)

4: *A Legend of Time, 1979.*

1   Manrique, D.A. (2001) 'Tomatito, el toque perfecto de Camarón.' *El País Semanal.* (6 April 2001)

2   Clemente, L. (1999) Asi que pasan viente anos. 20 muescas da "La Leyenda del Tiempo" por Luis Clemente. www.flamenco-world.com/magazine

3   *ibid.*

4   *ibid.*

5   *ibid.*

6   Manrique, D.A. (2006) 'Veneno contra corriente.' *El País Semanal.* (February 2006)

7   Gamboa, J.M. & Núñez, F. (2003) *Camarón vida y obra.* Madrid, Sociedad General de Autores y Editores.

8   Fernández Zaurín, L. & Candado Calleja, J. (2002) *Camarón, biografía de un mito.* Barcelona, RBA Libros.

9   Espínola, P. (1993) 'La herencia de la Ruina Negra.' *La Caña: Revista de Flamenco.* No.6 (Verano 1993)

10   Clemente, L. (1999) Asi que pasan viente anos. 20 muescas da "La Leyenda del Tiempo" por Luis Clemente. www.flamenco-world.com/magazine

11   Pachón, R. (1993) 'El flamenco según Santiago.' *La Caña: Revista de Flamenco*. No.6 (Verano 1993)

12   Pachón, R. (1994) Sleeve notes for *Camarón Nuestro*. Universal. (August 1994)

13   Pachón, R. (1993) 'El flamenco según Santiago.' *La Caña: Revista de Flamenco*. No.6 (Verano 1993)

14   Manrique, D.A. (2001) 'Tomatito, el toque perfecto de Camarón.' *El País Semanal*. (6 April 2001)

15   Clemente, L. (1999) Asi que pasan viente anos. 20 muescas da "La Leyenda del Tiempo" por Luis Clemente. www.flamenco-world.com/magazine

16   Pohren, D.E. (1992) *Paco de Lucía and Family: The Master Plan*. Madrid, Society of Spanish Studies.

17   Hentoff, N. (1960) Sleeve notes for *Miles Davis: Sketches of Spain*. CBS.

18   Marcos (2002) Script for 'Nightwaves'. BBC Radio 3. (27 June 2002)

19   *ibid*.

20   Clemente, L. (1999) Asi que pasan viente años. 20 muescas da "La Leyenda del Tiempo" por Luis Clemente. www.flamenco-world.com/magazine

21   Sáenz de Tejada, N. (1993) 'Los jóvenes flamencos: entre el viejo mundo y el volando voy.' *La Caña: Revista de Flamenco*. No.6 (Verano 1993)

22   Salazar, G. (1992) A Special tribute to Flamenco singer, Camarón de la Isla (trascription of English Language Service of Spanish National Radio programme) *¡Flamenco! The Journal of Flamenco Artistry*. Vol.1, No.8. (October 1992)

5: San Fernando's Rolling Stone, 1980–1987.

1   Espínola, P. (1993) 'Días de vinos y rosas. (Ános 80–90)'. *La Caña: Revista de Flamenco*. No.6 (Verano 1993)

2   Gamboa, J.M. (1993) 'Camarón en imagen: Cine.' *La Caña: Revista de Flamenco*. No.6 (Verano 1993)

3   Núñez, F. (1998) *Todo el flamenco. Camarón de la Isla. La esencia del cante*. Spain, EDILIBRO/ Club Internacional del Libro.

4   Espínola, P. (1993) 'Días de vinos y rosas. (Ános 80–90)'. *La Caña: Revista de Flamenco*. No.6 (Verano 1993)

5   *ibid*.

6   *ibid*.

7   *ibid.*

8   Fuentes, M.S. (1986) 'Camarón de la Isla.' *Jaleo.* Volume IX, No.2.
     (Summer 1986) (translating Contreras, M. (1986) Camarón de la Isla. El
     niño que fue un dulce. *El País Semanal* (11 May 1986))

9   Sevilla, P. (1986) 'The Enigma'. *Jaleo.* Volume IX, No.2. (Summer 1986)
     (translating Álvarez Caballero, A. (1986) 'Tres grandes cantaores.' *El País* (16
     May 1986))

10   Núñez, F. (1998) *Todo el flamenco. Camarón de la Isla. La esencia del cante.*
     Spain, EDILIBRO/Club Internacional del Libro.

11   Gamboa, J.M. (1993) 'Discografia: Cada día canta mejor.' *La Caña: Revista de
     Flamenco.* No.6 (Verano 1993)

12   Núñez, F. (1998) *Todo el flamenco. Camarón de la Isla. La esencia del cante.*
     Spain, EDILIBRO/Club Internacional del Libro.

13   Sevilla, P. (1986) 'Record Review: Te lo dice Camarón.' *Jaleo.* Volume IX,
     No.2. (Summer 1986) (translating Álvarez Caballero, A. (1986) 'Te lo dice
     Camarón.' *El País.* (16 May 1986))

14   Gamboa, J.M. (1993) 'Discografia: Cada día canta mejor.' *La Caña: Revista
     de Flamenco.* No.6 (Verano 1993)

15   Espínola, P. (1993) 'Días de vinos y rosas. (Ános 80–90).' *La Caña: Revista de
     Flamenco.* No.6 (Verano 1993)

16   García Plata, M. (2002) *Camarón de la Isla 1969–1992. Entre Tradición y
     Evolución.* Diputación de Cádiz.

17   Montiel, E. (1993) *Camarón. Vida y muerte del cante.* Barcelona, Ediciones B.

18   Lencero, C (2004) *Sobre Camarón. La leyenda del cantaor solitario.* Barcelona,
     Alba Editorial.

19   *ibid*

6: Echoes of the White Towns, 1988–1989.

1   Fernández Zaurín, L. & Candado Calleja, J. (2002) *Camarón, biografía de un
     mito.* Barcelona, RBA Libros.

2   Espínola, P. (1993) 'Días de vinos y rosas. (Ános 80-90).' *La Caña: Revista de
     Flamenco.* No.6 (Verano 1993) (citing Diario de Cádiz, 29 August 1989)

3   Márquez, H. (2002) 'Otra chispa de Camarón.' *Rolling Stone* (Spain) No.34
     (August 2002)

4   Rodríquez Sánchez, A. (1998) *Camarón. Se rompió el quejío.* Madrid, Nuer
     Ediciones.

5   Espínola, P. (1993) 'Días de vinos y rosas. (Ános 80-90).' *La Caña: Revista de*

Flamenco. No.6 (Verano 1993) (citing Espínola, P., Tiempo, 29 May 1989)

6   Marcos (1989) 'Cuaderno Flamenco.' *Guitar International*. (November 1989)

7   Espínola, P. (1993) 'Días de vinos y rosas. (Años 80–90).' *La Caña: Revista de Flamenco*. No.6 (Verano 1993)

8   Gamboa, J.M. & Núñez, F. (2003) *Camarón vida y obra*. Madrid, Sociedad General de Autores y Editores.

9   *ibid*.

10 Lencero, C. (2004) *Sobre Camarón. La Leyenda del cantaor solitario*. Barcelona, Alba Editorial.

11 Espínola, P. (1993) 'Días de vinos y rosas. (Años 80–90).' *La Caña: Revista de Flamenco*. No.6 (Verano 1993)

12 Peregil, F. (1993) *Camarón de la Isla. El dolor de un príncipe*. Madrid, El País Aguilar.

13 *ibid*.

14 Manrique, D.A. (2001) 'Tomatito, el toque perfecto de Camarón.' *El País Semanal* (6 April 2001)

15 Espínola, P. (1993) 'Días de vinos y rosas. (Años 80-90).' *La Caña: Revista de Flamenco*. No.6 (Verano 1993)

7: *The Last Goodbye, 1990–1992.*

1   Fernández Zaurín, L. & Candado Calleja, J. (2002) *Camarón, biografía de un mito*. Barcelona, RBA Libros.

2   Espínola, P. (1993) 'Días de vinos y rosas. (Años 80-90).' La *Caña: Revista de Flamenco*. No.6 (Verano 1993) (citing Espínola, P., Tiempo, 29 May 1989)

3   Marcos (1990) 'Bienal de Arte Flamenco VI – El Toque.' *Guitar International*. (November 1990)

4   Martín Martín, M. (1990) *Cultura. La coherencia artística de Tomatito. Diario 16* (18 September 1990)

5   Fernández Zaurín, L. & Candado Calleja, J. (2002) *Camarón, biografía de un mito*. Barcelona, RBA Libros.

6   Espínola, P. (1993) 'Días de vinos y rosas. (Años 80-90).' *La Caña: Revista de Flamenco*. No.6 (Verano 1993)

7   Espínola, P. (1993) 'Días de vinos y rosas. (Años 80-90).' *La Caña: Revista de Flamenco*. No.6 (Verano 1993) (citing Espínola, P., Tiempo, 29 May 1989)

8   Fernández Zaurín, L. & Candado Calleja, J. (2002) *Camarón, biografía de un mito*. Barcelona, RBA Libros.

9   *ibid*.

10   Peregil, F. (1993) *Camarón de la Isla. El dolor de un príncipe*. Madrid, *El País* *Aguilar*.

11   Blázquez, J.A. (1991) 'Naranjito, Aurora Vargas, Manolo Franco, Enrique Paredes y Javier Barón triufaron en el Auditorio.' *ABC*. (22 September 1991)

12   Huélamo, L. & Santander, F. (1992) 'Llanto por un gitano.' *Panorama*. (6 July 1992)

13   Jurado, M. (1992) 'Un potra de rabia y miel.' *El País*. (3 July 1992)

14   Font, C. (1993) 'Paco de Lucía rompe su luto.' *Panorama*. (5 July 1993)

15   Fernández Zaurín, L. & Candado Calleja, J. (2002) *Camarón, biografía de un mito*. Barcelona, RBA Libros.

16   Toro, J. (1992) 'Entrevista al doctor Rafael Rosell Costa.' *Sevilla Flamenca*. No.79. (July–August 1992)

17   Gamboa, J.M. & Núñez, F. (2003) *Camarón vida y obra*. Madrid, Sociedad General de Autores y Editores.

18   Fernández Zaurín, L. & Candado Calleja, J. (2002) *Camarón, biografía de un mito*. Barcelona, RBA Libros.

19   Silva López, J.L. (1992) 'Camarón para siempre.' *Candil*. Ano XV, No.82. (July–August 1992)

20   Bellver, J.M. (1992) 'Bulerías para alcanzar el cielo.' *Cambio 16*.(25 May 1992)

21   Huélamo, L. & Santander, F. (1992) 'Llanto por un gitano.' *Panorama*. (6 July 1992)

22   Bellver, J.M. (1992) 'Bulerías para alcanzar el cielo.' *Cambio 16*. (25 May 1992)

23   Espínola, P. (1993) 'Días de vinos y rosas. (Ános 80-90).' *La Caña: Revista de Flamenco*. No.6 (Verano 1993)

24   *ibid*.

25   *ibid*.

26   Huélamo, L. & Santander, F. (1992) 'Llanto por un gitano.' *Panorama*. (6 July 1992)

27   Perejil, F. (1992) 'Los últimos días de un principe.' *El País*. (3 July 1992)

28   *ibid*.

29   Toro, J. (1992) 'Entrevista al doctor Rafael Rosell Costa.' *Sevilla Flamenca*. No.79. (July–August 1992)

30   Perejil, F. (1992) 'Los últimos días de un principe.' *El País*. (3 July 1992)

31   'Gente. Homenaje a Camarón.' *ABC*. (July 1992)

32   Perejil, F. (1992) 'Los últimos días de un principe.' *El País*. (3 July 1992)

33   Manrique, D.A. (2001) 'Tomatito, el toque perfecto de Camarón.' *El País*

Semanal. (6 April 2001)

34   Primo, J. (2001) 'Tomatito: Azul y rojo de geranios.' *Alma 100.* No.26 (July/ August 2001)

35   Manrique, D.A. (2001) 'Tomatito, el toque perfecto de Camarón.' *El País Semanal.* (6 April 2001)

36   Font, C. (1993) 'Paco de Lucía rompe su luto.' *Panorama.* (5 July 1993)

8: A Gigantic Creation of the Spanish People

1   Stainton, L. (1998) *Lorca. A Dream of Life.* London, Bloomsbury.

2   *ibid*

3   Blas Vega, J. & Ríos Ruiz, M. (1988) *Maestros del Flamenco.* Barcelona, Planeta de Agostini.

4   Álvarez Caballero, A. (1995) *La Discoteca Ideal de Flamenco.* Barcelona, Editorial Planeta.

5   *ibid.*

6   Blas Vega, J. & Ríos Ruiz, M. (1988) *Maestros del Flamenco.* Barcelona, Planeta de Agostini.

7   Bendala Lucot, M. (1983) *Sevilla.* Leon, Editorial Everest.

8   Lencero, C. (1992) Sleeve notes for *El Ángel.* Productora Andaluza de Programas S.A./ RTVE Musica (September 1992)

9   Bendala Lucot, M. (1983) *Sevilla.* Leon, Editorial Everest.

10   Blas Vega, J. & Ríos Ruiz, M. (1988) *Maestros del Flamenco.* Barcelona, Planeta de Agostini.

11   Álvarez Caballero, A. (1995) *La Discoteca Ideal de Flamenco.* Barcelona, Editorial Planeta.

12   Sevilla, P. (1999) *Queen of the gypsies. The Life and Legend of Carmen Amaya.* San Diego, Sevilla Press.

13   *ibid.*

14   *ibid.*

15   Howson, G. (1965) *The Flamencos of Cádiz Bay.* London, Hutchinson & Co.

9: The New Che, 1993–2005

1   Muñoz, D. (1993) 'Camarón renace al ano de su muerte en un libro que recoge su voz.' *La Vanguardia.* (4 July 1993)

2   *ibid.*

3   Gott, R. (2006) 'Poster Boy.' *The Guardian.* (3 June 2006)

4   *ibid.*

5   Marín, K. (2006) 'Manuel Chaves. "El PSOE me lleva a toque de corneta"'
     El País. (28 May 2006)

6   Acal, M. (2000) 'Camarón de la Isla. ¿cuarta Llave del Cante?' *El Candil.*
     No.130 (November/December 2000)

7   Espínola, P. (1993) 'La herencia de la Ruina Negra.' *La Caña: Revista de
     Flamenco.* No.6 (Verano 1993)

8   *ibid.*

9   *ibid.*

10   Márquez, H. (2002) 'Otra chispa de Camarón.' *Rolling Stone* (Spain). No.34
     (August 2002)

11   Bueno, A. (2002) 'Camarón.' *El Mundo. Revista* No.127 (March 2002)

12   Boyero, C (2002)' Las Comparaciones no siempre son odiosas. Camarón y
     Billie Holiday.' *El Mundo. Revista* No.127 (March 2002)

13   Molina, M. (2003) 'El Ayuntamiento de San Fernando crea una ruta para
     visitar los lugares claves en vida de Camarón.' *El País.*
     (26 October 2003)

14   Castro, C (2002) 'Turismo: Un paseo por la vida de Camarón, leyenda viva
     del flamenco.' *Diario de Cádiz.* (4 February 2006)

15   Bueno, A. (2002) 'Camarón.' *El Mundo. Revista* No.127 (March 2002)

16   *ibid.*

17   Manrique, D.A. (2006) 'Veneno contra corriente.' *El País Semanal.* (February
     2006)

10: The Flamenco Christ, 2005-2006.

1   Zenit Comunicacion (2005) Press Pack. Una produccion de Monoria
     Films. *Camarón.*

2   San Sebastián Film Festival (18 September 2005) Velodrome: Camarón
     http://sansebastian.mister-i.com

3   Flamenco World/S.C. (February 2005) Shooting begins of *Camarón* by
     Jaime Chavarri, the first film about the legendary cantaor. www.flamenco-
     world.com

4   F.-Santos, F. & García, R (2005) 'Cultura. El cine indaga en dos mitos de la
     música.' *El País.* (18 September 2005)

5   Díaz, F. (2005) 'Cultura. Los islenos se vuelcan de nuevo con "Camarón, un

mito"'. *Diario de Cádiz*. (21 April 2005)

6   Stills, B. (2005) 'Film may end in a flamenco feud.' *The Guardian*. (25 February 2005)

7   Telecinco (September 2005) 'Demandan a los productores de "Camarón" por incumplimiento del contrato por el guión.' www.telecinco.com

8   Dupagne, M-F. (February 2006) News. Rotterdam 2006. Official Competition. 'In search of the Legend of Time.' www.cineuropa.org

9   Vidal, N. (June 2006) 'La leyenda del tiempo.' www.fotogramas.wanadoo.es

11: The Long Journey.

1   Grande, F. (1976) Sleeve notes for *Persecución*. Fonogram. S.A.

2   *ibid*.

3   Borrow, G. (1846) *The Zincali or An Account of the Gypsies of Spain*. London, John Murray.

4   Grande, F. (1976) Sleeve notes for *Persecución*. Fonogram. S.A.

5   Clébert, J.P. (1963) *The Gypsies*. London, Vista Books.

6   Christie, G.J. (1994) 'I Congreso Gitano de La Union Europea.' *¡Flamenco! The Journal of Flamenco Artistry*. Vol.2, No.5. (Fall–Winter 1994)

7   Rincón, R. (2005) 'Noche de terror en Cortegana.' *El País*. (18 January 2005)

8   Euroresidentes (2 March 2005) 'Spain's football coach fined for racist comments' www.euroresidentes.com

9   Mujer Hoy (2005) Tu opinas en mhmujer.com. (27 August–2 September 2005)

10 Serrano, S. (2006) 'Opinión. Una Niña gitana y gordita.' *El País*. (29 January 2005)

11 de Cozar, A. (2006) 'Cultura. El diccionario impertinente.' *El País*. (25 June 2006)

12 Alcaide, S. & de Sandoval, P.X. (unknown) 'Gitanos, a cuestas con su topico.' *El País*.

13 Ortega Dolz, P. & Oleaque, J. (2006) Domingo. '¿Gitanos de clase media? Si, y son mayoría.' *El País*. (12 March 2006)

14 Pohren, D.E. (1962) *The Art of Flamenco*. Sevilla, Society of Spanish Studies.

15 Gay y Blanco, P. (1999) *Gypsies in Madrid. Sex, Gender and the Performance of Identity*. Oxford, Berg.

16 *ibid*.

17 Fraser, A. (1992) *The Gypsies*. Oxford, Blackwell.

18 Ortega Dolz, P. & Oleaque, J. (2006) Domingo. '¿Gitanos de clase media?

Si, y son mayoría.' *El País*. (12 March 2006)

19   Malagón, C. (2006) 'La precariedad marca la actividad de los gitanos que tienen empleo.' *Diario de Cádiz*. (16 July 2006)

20   Lee, L. (1955) *A Rose for Winter*. Middlesex, Penguin.

21   Howson, G. (1965) *The Flamencos of Cádiz Bay*. London, Hutchinson & Co.

22   Jacobs, M. (1994) *Between Hopes and Memories. A Spanish Journey*. London, Picador.

12: Fifteen Years Without 'Our José'

1   RTE Television (1992) Tribute to Camaron.

Appendix A

Transcription of the interview with Rancapino conducted in Spanish.

Marcos: ¿Ha visto la película de Camarón? ¿Qué opinión le merece?

Rancapino: Hombre, hay cosas que están bien, pero no, no es Camarón. Camarón era otra cosa. Era totalmente otra cosa.

Marcos: ¿Por qué?

Rancapino: Porque Camarón tenía otras hechuras de costumbres, otras maneras; era muy tímido. Después hay una combinación que dice Camarón en la película 'mi mamá, mi papá' Mentira, Camarón nunca dijo esa palabra. Nunca llamaba a su madre mamá, la llamaba omá, o opá, pero no mama ni papá. Muchas cosas que no van. Ha salido lo mínimo de menos importancia de Camarón.

Marcos: Entonces ¿Tiene problemas con la representación de Camarón?

Rancapino: De lo que era Camarón, hombre claro, ya que haces una película de Camarón debes de hacerla tal y como era Camarón y haber buscado personajes que vivieron con él y que muchas cosas, muchas cosas, muchísimas que no salen ahí. Pero no se trata de cosas feas, sino sus formas en el tiempo taurino que él tenía. Cuando toreaba, aficionado a los toros nos íbamos los dos a torear a los tentaderos, cuando íbamos a la Línea, cuando no conocía a la Chispa que se la presente yo y muchas cosas, pero bueno …

Marcos: Entonces ¿Cuáles son sus primeros recuerdos sobre Camarón?

Rancapino: Mis primeros recuerdos de chicos los dos son desde que tenia
Camarón 14 años y yo 16 y me lo llevaba yo a la Venta de Vargas y
entonces me decía María y Juan Vargas, me decía "por favor no traigas
más a este niño aquí que me van a cerrar la venta" y yo le decía no
"yo ahora me lo llevo" y entrábamos en las fiestas y la gente se volvía
loca con él escucharlo cantar na' más. Era un genio. Y de ahí nos
íbamos errantemente aquí a Cádiz, nos veníamos al "Burladero", un
bar que era de unos gitanos que eran carniceros, que eran familia de
Caracol, y entonces ahí en el burladero paraba Aurelio Sellés, paraba
Pericón, paraba tío Agustín, que era el dueño del bar y nos llamaba
a nosotros "anda, dale un fandanguito a tío Aurelio". Entonces le
cantábamos un fandango a tío Aurelio y a los amigos que estaban allí
y nos daban una peseta y nos íbamos a hacer una fotografía.

Marcos: ¿Y usted cantaba con Camarón en el tranvía de Cádiz, no?

Rancapino: No. Eso es mentira total. Camarón nunca cantó en los tranvías, ni
en los trenes, ni pidió nada; mentira. Yo, si conocía a la gente, me
llamaban, cantábamos y nos daban un dinero en los bares o en las
fiestas o en las cuevas Pájaro Sur en la Venta de Vargas.

Marcos: ¿Y por qué ahora la figura de Camarón crece con el paso del tiempo?

Rancapino: Crece, hombre Camarón era un genio. Era un cantaor irrepetible y
entonces Camarón tenía una musicalidad distinta a todos los cantaores
habidos y por haber. Él no se parecía cantando a nadie. Cantaba por
Camarón, ¿comprende?

Marcos: ¿Y por qué se le ve como otro Che Guevara?

Rancapino: Hombre porque es un genio, porque Camarón improvisaba cantando
y tenia una musicalidad distinta a todos los cantaores del siglo pasado,
de éste y del que va a venir; de todos los siglos.

Marcos: ¿Y usted cree que Camarón fue explotado económicamente?

Rancapino: Si, Camarón ha sido explotado por muchísima gente.

Marcos: ¿Y la situación de la Chispa?

Rancapino: Hombre la Chispa … Camarón le dejó dinero que eso lo se yo.
Entonces como era un genio, pues todo el mundo va buscando
también negocio; uno por un libro, otro porque quiere grabar
cosas que tenia antiguas que no estaban a la comercialización, para
comerciar, ¿no?

Marcos: Entonces ¿Le trae recuerdos el entierro de Camarón?

Rancapino: Hombre por favor, eso para mi fue un palo muy gordo, porque
Camarón y yo siempre estábamos juntos toda la vida y luego la
Chispa porque fuí yo el que lo llevé, me lo llevaba a la Línea con

12 años con pantalones cortos y al mismo tiempo Camarón ha sido, para mí ha sido. . . no veas, siempre íbamos juntos a todos los lados. Ya en Madrid estaba parando en una casa del chico de un palmero, de Bambino y ahí parábamos la Fernanda, la Bernarda, Pansequito, Turronero, Camarón y yo; y pagábamos 50 pts por cada uno para comer un puchero que nos ponían con agua y Camarón trabajaba entones en Torres Bermejas y yo trabajaba en el cuadro y Camarón de figura y de ahí se enamoro una mujer de Camarón, Mari Paz. Tuvo una niña de Camarón. Entonces nos fuimos a Dr Fleming en Madrid. Ahí vivíamos Mari Paz, Camarón y yo, ¿comprende? Y de ahí pues le salió hacer la película de "Casa Flora" que trabajaba Camarón con Máximo Valverde, Lola Flores, Paquita Rico, Conchita Piquer y una serie de artistas muy grandes. Camarón en la época del 66 al 69 estaba en Madrid, en Torres Bermejas, y venía Ricardo Pachón a verlo y decía Camarón "osú que pesado es este tío", pero después Ricardo seguía y seguía.

Marcos: ¿Qué piensas sobre la relación artística de Paco y Camarón?

Rancapino: Hombre, eso han sido dos genios del Flamenco. Paco ha sido un genio en la guitarra, una de las guitarras más adelantadas que ha habido también del siglo pasado, éste y él que va a venir como Camarón en cuanto al cante, ha sido el cantaor más grande que se ha conocido con esa edad. Los Lucía le han ayudado a Camarón y Camarón le ayudo a los Lucía, comprende?

Marcos: Entonces ¿Qué ha hecho Camarón para mejorar la imagen del pueblo gitano?

Rancapino: Hombre mucho, mucho, Camarón ha dado mucho al flamenco y el pueblo gitano está muy contento con Camarón porque Camarón cantaba muy bien. Camarón le ha dado mucho a la música Flamenca, prueba evidente es que no hay ni un niño gitano que no tenga un disco de Camarón, ¿comprende?

Marcos: Cuál es la realidad entre Camarón y la droga?

Rancapino: Camarón era un genio y Camarón como Elvis Presley, como John Lennon y como. . . Camarón era un genio y entonces se tenía que estimular para él venirse arriba como los genios, como todos esos artistas no?

Marcos: Pero usted es artista también …

Rancapino: No hombre no. La droga es muy mala. Se comprende que es muy mala, pero Camarón desde que era un niño pequeño andaba por las calles de San Fernando errantemente y por Cádiz.

Appendix B

Transcription of the interview with Enrique Montiel conducted in Spanish.

Marcos: ¿Has visto la película de Camarón un mito? ¿Qué opinión le merece?

Enrique: Me parece espantosa. No me ha gustado absolutamente nada.

Marcos: ¿Por qué?

Enrique: No me ha gustado nada porque es una película falsa. Es una película que está descompensada, donde se ha producido una especie de división entre la puta paya y la gitana virginal. Cuando la paya de la película que se llama Isabel quieren que sean muchas payas, ¿no? Pero lo cierto es que Camarón tuvo una relación como yo puse en mi libro con Mari Paz de la cual tiene una hija que se llama Juana que vive en Barcelona y solamente por respeto a Mari Paz y por respeto a su hija. Esa parte de la película me parece verdaderamente fatal. Después la película no profundiza en la figura interior de Camarón. Camarón era un artista excepcional y todos los artistas excepcionales tienen una gran riqueza interior que ahí no aparece para nada. Me parece que se le ha dado al mundo de la droga en la película una dimensión que no debería tener. Cuando hablamos de Camarón, que hablamos de un adicto o hablamos de un músico ¿no? Entonces bueno, qué influencia tuvo la droga en la música de Camarón.

Después hay varias cosas qué me molestaron muchísimo, por ejemplo la figura de Paco de Lucía en la película; un tipo afeminado

con una melenilla así … medio maricón, bueno la verdad el actor no
me ha gustado nada. Además un tipo muy blando cuando Paco es un
hombre de una fuerza extraordinaria. Me parece que en la película no
está alguien fundamental en la biografía de Camarón que es Ricardo
Pachón. Fue el que hizo La Leyenda del Tiempo el que hizo Soy gitano
y el que participa en la zona de Camarón de la Isla más rupturista y
más original, ¿no? Es decir, hay partes que bueno están bien reflejadas.
Yo creo que todo esto tiene que ver con el guión, que lo ha hecho
el guión al parecer, vamos, el guión esta inspirado fundamentalmente
en la información que le proporciona, yo pienso, Candado. Entonces
Candado tiene conocimiento de la parte digamos del viaje … del final
de la vida de Camarón. Es decir, cuando Candado está en Los Estátos
Unidos con Camarón. Candado está en Santa Coloma y eso es una
dimensión en la película que por cierto, sin embargo no han querido…
yo creo que el guión se ha hecho un poco a la imagen y semejanza
de la viuda. Quiere decir que la viuda es la que ha condicionado
completamente el guión. Me parece un error enorme. Ella me llamó
por teléfono a mí, lo que pasa es que yo no entendí muy bien aquella
llamada. Me llamó por teléfono bastantes meses antes.

Marcos: ¿Usted ha hablado con algún director?

Enrique: No, no a mi no me ha llamado Chavarri. Si no me ha llamado, yo no
llamo, pero ella si me llamó. Me llamó La Chispa por teléfono para
darme las quejas del guión que ha hecho Candado y el amigo no,
no, no, ella me dijo que no le gustaba el guión. Literalmente me dijo
que lo había tirado para atrás el guión. Después he sabido que han
habido problemas con el guión, con el guionista y con Chavarri, pero
me han dicho luego que seguramente La Chispa me llamo a mí para
que yo hubiera participado en el guión. Desde luego si yo hago ese
guión no hubiera hecho el guión que salió. Entonces el guión que le
presentaron a ella 'lo tiré para atrás porque no me gustaba' me dijo,
pero a mi no me pidió La Chispa ¿'oye por qué no' … y yo no dije
nada porque yo no entendí bien. No me comentó. Si ella hubiera sido
clara conmigo. Si ella me hubiera dicho mira tal, yo quiero que hagas
el guión, pero bueno no me dijo nada. En definitiva la película no me
gusta nada. Es mi opinión.

Marcos: ¿Cuáles son sus primeros recuerdos de Camarón?

Enrique: Bueno pues yo lo he contado alguna vez. Yo tengo hoy la edad que
tendría Camarón hoy, es decir, Camarón nació en diciembre del 1950
y yo nací en mayo de 1951. Nacimos en el mismo pueblo, estudiamos

en el mismo colegio lo que pasa es que claro yo estudié hasta la
universidad y él … Entonces yo el primer recuerdo que tengo de
Camarón es el recuerdo de un niño que canta en un bar.

Marcos: ¿En la venta de vargas?

Enrique: No, en la venta de vargas no. Canta en lo que se llama en el lenguaje
slang, argot, un Güichi que era un bar muy modesto que había en el
castillo.

Marcos: ¿Y que edad tenía Camarón?

Enrique: Camarón podría tener 6 años. Claro es que yo voy por la calle, porque
los niños de esa edad nos bañábamos en el agua del puente del Zuazo,
y entonces pasábamos por allí y en el castillo se daban peleas de
gallos, las gentes ¿no? Entonces recuerdo que entré a ver una pelea
de gallos junto con todo el mundo y ví que había un alboroto en el
Güichi, en el bar de bebida que había, bar de vino, pero muy humilde,
muy modesto y ví que había un niño subido en una mesa cantando
y entonces pues bueno, yo me quedé mirando al niño porque yo
era otro niño también con 6, 7, 8 años y luego claro, luego cuando
Camarón fue Camaron ya prácticamente pocos años después, dije
ya "Ah ¿este es el niño que cantaba no?" Así es que ese es el primer
recuerdo que tengo yo de Camarón y luego tuve con él mucha
relación evidentemente hasta su muerte.

Marcos: Entonces, ¿por qué ahora la figura de Camarón crece con el paso del
tiempo?

Enrique: Bueno, ya lo hemos dicho algunos. Yo eso lo dije hace muchos años.
Camarón cada día canta mejor. Yo soy el productor del último disco
de Camarón, La Venta de Vargas. La grabación se hizo en La Venta de
Vargas en un 4 pistas. Grabación de Juan Vargas, pero Ricardo Pachón
y yo hemos hecho la producción de ese disco.

Marcos: ¿Por qué se le ve como otro Che Guevara del flamenco?

Enrique: Bueno eso es un invento de Pachón. Bueno más que de Pachón, de
un diseñador de Sevilla que se le ocurrió coger el retrato del Che para
ponerlo en la Antología Inédita que hizo Pachón en el año 2000

Marcos: ¿Qué significa para Camarón el pueblo gitano?

Enrique: Bueno, Camarón era para los gitanos el Dios, o sea, Camarón era el
rey de los gitanos, como el Che no porque los gitanos no tienen una
gran conciencia política. Tienen conciencia de pueblo y de etnia, pero
no tienen una conciencia política. El gitano desconfia de todos los
políticos, tiene motivos claro. Todos los políticos los han perseguido y
por lo tanto no tiene una conciencia política. La conciencia que tiene

es que hay que estar lejos del poder.

Marcos: ¿Entonces usted cree que Camarón fue explotado económicamente
            alguna vez?

Enrique: Yo pienso que no. Camarón desde muy niño como era un genio
            siempre tuvo dinero. Siempre cantó donde le dio la gana. Aparte, que
            él era un hombre de gran humildad. A él le daba igual comerse un
            plato de puchero o unas lentejas y no quería más. Él realmente no ha
            hecho por atesorar dinero, ni tener casa ni propiedades. Él vivir la vida
            y reírse mucho y ser feliz como el lo canta además porque el hace
            muchos cantes autobiográficos 'vivir y soñar yo solo busco mi libertad'
            cantó.

Marcos: ¿Le trae recuerdos el entierro de Camarón?

Enrique: Claro, yo estuve allí. Yo estuve en ese entierro. Fue terrible y fue
            algo impresionante. Yo estuve a pie de la fosa. Cuando yo estaba
            sobrecogido completamente haciá un calor enorme, una luz de La
            Isla que es una luz de julio del mediodía, rebotaba en las paredes
            blancas del cementerio, no? Y yo vî como depositaron el ataúd en la
            fosa y como un gitano con la camisa hecha jirones gritó ¡'no te vayas
            Camarón!, ¡no te vayas!' yo vî el dolor de la familia, de su viuda, de
            sus hermanas, de sus hermanos, Pijote, Manuel, Remedios, Isabel, El
            Metepata y …

Marcos: ¿Ha visto el rostro de Paco, con miedo?

Enrique: No, de miedo nada. Descompuesto de dolor y de probablemente
            también de impotencia porque unos imbéciles se metieron con él.
            Una gran injusticia que han cometido con Paco.

Marcos: Entonces que piensa sobre la relación artística de Paco y Camarón?

Enrique: Bueno fue una relación … gracias a esa relación el Flamenco avanzó
            mil años, o sea, la relación de Camarón y Paco fue como un milagro,
            milagro total para el flamenco.

Marcos: ¿Qué ha hecho Camarón para mejorar la imagen del pueblo gitano?

Enrique: No entiendo muy bien la pregunta, ¿por qué? ¿Cual es la imagen
            del pueblo gitano? Hay que tener mucho cuidado con identificar
            a un pueblo con una imagen porque, ¿cuál es la imagen del pueblo
            inglés? El pueblo inglés, tiene una imagen? ¿Soló una imagen? ¿Existe
            un pueblo? En Inglaterra la imagen es muy mala. Un gitanillo le
            preguntó a Camarón un día, digo José, porque el era muy amigo de
            los Payos yo le pregunte a el 'José a ti que te parece que una niña tuya
            se case con un payo' dice 'como se va a casar mi niña con un payo'. Si
            es que no le entraba en la cabeza, que su hija se casara con un payo.

Entiendes el chiste ¿no? ¿Como se va a casar mi hija con un payo?
¡Cómo se te ocurre! Mi hija se tiene que casar con un gitano puro.
Ahora, la imagen de los gitanos, pues hay muchas clases de gitanos
como muchas clases de payos.

Marcos: ¿Desde que usted escribió su libro hace 13 años, se ha publicado algo
nuevo en libros posteriormente o añadiría algo más a su libro?

Enrique: ¿Se han publicado 2 libros, para mi gusto dos libros que tienen mucho
interés, ¿no? Se ha publicado un libro de Gamboa y Núñez que
era el libro que yo siempre dije que faltaba que era el libro de un
musicólogo, donde hay un estudio de todos los discos de Camarón,
canción por canción.

Marcos: ¿Un libro para especialistas?

Enrique: Ese es un libro muy importante. Y luego se ha publicado un libro
que a mí me gusta mucho y está muy bien escrito que es el libro de
Carlos Lencero.

Marcos: ¿Qué pone que sea diferente de su libro?

Enrique: No es que todos han copiado de mi libro. Todos han copiado de mi
libro. Yo lo puedo demostrar, que todos han copiado de mi libro. Yo lo
puedo demostrar. Todos, por eso si quieres mirar bien búscate mi libro
que alguien te lo preste y ... es que yo saque cosas de Camarón que
nadie sabía. Yo conté la infancia de Camarón, que nadie la sabía mejor
que yo. Yo conté por ejemplo el que era el scoop del nacimiento de
su hija secreta era yo. Yo soy el que cuenta lo que son los primeros
20 años y los últimos 20 también, o sea, que todos han copiado de
mi libro, todos. A parte yo he escrito otras muchas cosas también de
Camarón ¿eh? Artículos, reportajes. ¿He publicado muchas cosas, eh?

Marcos: ¿Cuál es la realidad sobre el problema de las drogas de Camarón?

Enrique: Bueno pues Camarón, Camarón, la realidad es que es muy
complicado, o sea, habría mucho que hablar. Camarón era una persona
en cierto modo ignorante como tantísimas personas que en los años
sesenta eran ignorantes. Entonces Camarón fumaba, fumaba cigarrillos
realmente el murió del tabaco, murió del tabaco, de Winston. Si
fumaba 3 paquetes al día o 4. Cuatro cajetillas de Winston.

Marcos: ¿No de la droga?

Enrique: No, nada, nada. Además eso ésta demostrado en la ficha médica
todo, pero en la época esa en el mundo del arte empezó a fumarse
la marihuana y el chocolate; claro todo el mundo fumaba maría
y ñchocolate, entonces alguien un día, yo sé quién es ese alguien
además, pero no lo voy a decir, le dijo prueba esto, esto es mejor que

el jamón. Le dijo literalmente 'esto es mejor que el jamón'.

Marcos: ¿Chocolate?

Enrique: Si, esto es mejor que el jamón. Entonces Camarón tomo la cocaína. La cocaína para un artista que ... entonces él empieza a tomar la cocaína que era fantástico pero claro él ... todos, es que a mí me gustaría que me dijeras de algún artista de esa época que no tomara la cocaína en esa época. Estoy hablando de los años setenta. Es que un flamenco se metía en una fiesta y podía estar dos días sin dormir cantando, ¿me explico? Pero vamos la droga del flamenco era el aguardiente que es lo que le gustaba a Camarón, el aguardiente.

Marcos: ¿Anís del mono?

Enrique: No, no del Mono. Aguardiente de Huelva. El anís es dulce, el aguardiente es más fuerte. Ese era el que le gustaba a Camarón, el aguardiente de Huelva, pero bueno este fue el proceso, entonces otro día pues alguien le dio la heroína y la fumó. Él nunca se metió la inyección. Nunca se pinchó, jamás. Siempre la fumaba. Entonces fumó eso y llegó un momento en que se encontró que aquello empezó a pasarle cuenta, factura y a partir de ese momento la vida de Camarón fue una lucha contra eso. Entonces como esa lucha fue una lucha noble, me parece muy mal que eso sea la anécdota de Camarón. Cuando se habla de la droga de Camarón hay que hablar siempre de su lucha contra la adicción por respeto, él lo dijo, a mis hijos y al pueblo gitano. Él estaba viéndolo. La cantidad de gitanos que estaban cayendo.

Marcos: Háblame un poquito sobre Abbey Road y Camarón

Enrique: Camarón fue allí a Londres con Ricardo Pachón para grabar "soy gitano". Entonces recuerdo que tenía toda la orquesta ya preparada pagada por Universal y Camarón llegó tarde, entonces Universal tuvo que pagar otro día más a la orquesta, porque eso es lo que pasaba con Camarón, que era un artista genial, pero era un hombre rebelde, ¿no? Pero por supuesto que estuvo allí, por supuesto que grabo, sí, sí.

Select Bibliography

Blas Vega, J. & Ríos Ruiz, M. (1988) *Maestros del Flamenco*. Barcelona, Planeta de Agostini.

Fernández Zaurín, L. & Candado Calleja, J. (2002) *Camarón, biografía de un mito*. Barcelona, RBA Libros.

Gamboa Rodríquez, J.M. & Núñez, F. (2003) *Camarón Vida y Obra*. Madrid, Sociedad General de Autores y Editores.

García Plata, M. (2002) *Camarón de la Isla 1969–1992*. Entre Tradición y Evolución. Diputación de Cádiz.

Grande, F. and Zaafra, D. (1998) *Paco de Lucía and Camarón de la Isla*. Madrid, Caja Madrid and Lunwerg.

Lencero, C. (2004) *Sobre Camarón. La leyenda del cantaor solitario*. Barcelona, Alba Editorial.

Montiel, E. (1993) *Camarón. Vida y muerte del cante*. Barcelona, Ediciones B.

Núñez, F. (1998) *Todo el flamenco. Camarón de la Isla. La esencia del cante*. Spain, EDILIBRO/Club Internacional del Libro.

Peregil, F. (1993) *Camarón de la Isla. El dolor de un príncipe*. Madrid, El País Aguilar.

Rodríquez Sánchez, A. (1998) *Camarón. Se rompió el quejío*. Madrid, Nuer Ediciones.

Sánchez, T. (2002) *Camarón. Antología*. Spain, Ópera Prima.

The following journals, who published dedicated editions to Camarón, were also consulted: *Candil* No.82, July–August 1992, *Sevilla Flamenca* No.79, July–August 1992, *La Caña* No.6, *The Journal of Flamenco Artistry* Vol.1 No.8, October 1992, *El Olivo* Autumn 1992 and *Camarón cinco anos después* 1997.

Further Reading

Brenan, G. (1957) *South from Granada*. Cambridge University Press.

George, D. (1969) *The Flamenco Guitar*. Seville, Society of Spanish Studies.

Hecht, P. (1994) *The Wind Cried*. The Bold Strummer.

Howson, G. (1994) *The Flamencos of Cádiz Bay*. The Bold Strummer.

Jacobs, M. (1999) *A guide to Andalusia*. London, Viking.

Lalaguna, J. (1999) *Spain. A Traveller's History*. Gloucestershire, The Windrush Press.

Perez Reverte, A. (1995) *The Seville Communion*. London, Harvill Press.

Pohren, D.E. (1999) *A Way of life*. University of Hertfordshire Press.

Preston, P. (1986) *Concise History of the Spanish Civil War*. London, Harper Collins.

Sevilla, P. (1999) *Queen of the Gypsies. The Life and Legend of Carmen Amaya*. San Diego, Sevilla Press.

List of Illustrations

9   The gypsy Tomatito who first met Camarón when he was fifteen years old and went on to be recognised as *his* guitarist. ©José Lamarca

10 Despite his battle with ill health, Camarón remained flamenco's highest paid, most innovative and respected singer. ©Agencia EFE/B. Rodriguez

11 Mario Pacheco's grainy over-exposed photograph provided the perfect sleeve for the album *La Leyenda del Tiempo* (1979). Now viewed as the *Sgt. Pepper* of flamenco but returned to the shops by conservative gypsies. Reproduced courtesy of UNIVERSAL MUSIC SPAIN, SL. Madrid-España

12 On the fourth anniversary of Camarón's death in 1996 his image was immortalised on a Spanish postage stamp. ©Correos, España

13 A rare example of the singer's signature, collected from his trip to Morón de la Frontera's Gazpacho festival.

14 To the end of his life Camarón remained a very unassuming, introverted and private person admitting very little in public. ©Agencia EFE

15 Controversially Camarón was posthumously awarded the *Llave de Oro* in 2000 and was later joined by Fosforito, pictured right, as one of only five artists in 150 years to receive this honour. Manolo Caracol, centre, once snubbed Camarón and lived to regret it. *Figuras de la Canción Vol. VIII* (1973) reproduced courtesy of UNIVERSAL MUSIC SPAIN, SL. Madrid-España

16 Since his death the reproduction of Camarón's image on everything from flags to cigarette lighters has become a highly lucrative business. ©Marcos/ Andrew Beck

17 The maestro Pepe Martínez, one of flamenco's old guards, who became a reluctant fan of Camarón. ©Estate of Pepe Martínez

18 Inspired by Camaron's flamenco revolution Marcos performs with his sister Claire. ©Douglas Denton.

Index